THE MERTON ANNUAL

7

THE MERTON ANNUAL

Studies in Culture, Spirituality, & Social Concerns

THE MERTON ANNUAL publishes articles about Thomas Merton and about related matters of major concern to his life and work. Its purpose is to enhance Merton's reputation as a writer and monk, to continue to develop his message for our times, and to provide a regular outlet for substantial Merton-related scholarship. THE MERTON ANNUAL includes as regular features reviews, review-essays, a bibliographic survey, interviews, and first appearances of unpublished, or obscurely published, Merton materials, photographs, and art. Essays about related literary and spiritual matters will also be considered. Manuscripts and books for review may be sent to any of the editors.

EDITORS

Michael Downey
Theology Department
Bellarmine College
2001 Newburg Road
Louisville, KY 40205-0671

George A. Kilcourse
Theology Department
Bellarmine College
2001 Newburg Road
Louisville, KY 40205-0671

Victor A. Kramer
English Department
Georgia State University
University Plaza
Atlanta, GA 30303-3083

Volume editorship rotates on a yearly basis.

ADVISORY BOARD

THE MERTON ANNUAL

Studies in Culture, Spirituality, & Social Concerns

Volume 7   **1994**

Edited by

Victor A. Kramer

A Liturgical Press Book

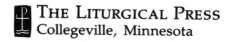

THE LITURGICAL PRESS
Collegeville, Minnesota

Cover design by Ann Blattner. *Artwork:* "Jerusalem" by Thomas Merton.

"Vocations to the Lay Apostolate" by Thomas Merton. Copyright by The Trustees of the Merton Legacy Trust.

ISBN 0-8146-2251-8

1	2	3	4	5	6	7	8	9

The Merton Annual

Volume 7   1994

* * *

A Review Symposium of
Ace of Freedoms: Thomas Merton's Christ
by George Kilcourse

Symposium Participants:

* * *

Introduction

Solitude Leads toward Apostolate in and for the World

Victor A. Kramer

A common theme present in much contemporary scholarship about Thomas Merton and a striking pattern woven into this volume of essays is an awareness of the paradoxical fact of both spiritual ascent and descent along with a sense of the transcendent. At the same time this is an awareness of the immanence of God's presence within the very fragments of a world constantly changing. This is a rhythm pulsating at the core of all genuine monasticism. Such a dual awareness is always at the heart of all solitaries who seek beyond themselves.

This gathering of essays about Thomas Merton continues patterns introduced in preceding volumes, and especially in volume 6 (1993). There we selected essays that reflect his importance, not only as a monk and writer who was aware of the importance of monasticism and contemplation for himself, but as a fundamental cultural need which has meaning for all persons. Merton's life and writing, therefore, reminds persons in varied circumstances of a continuing need for solitude, yet also of the call for building connections with others. The studies selected here have grown out of various contemporary currents that have generated realizations about balancing contemplation and action—always a combination that persons have to keep working on diligently to achieve. With this in mind, it seems especially fitting that we have been able to include in this volume the earliest known essay by Merton in relation to this subject. The Merton Legacy Trust has generously allowed this unpublished essay to be included here, and we are appreciative of this permission, which allows us to continue our tradition of printing unpublished, or obscurely published, primary Merton material.

This draft essay by "Thomas James Merton" was focused upon the lay apostolate at a time when laypersons were often, more or less, expected to remain quiet. Yet clearly what this premonastic Thomas Merton articulated in his 1941 article remains of value for monastics, for all seekers, indeed for all religious persons today. We also recognize a half century later that the needed balance of contemplative and active threads in life, woven into an integrated whole, may be even harder to accomplish in 1995. The thrust of many of the pieces included in this gathering reminds us, as one of the contributors to the review-symposium included here explicitly suggests, that we must remember (by way of Richard of St. Victor) in relation to Merton's developing thought that "[a]scent is followed by descent. Escape from the world is followed by return to the world."

Merton's heretofore unpublished essay about the lay apostolate remains of value for many reasons. As its editor, Patrick F. O'Connell, wisely speculates, this early essay contains embedded at its core the seeds of Merton's own inevitable involvement with apostolic Christianity and therefore with our larger world. It is that continuing involvement throughout his monastic career as a commentator, and later as a catalyst, that allows him to remain of considerable interest to many different readers today, and especially to those who live beyond the confines of a monastic enclosure. One of the continuing paradoxes of Merton's writing is that it makes clear that separation and solitude experienced within an enclosure bring one's focus right back to basic issues about the world.

The General Meetings of The International Thomas Merton Society (1989, Louisville; 1991, Rochester; 1993, Colorado Springs) have clearly demonstrated the living connections between solitude and action. These connections have been sustained at meetings that are extended moments when hundreds of persons gather to recognize Merton's value for an enormous range of readers and seekers. This is manifested by scholars with specialized interests (and sometimes extremely specialized topics of inquiry), but also in the range of readers for whom Merton lives as a model for spirituality. The Society meetings allow this diversity of persons to meet, discuss, and appreciate Merton in a variety of ways. The five papers, revised here from presentations at the 1993 meeting, reflect Merton's wide appeal to laypersons and specialists. Value is derived from careful and specific analysis of Merton's themes and language, but also other values are exhibited because of the common enthusiasm for a monk who will not remain isolated.

One of the principal features at the 1993 meeting was the sponsorship of a "Springboard" address by William H. Shannon about Merton's "Notes for a Philosophy of Solitude." This key examination of the need all persons have for solitude first appeared in Merton's *Disputed Questions*. Shannon's examination of this fundamental inquiry by Merton stressed Merton's understanding of the need for balance of solitude within a framework that must adequately integrate solitude into a still larger life. Shannon's presentation stimulated many response papers and considerable discussion. Both of the revised papers chosen for inclusion here, by David Belcastro and Patrick Eastman, provide ways for contemporary readers to become attuned to Merton's complex and developing attitudes concerning solitude, but also its dangers. We are, therefore, reminded of a basic need to embrace a world beyond the one that may seem to exist in individual separateness.

Three additional papers that have grown out of the 1993 I.T.M.S. meeting are included here. They are about Merton as a critic who absorbed much that was in the air because of "New Critical" tendencies in the 1930s; about his awareness of and uses of rhetoric and his personal development of rhetoric in the 1950s; and, finally, about his own successful development of images about the self in his later poetry, especially in the 1960s. In their concentrated ways these three examinations remind us that Merton remained a careful user of language throughout his career and that he was able to absorb traditions well and then to build beyond any simple mirroring. Merton's job, we see, was always to bring tradition into line with the present moment. In this regard he was constantly building on insights he absorbed in key sources, in T. S. Eliot, for example, who stressed an ideal of an extinction of personality. But Merton was also learning because of his monastic career that it was also (paradoxically) through an awareness of selfhood that one builds fresh insights and learns to forget about the self.

Each of these scholarly examinations provides paradigmatic patterns that might well be extended to other parts of Merton's canon. He was a lifelong critic who absorbed other critics; a rhetorician who finally sensed he must rely upon his own personal rhetoric; and an original poet who found self through a systematic forgetting of self, as I have argued in a recent article in *Cross Currents*.

Another valuable group of essays included here comes out of the 25th Anniversary Thomas Merton Symposium-Celebration, held at St. John's University in New York in October 1993. These diverse pieces are further reflections of contemporary commentators' recognition of Merton's continuing skill at absorbing traditions but also in moving on. In papers at that meeting Merton was investigated as a cultural critic. Merton embraced the monastic life but not just for himself, rather for others too, and thus he had to be a critic of culture. Appropriately, at the opening address for the St. John's University meeting (not included in this volume), Mary Jo Leddy talked insightfully about Merton's concerns with community and about related questions in contemporary society as various experiments in today's communities evolve and change. Her comments, which were built on Merton's insights, help remind us of the need to move on and to adapt: new "Catholic Worker" Houses; a *Sojourners* community in Washington, D.C., reacting to changing political needs; Leddy's own involvement in Romero House in Toronto, a residence for refugees.

In a parallel vein, the keynote address by Robert Morneau and a response by Sandra Schneiders extended reflections about Merton's gifts for today's audiences. Robert Morneau stressed Merton's poetic abilities, and rightly so, as his fundamental way of revealing the spiritual *for others*. Interestingly, the response to this analytical talk by Sandra Schneiders emphasized the complexity of Merton's poetry but also the equally important—and very simple—fact that he "was a man of prayer." Both of these addresses, included here, are, finally, manifestations of Merton's prayerfulness. We sense that it was prayer that made his best poetry. We also sense that Merton's poetry often remains unread, perhaps because of contemporary culture's haste and concern for the expedient, which makes it unprayerful.

The sophisticated study of the eight poems that make up Merton's "Freedom Song Cycle" by Patrick F. O'Connell (also derived from a presentation at St. John's) is further proof of the nature of Merton's ability to build on his love of tradition (here, especially the Old Testament) while doing so in ways that make it necessary for him to speak with an immediacy about the contemporary era. These are songs of urgency about the Civil-rights movement of the mid-1960s. They are poems that are successful precisely because they move beyond stereotypes to suggest a universal dimension of compassion for all persons who have been ignored and who are struggling for justice. These songs are, paradoxically, about how the true self is formed (with others) when the "false self" is forgotten. One learns, Merton reminds us, and in so doing learns to inspire and teach others.

Another example of Merton's continual reaching out, and how his reaching out through friendship lives into the present moment, is the interview conducted for this volume with Ron Seitz. Seitz knew Merton in the later years of the monk's life, and in our interview Seitz explains how his memory and knowledge of Merton has been carried over into his own writing. (This *Annual* also contains a review of Seitz's recent book, a "memory song" about Merton.) We suspect that there are many others who knew Merton well, especially in the final years of his life, persons who were also changed by his presence. We hope to identify more of these persons and continue the interview process, which has been an ingredient in all previous *Annuals*. Thus the influence of others, like Seitz, via Merton, such as Mary Luke Tobin (vol. 2) and Jack Ford (vol. 6) will also be documented.

The bibliographical review-essay for 1993 by fellow editor George Kilcourse surveys major work by, and related to, Merton during the preceding year. This essay is not meant to be a catalogue of all items written about Merton. (Such an inclusive list is found in the quarterly *Merton Seasonal*.) In the *Annual* bibliographical review-essays, which will be rotating year by year in authorship among the editors of the *Annual*, we plan to be speculative. It is hoped that as trends in scholarship are noted, we may alert readers and that then further scholarship can be built upon insights accomplished by others and reported upon here.

Similarly, it should be noted that the books chosen for review in volume 7 are not only books by, or about, Merton. As in immediately preceding volumes we have attempted to choose books for review that demonstrate that Merton's concerns live on into the present moment. Thus, appropriately, Glenn Hinson's work (represented in vol. 6 through his study of Douglas V. Steere) is further represented in the review included here of his recently edited collection of essays about ecumenical spirituality. Hinson (just as Ron Seitz) literally learned from Merton in an ecumenical setting when he was invited to come with his students to Merton's Mt. Olivet retreat in 1960. The fruit of that work is now being manifested in the continuing ecumenical work of Hinson and others. Similarly, Kathleen Norris' *Dakota* is also reviewed here because it so clearly strikes chords that would resonate for Merton. We are reminded that there are many approaches to basic spiritual questions, and that persons from many different backgrounds continue to raise questions that today parallel Merton's prophetic interests, not the least of which is the common theme that holds this volume together—the need for balance and alternation between genuine solitude and a genuine reaching out.

With that in mind, we have also chosen to include a review-symposium in this volume about the recently published study *Ace of Freedoms: Thomas Merton's Christ*, written by one of our editors. This book is also the subject of a review-symposium in another journal, *Horizons* (Fall, 1994). The diversity of enthusiastic approaches to Kilcourse's study helps us to see that Merton's prophetic concerns, yet sometimes enigmatic expression of those concerns, live into the present era. As Merton matured, above all he was perhaps less sure of definite answers, but his awareness of Christ, the Church, and his compassionate concern for others with their diverse traditions alerted him to the contemporary scene. Through his sustained attention we are made more aware of the presence of God in a shattered world. All the participants in this review-symposium stress an awareness of the surprising presence of the divine in a world sometimes only to be beheld in fragments.

The reviews and review-symposium for this volume were ably co-coordinated by Michael Downey. As is the case with volume editorship of the annual and with bibliographical review essays, each year's duties are rotated on a three-year cycle among the editors. We hope this rotation of responsibility provides a freshness of insight year by year for each of these major tasks.

Victor A. Kramer
Editor, *The Merton Annual* 7 (1994)

Vocations to the Lay Apostolate

Thomas James Merton
Edited by Patrick F. O'Connell

Editor's Note

Shortly before leaving St. Bonaventure College for the Abbey of Gethsemani in December 1941, Thomas Merton gave a miscellaneous collection of his papers to Richard F. Fitzgerald, a seminarian from the Erie, Pennsylvania, diocese who was studying at St. Bonaventure's Christ the King Seminary. In June 1974 these materials were returned by then Msgr. Fitzgerald to St. Bonaventure and now form part of the Friedsam Memorial Library's Merton archives. Included in this "Fitzgerald File" is a ten-page typescript entitled "Vocations to the Lay Apostolate," by-lined "Thomas James Merton" at its conclusion. (Merton frequently used "James," his confirmation name, in signatures in the years following his conversion.)[1] Though the article is undated, internal evidence provides a fairly clear indication of when it was written. The only datable reference is to the fall of France in June 1940, but the extensive discussion of Catherine de Hueck and her Friendship House apostolate strongly suggests that the piece was written after the baroness had visited St. Bonaventure on August 4, 1941, and probably after Merton had spent the latter half of August at Friendship House in Harlem. The most likely time of composition was after he returned to the college from a retreat during the week following Labor Day, 1941, at Our Lady of the Valley Monastery in Rhode Island, where he had gone to try to discern if he should work full time at Friendship House. If Michael Mott is correct in supposing that this was one of "the articles and stuff I had lying around," which Merton says in an October 6, 1941,

---

1. William H. Shannon, *Silent Lamp: The Thomas Merton Story* (New York: Crossroad, 1992) 97.

1

letter to Catherine de Hueck that he is going to send to Mary Jerdo at Friendship House,[2] then it was probably written sometime in September 1941. It must have been finished, at any rate, before Merton once again began considering religious life as an option for himself: though the voice in the essay is public rather than private, the author clearly includes himself as one of those called to the vocation of lay apostle.

The typescript provides some interesting documentation concerning Merton's writing methods at the time. The kinds of corrections he makes suggest that he is composing directly at the typewriter, since he frequently alters his wording as he proceeds. There are about thirty-five instances (not including the occasional typographical errors immediately caught and corrected) when he x-es out words and rewrites on-line directly afterward. Most of these consist of one- or two-word changes and are mainly stylistic: for example, "society" becomes "community"; "come" becomes "penetrate"; "teach" becomes "preach"; "centered" becomes "founded"; "parties" becomes "persons." At times the alteration permits expansion of a thought: where Merton originally wrote ". . . to study books of philosophy or religion," he canceled the last word and then added "speculate about religious questions . . ."; after writing "the prophetic laceration of the lukewarm," he canceled the last two words and continued with "materialistic and lukewarm Catholics . . ."; "could also learn much from them" is canceled and replaced by "would do well to study at least our best philosophers"; the canceled "And there is a better term than good Catholic" is followed by "And a better word for 'good Catholic' is saint, . . ." On occasion, the cancellation is not replaced: contrasting religious and lay vocations, he mentions that those called to priesthood "will have much guidance," and in apparent contrast originally wrote, "We have no other person, generally" and then interlined "mortal" before "person" but canceled all of this and made no further reference to spiritual direction. In one instance, in the opening paragraph, the alteration appears to represent theological reconsideration: ". . . from the moment of his first communion and especially confirmation" is changed to "from the moment of his confirmation, (if not before)," apparently to associate the lay apostolate more specifically (though not exclusively) with the latter sacrament. The evidence of

2. Michael Mott, *The Seven Mountains of Thomas Merton* (Boston: Houghton, Mifflin, 1984) 194, 598. The nucleus of the essay can be found in a Journal passage from August 21, where Merton writes, "Reading Bloy's 'L'Invendable' it is quite clear to me that what he was doing was a kind of 'Lay Apostolate' (a fancy term I don't like much); he had a definite vocation to write what he wrote—nobody knows, or can measure, the tremendous value of his writing, as apostolate. If he only converted one man, it would justify his whole life. But he converted Maritain and a pile of others, and was crucified for how many?" *St. Bonaventure Journal* (unpublished), p. 182.

these revisions suggests a concern for precision but also a process of rethinking as he is composing.

Another set of revisions consists in interlineations above canceled material; many of these changes are relatively inconsequential, such as "no little" for "a lot"; "apostolate" for "apostles"; "his" for "the"; it is impossible to determine at what stage of composition such changes were made. Other alterations of this type seem to represent more significant revising and may have been added after the initial draft was completed. For example, the statement that "social work is inevitably submitted to the control of local parish priests and their bishop" may have sounded too negative on rereading, and "hastens to submit itself" is interlined above the canceled "is inevitably submitted" (though the context still suggests Merton's lack of strong sympathy for the situation described). A number of these changes are to be found in the paragraphs concerning Leon Bloy, and both the frequency and the types of alteration indicate they may have been made together: in a couple of cases the language is toned down: "attacked" becomes "criticised"; "fought by" becomes "looked at askance by"; in another instance, the generalized "souls" is changed to "sad, Godless men"; "foresees" becomes "hopes for" in reference to increased numbers of devout laypeople, an alteration suggesting less certainty about the outcome; the longest such change occurs in the same sentence: "who will offer up all their prayers and works without exception" is substituted for "devoted to works of prayer and penance all offered up," though in this instance the rationale for the revision is less evident.

The essay also provides some insight into Merton's state of mind in the months previous to his decision to become a Cistercian. His degree of commitment to the Christian life is obviously quite deep: the influence of his pivotal conversation in the spring of 1939 with Robert Lax, to be recounted in a famous passage from *The Seven Storey Mountain*,[3] is evident here in his preference for "saint" over "good Catholic" as a description of the dedicated Christian, and in his assurance that "anything we desire, in this realm, we can have, . . ." What the Second Vatican Council would later describe as the universal call to holiness (see especially "The Call of the Whole Church to Holiness," chapter 5 of the Dogmatic Constitution on the Church) is already very much a part of Merton's understanding of the Christian life in 1941. When he writes, "To have a 'lay vocation' means to be impelled, by an insatiable desire to see God, to do acts by which are realised the infinite values that God has implanted in our souls, our personalities," not only does the concluding image foreshadow the opening words of *Seeds of Contemplation*,[4] but the entire

3. Thomas Merton, *The Seven Storey Mountain* (New York: Harcourt, Brace, 1948) 237–38.
4. Thomas Merton, *Seeds of Contemplation* (Norfolk, Conn.: New Directions, 1949) 17.

sentence suggests an intense personal attraction to such vision. But the article also reveals the unsettled state of Merton's mind at the time of writing: "We are still restlessly trying to find out what it is we are called upon to do" is expressed generally, as applying to all those with lay as opposed to priestly vocations, but has the ring of personal experience, as does the conclusion of the same paragraph: "We develop this secret life, because we have to, we need it terribly, we want much more than this. What is there for us?"

He goes on to distinguish between active and contemplative lay vocations, and there is little doubt which is more attractive to him. Though the Friendship House apostolate is praised highly and held up as a model of the active apostolate, there is evident a certain lack of enthusiasm for this life on the writer's part, as when he mentions that the communal aspect of such a life, along with the ecclesiastical control involved, "brings up problems which the contemplative lay apostle need not fear: problems of organisational conflicts, and disappointments that they bring with them, which all add to the trials of this kind of life." Though he hastens to add dutifully that "[e]ach type of lay vocation naturally involves its own difficulties which the zealous servant of God not only expects but even welcomes," the tone here does not suggest someone who is eager to embrace that sort of life. (With hindsight, the reader may note that the problems the author detects with regard to active lay communities are remarkably similar to those he will later encounter in a contemplative monastic community.) Merton seems much more attracted by the example of the lay contemplative, which he finds represented by Jacques Maritain and especially Leon Bloy: the model here is not that of the person who lives an inconspicuous life of prayer in the midst of contemporary secular society, but of one who prophetically confronts by word and example the infidelities of that society and witnesses to a radically different way of life.

Merton's notion of a lay contemplative is clearly one that is compatible with being a writer, in fact virtually presupposes it. The "twofold" function of the lay contemplative vocation is described as "to teach and edify those who have no idea what Christianity is really all about" and to "clarify Christian ideas for Christians themselves who also are always in need of edification and mental stimulation." Though he does subsequently make room for "[h]undreds of other examples" of lay contemplatives who do not write or "teach in big speeches," such as Louis Martin, it is evident that his own leanings are toward a role that is both deeply contemplative and quite public. Thus the essay provides some hint of what direction Thomas Merton's life might have taken had he remained a layperson. But it is not without significance that in the final sentence of the article the Trappists make a brief appearance, an indication that perhaps the author is not completely resigned to life as a layman—though of course he shows no awareness of how much of his conception of the role of the lay contemplative he would bring with him, and fulfill, as a monk who remained very much a writer.

This edition of Merton's hitherto unpublished essay prints only the final version of the typescript; it silently corrects typographical errors, the occasional misspelling, and misspacings, and it regularizes punctuation according to commonly accepted practice. The two substantive changes, "now" for "not" in the sentence beginning "The idea of what a 'lay vocation' can mean . . ." and "to" for "by" in the sentence beginning "Each type of lay vocation . . ." are both required by the sense; in the sentence beginning "The answer will be quite different . . ." the word "we" is added before "possibly." The editor would like to express his gratitude to the staff of the Friedsam Memorial Library of St. Bonaventure University, especially Mrs. Lorraine Welsh, assistant university archivist, for making this article available; to the trustees of the Merton Legacy Trust and their representative, Mrs. Anne H. McCormick, for permission to publish it; and to Grace Davies and Anita Smith, archivists of the Nash Library of Gannon University, for assistance in obtaining information concerning Rev. Richard Fitzgerald.

Vocations to the Lay Apostolate

It may as well be said at once that every Catholic has a vocation to be a lay apostle. The terms are unfortunate in being those big, abstract words that seem essential to all discourse about anything serious in this age of jargon: but what do these words mean? Every Catholic, from the moment of his confirmation, (if not before) becomes, by God's grace, a lay apostle. There is no such thing as being a practicing Catholic and *not* being a lay apostle, to some extent. And further, what does it mean to be a lay apostle? How much can it mean? Everything: the notion rises as high as sanctity, but its starting point is the minimum requirement of Catholic life. Anyone who ever said a prayer, offered up the smallest sacrifice for anybody else, was, at that moment, a lay apostle.

Therefore a discourse on "Vocations to the lay apostolate" will necessarily sound pretty much like a discourse on being a good Catholic. And a better word for "good Catholic" is saint, a term which some people are apparently scared of, out of a totally false delicacy. Is it any more presumptuous to want to be a saint than to want to be a good Catholic? Is it any more difficult to desire? And anything we desire, in this realm, we can have, if we pray for it patiently and humbly. And since this is so, is there any other conclusion to be drawn except that the only reason why we aren't all saints is that most of us never tried to be, never even thought of asking to be.

Everybody who was ever confirmed has been certainly called to the lay apostolate, and actually, so have all the others too, in a less definite and forceful sense: but they are all called to this work.

However to make this classification of "lay Apostle" as broad as this, is to make it a little vague, and it will not be comprehensible until we narrow it down at least to those who are conscious of the responsibility that has come upon them. They have taken up their crosses already, without knowing it: but they are obscurely aware that something has been imposed upon them, and they begin to seek, with a kind of inner craving, to find out what it may be.

Some of them find that they have vocations to the priesthood, then. They are luckier than the rest of us. For them, from now on, everything is definite, is settled for them, they will have much guidance. And as for us? We are still restlessly trying to find out what it is we are called upon to do. We go to mass, go hungrily to the sacraments, and we pray when we can, and we read things that feed our love of God, and we read the lives of people who have loved Him before us. Sometimes we work out some sort of a private religious life for ourselves, with daily Mass, a rosary, or stations of the Cross sometime during the day. Perhaps we attempt some mental prayer, some meditation, every day at a set time. We develop this secret life, because we have to, we need it terribly, we want much more than this. What is there for us?

The men and women who do all these things, or things like them, who pray, or devote themselves no little to others, or love to study books of philosophy or speculate about religious questions, sing religious music, anything, are all of them ready to be made conscious of the meaning of their ''lay apostolate,'' which they have already, without knowing it, been led to begin. Because the lay apostolate is nothing more than the life of one who desires to see God, and wants to know Him. Secretly, they are always saying, in their prayers: ''Show me what I am to do.'' ''Tell me what You want of me.'' ''How do I follow you? What does that mean?''

How can the general words of Christ be reduced to fit our particular cases? The answer will be quite different for each one of us, and it will amount to our doing no more than what we can do, but to do that as well as we possibly can. And how does a Christian do anything well? By giving himself over to the direction of God's infinite will, for only God fulfills and perfects all things, and we ourselves have no strength of our own to turn anything to any real use. The best we can do with our own resources, is to exploit material values, which, however, are not real values. And the values we are called upon to perfect are the moral values in our own personality and in the persons of all we live with.

To have a "lay vocation" means to be impelled, by an insatiable desire to see God, to do acts by which are realised the infinite values that God has implanted in our souls, our personalities. It means to desire not only to become more real and more perfect ourselves, but to help all those around us to realise themselves in good acts and good lives. This, so far, is the same as the priestly vocation, from which it is only distinguished by the fact that this vocation does not involve leaving the world in any special sense (although a lay person can take a vow of chastity or of poverty or of obedience too, there is nothing to stop him); on the contrary, the lay apostle is one who lives outwardly the same life as all the other laymen, no matter how different his life may be, in secret, from theirs. He is subject to all their insecurities, all their worries, and all their ordinary temptations, and he has none of the advantages that a priest has, spiritually. If he wants to lead a religious life, he has to make time for it, and carry it on in the thick of the world's commotions: and no one will grant him any concessions for it. He had best keep most of it secret, or be called not a saint but an idiot. (It is much better to be called an idiot.)

The idea of what a "lay vocation" can mean is now getting a little more precise, and it is time to make an important distinction, which arises here as well as in religious vocations: the distinction between the active and the contemplative life. In lay vocations also, the contemplative is the better vocation ("Maria meliorem partem elegit") but also the rarer. However, there is no purely contemplative "lay vocation," since the layman remains in the world, and such a thing is impossible. His vocation is strictly tied up with all the confusion of a heterogeneous human community. All Christian vocations are to some extent social: even the hermits in the Thebaid had their disciples. The presence of two persons is essential to the virtue of charity. But the lay contemplative vocation is social in the widest sense, almost as wide a sense as the active lay vocation is. The lay vocation necessarily means apostolate, communication, and the one advantage it has over the priesthood is that the layman reaches places in the darkness of our chaotic society where a priest could never penetrate.

The lay apostle has to teach, but it is well to point out that the most effective and the most fundamental way to teach the Christian way of life (because that is what we are to preach: "Christ crucified") is by example rather than by word. Words are essential, but example comes first.

There are no doubt hundreds of enthusiastic Catholics (but not enough even of these) who keep going the interminable arguments about religion that enliven gatherings of men everywhere, always to less purpose than one would think. These arguments are certainly valuable in strengthening the convictions of those who propound them: but the other arguers are much sooner impressed by the example of a person like Catherine de Hueck than by any polite argument handed out by someone in whom they recognise their own colorless and rather unavailing way of life.

Both the contemplative and the active vocation will, then, have a common basis: they will consist in a strong desire to see God, and they will manifest themselves in acts before words: these persons go about, now, so absorbed in their work of pleasing God by the sanctification of themselves and by works to help sanctify others, that, without knowing it, they have kindled a "light which so shines before men that they glorify Our Father Who is in Heaven."

The distinction between the active and contemplative vocation is laid down by the individual's own talents, his abilities, what he already knows how to do, his skills, the way of life, perhaps, which he already follows.

For the great majority of Catholic laymen, the lay vocation means continuing to live whatever life they live, provided it is the exercise of some honest skill, and not something that involves continual sharp-practise at the expense of rivals (as too many businesses do) but in continuing their way of life, these people devote themselves to God, following the familiar lines of Catholic Action laid down in the Encyclicals of Pius XI. The Catholic who lives by some skill he can be proud of, who is a real craftsman, a real producer of good things and not some kind of a drudge connected with a machine or an office, a unit in a money making organisation, that Catholic is a rare man, and one of unusual good fortune, because he possesses a talent which he can devote entirely to God.

Most of us have jobs which can only be offered up to God as a kind of penance. For us it is necessary to divide our lives between the purgatory of our servile work and the things we really want to do. Like the people of the world who run from the office to their various methods of deadening all thought of the office, we too go now to some other occupation, and try, in it, to make up for not having served God the rest of the day. We teach a little Catechism. We go out street-speaking perhaps. Or perhaps we only make some kind of compromise between serving God and amusing ourselves: we organise dances and basketball games in the Parish Hall. It all has something more or less remote to do with the lay apostolate, and the active lay apostolate.

What the active lay vocation means in its full sense is now being made clear to many Catholics by the work and influence of Catherine de Hueck, for example, and those who have offered themselves to share the life of voluntary poverty and works of mercy at the Friendship Houses of Harlem and the slums of Toronto. For these workers, the lay apostolate is based on an elementary form of community life, centered upon daily mass and communion, living together in poverty, working together, and reciting compline together in the evening. The whole of the life is work, and there is only a minimum of prayer attached to it, because Baroness de Hueck deliberately and jealously guards her communities from becoming in any way unlaicised, and turning into communities of religious sisters and brothers, instead of plain lay-people. This communal aspect that can be taken by the active lay vocation, together with the fact that social work hastens to submit itself to the control of local parish priests and their bishop, brings up problems which the contemplative lay apostle need not fear: problems of organisational conflicts, and disappointments that they bring with them, which all add to the trials of this kind of life. Each type of lay vocation naturally involves its own difficulties which the zealous servant of God not only expects but even welcomes, so strong is his desire to please Christ in all the opportunities he sends them, of work or of trials.

As opposed to the active lay apostolate, the contemplative lay vocation is exemplified quite clearly by a man like Jacques Maritain, and even more clearly by the life of the man who in his lifetime converted Maritain: Leon Bloy.

Leon Bloy, too little known in this continent, is one of the most interesting figures in French literature of the turn of the century and the time of the First War.

He was fortunate in having a real skill he could devote to God, Whom he served all his life, in poverty, with an impassioned and apocalyptic eloquence. Now that Bloy is dead, the many Journals and letters into which he poured most of his intense creative effort, show clearly to any one who sees the man's whole life in perspective, how his vocation worked itself out, and how the Providence of God was using Leon Bloy for the salvation of sad, Godless men and the prophetic laceration of materialistic and lukewarm Catholics in France and everywhere else.

Bloy's vocation as a lay apostle was founded on one principal source of inspiration: the Apparition of the Blessed Virgin at La Salette, in which were made certain prophecies, since most horribly fulfilled (like the Fall of France), accompanied by the most clear and unequivocal warnings that were, Bloy always contended, suppressed by interested persons. In any case, even those parts of the warnings of La Salette which all the world knew were significant and important enough in themselves, and Bloy starts out from them to repeat over and over again his accusations against those Catholics who had forgotten the Doctrine of the Mystical Body of Christ, and had come to live as if the Church were synonymous and coextensive with the Middle Class, and the ideals of Christian Charity were only another, less clear way of expressing the virtues of commercialism. Bloy's life was a life of great poverty and suffering, a suffering increased, for him, by the fact that it had to be shared by his wife and children. His whole career was a long succession of malevolent attacks by not only those of the Catholic bourgeoisie who took offense at his indictment of their pious self-indulgences, but those of the radical and atheistic groups which he criticised with even less mercy.

Yet Bloy refused to write anything but what he knew; he had to write about what he believed. He consistently turned down opportunities of money-making assignments in order to write journals and pamphlets which always somehow found a publisher but never made any money. Curiously, though, his writings always seemed to fall into the hands of those who most needed them, and Bloy led into the church many remarkable souls, not the least of them being Jacques and Raissa Maritain.

Bloy, again, and his whole family, based their whole lives on daily communion at a time when, in spite of the fact that the Popes were trying to get this practise universally accepted, it was still looked at askance by inexplicable prejudice on the part not only of laypeople but even certain of the clergy. Bloy's life was one of poverty and of begging and of writing for God and not for money. It also included a considerable amount of prayer and meditation. Perhaps Bloy even read the Divine Office, or the Little Office, anyway, each day. In any case, speaking of the lay vocation, in this more contemplative sense, he hopes for a time when there will be many laymen who will offer up all their prayers and works without exception to the Mother of Sorrows for the souls in Purgatory and for the conversion of sinners, and who will, among other things, read the Divine Office from day to day.

The function of the contemplative lay vocation of Catholics is twofold: besides the fact that this Catholic must also first of all be, by his devoted service of God in prayers and merciful works, a light shining before men, his actual teaching will take one of two directions, and perhaps both. On one hand, it will tend to teach and edify those who have no idea what Christianity is really all about; on the other hand it will clarify Christian ideas for Christians themselves who also are always in need of edification and mental stimulation.

The work done by two good philosophers, like Maritain and Gilson—men who are read and respected by non-Catholic philosophers perhaps even more than they are appreciated by ordinary educated Catholics (who nevertheless could learn much from them)—is an example of valuable and far reaching Catholic Action. This applies also to the work and art criticism of Eric Gill, to the historical studies of Christopher Dawson, to the novels of Graham Greene (to a minor extent), which all are especially good kinds of Catholic Action because they reach out beyond the boundaries of Catholicism and spread Christian ideas where our conventional writers and the thinkers more popular within our ranks cannot make them reach: that is, among the intellectuals outside. We too, inside the limits of what is too often merely a Catholicism in the cultural sense, would do well to study at least our best philosophers.

Hundreds of other examples of this type of lay vocation can be named, including great numbers who had nothing to write or nothing to teach in big speeches: yet consider Louis Martin, who was a most saintly man, and will certainly someday be canonised, who lived a holy retired life himself, which he entirely devoted to shaping the souls of his daughters to an even more perfect love of God than his own. He was the father of St. Therese of Lisieux whose own ''little way'' to sanctity forms a perfect and simple and intelligible foundation for the life of any lay apostle, since its essence is the perfection of spiritual childhood, of humility, that consists in submitting every part of our life entirely to God, and thereafter refusing Him nothing, not even the *smallest* sacrifice we can give Him: and none is too small to please Him.

   The world today can only be saved by saints, and every one of us should be praying daily to God to give us an army of them to help us. Jacques Maritain has said, somewhere, where he thinks these saints will appear: first, in the strict contemplative orders, but second, and perhaps more important, among the poorest of the laity: in other words, in the slums, in the concentration camps, on the forced labour gangs, in the bomb shelters, in the Harlems of our "civilization." And when they do come it will be because there were Catherine de Huecks and Leon Bloys among them, and it will be because of the prayers of Trappists and Poor Clares, not excluding the unnoticed, but not to be despised, prayers and works of those countless priests and laymen whose unhappy privilege it is to be members of the vast and unheroic and profoundly mediocre middle class.

The Dangers of Solitude*

Patrick Eastman

Growing up in England, and I refuse to say how many years ago, I remember a particular candy that we loved. I think it was called a "canon-ball," but essentially it was a sphere about the size of a marble, which, when sucked, would gradually release a fizzy fruit-flavored sherbet into one's mouth. However, if one bit into it there was a sudden release tantamount to an explosion in one's mouth frequently beyond containment, so that the frothing juice flowed down one's chin. An innocent looking candy with an explosive effect! In Thomas Merton's essay "Notes for a Philosophy of Solitude" I would suggest we have something similar. An innocent looking piece, but as one bites into it one becomes aware of its explosive content.

My reflections here are to address the dangers of solitude, and I begin by indicating what I hope to achieve and how I intend to pro-

* The five papers that constitute the following section are revisions of presentations made at the Third General Meeting of the International Thomas Merton Society at Colorado College, June 8–10, 1993. One of the principal speakers for that meeting was William H. Shannon, who used Merton's essay "Notes for a Philosophy of Solitude" as the basis for his major address about that subject. An expanded version of that speech appears in *Cisterian Studies Quarterly*.

Various speakers prepared responses to Shannon's paper. Two of those responses have been revised for publication here. These essays, by David Belcastro and Patrick Eastman, demonstrate that Merton's thinking about the need for solitude stimulated discussion along a wide range of issues. Interestingly, within the context of needed balance between contemplative withdrawal and involvement in (and for) a wider world, Shannon, and his respondents, stressed that solitude should never be only for the solitary self. Paradoxically, solitude is always a means of building connections with, and for, others.

ceed. First let me say that I do not intend to present a detailed analysis of Merton's essay. I wish rather to indicate how Merton's article stands firmly within the Christian tradition, not merely for monks but in a sense within the spirituality of all people. (Parenthetically it can also be noted that the vocation to solitude is a universal call and is clearly not restricted to monks or to the Christian tradition.) I shall say something about the Christian spiritual tradition and the way Merton's article can be located within it, and then I hope to show how we are called to embrace this essential feature of spirituality with all its inherent danger.

It is well known that Merton frequently had trouble with the censors, and this was no exception. There are two issues that arise out of that controversy, which are pertinent to our discussion here. First, there is the tension between the eremitic and the cenobitic lifestyles. This is an age-old issue that goes back to some of the earliest times in the Christian Church. The eremitic life is recorded positively for us in Athanasius' account of the life of Antony and the cenobitic life is given its ratification from the *koinōnia* of Pachomius. The two different lifestyles are portrayed as prime examples of the way to engage in the spiritual journey. Both are seen as a refining process, but through Evagrius' writing in the fourth century and copied into the writings of John Cassian in the fifth the tension continues, giving way ultimately to an underlying acceptance of the superiority of the solitary life. Basil, on the other hand, clearly favors the cenobitic tradition. Each of these aforementioned great writers have, as you may well know, influenced St. Benedict, and to a certain extent the tension is still there in his Rule, but the shift from Cassian is that within the tension it is the cenobitic life that now claims priority. The Cistercian reform of Benedictine monastic life of the twelfth century was an attempt to once again affirm the value of a desert spirituality, most explicitly expressed by the solitary life. The initial reform and the subsequent reform of LaTrappe endeavored to establish an eremitical element to the life within the context of community. I believe the problems the censors had with the text under examination here reflects clearly the tension between the communal and solitary life, which has been there throughout the history of Christian spirituality.

I mentioned earlier that there are two issues that I perceive raised in this censor problem. The second one seems to be that of power and control. And in this I think we are led right to the explosive heart of the article. This is precisely where the danger lies. Notice here that I have used the singular because I see not "dangers" in the solitary life so much as a single danger, which can manifest itself in all sorts of ways. The danger is portrayed in the *Life of Antony,* to which I have already referred; it was there for Merton as it is there for contemporary hermits or indeed for us all. Apart from a short stay in a hermitage a few years ago I have had no personal experience of the solitary life. Even that short immersion was very demanding and can be typified as a time of real struggle rather than a nice rest with some peace and quiet. But without any real experience myself, I asked three people who live as hermits today what their thoughts were on the dangers of solitude. Out of their remarkably varied experience there emerged one central danger under which all the other items could be subsumed. The real danger is the carrying of one's ego-centeredness into the solitude. This could manifest itself in terms of moving away from a Christ-centeredness, or an overwhelming abhorrence of one's sinfulness with an inordinate desire for penance or a constant concern about one's contribution to community and society.

I want now to take us behind this danger of ego-centeredness to ascertain its provenance. In order to do this we need to look at Scripture. If we examine the creation stories in Genesis carefully we notice the temptation to which Adam and Eve, as representatives of all humanity, surrender. They are tempted to be "like God," in other words to be a "self-creation" rather than a creature. We might say that this ego-self claims an illegitimate autonomy rather than existing as a true self under the authority of and in union with the creator God. But this ego-centered self, or perhaps we can use Merton's term of the "false self," has no real identity. It is nothing more than an illusion. So how, one might ask, does this false self establish its identity? I think we can get some answer to this if we look at the gospel account of Jesus' own first solitary experience. After his baptism we read that the Holy Spirit leads Jesus out into the wilderness. It may be worth noting here that Jesus is led by the Holy Spirit, and that the call to the solitary life throughout the ages is always God's initiative. Indeed, we must never forget that the ONLY authentic orientation in the spiritual journey is where God initiates and the human person responds.

We also do well to remember the place of the wilderness in the Hebrew Bible. As Dianne Bergant pointed out in a recent article in *The Bible Today,* "It is clear from the way the wilderness is depicted in the

Bible that it was a place to be feared rather than treasured."[1] The desert, while being a place of encounter with God, also represents the place of radical dependence upon God rather than on self. It is the place of the demons that can only be overcome by a surrender to God. It is, in other words, a dangerous place to be. So solitude, as experienced in the desert, is even recognized in our Sacred Scriptures as being dangerous. If we proceed with our examination of the pericope on Jesus' experience in this dangerous wilderness we hear that he is tempted three times. Now I personally think there is more to these three temptations than it being just a nice story about the way Satan tempted Jesus. Is there not something of a universal paradigm here with the story conveying something fundamental to the whole human condition? Let us look at the three temptations again. First, Jesus is tempted to turn stones into bread. Does bread here represent security or possessions? The second temptation is to jump off the Temple roof and win the esteem of all the people through such an impressive show. The third temptation is to worship Satan in order to gain power and control. So the temptations are to possessions, prestige, and power. None of these things are bad in themselves but only become a problem when they become compulsive and are used to give identity to this false self. The false self usurps the energy associated with possessions, power, and prestige to create identity from what it has or does as a separate entity.

The distractions to which Merton refers in his notes on solitude surely emanate from this ego-centeredness struggling to create an illusion of its own existence apart from God. One of the greatest yet almost totally unrecognized spiritual writers of the fourth century was Evagrius Ponticus. Drawing from the philosophical tradition of theology that he learned from Origen and from his own experience in the Egyptian desert, he demonstrates how these three energy centers manifest themselves in eight harmful thoughts (these are the basis of what eventually emerge through Thomas Aquinas as the seven deadly sins). Evagrius lists them as Pride, Avarice, Impurity, Vainglory, Gluttony, Anger, Sadness, and Acedia. John Cassian takes over the ideas of Evagrius, and through him they enter into the whole Western monastic tradition. Now the way to overcome these thoughts that emerge

---

1. Dianne Bergant, C.S.A., "The Desert in Biblical Tradition," *The Bible Today*, vol. 31, no. 3 (May 1993) 138.

into the consciousness, says Evagrius, is through *lectio divina,* recitation of the psalms and the pure prayer of silence in stillness. Here the Christian West is linked to the Hesychast tradition of Eastern Christendom, and both traditions demand a silence, stillness, and solitude for the exigencies of the ego-centered false self to be diminished. So we may say that the distractions and the dangers to which Merton refers relate to the eight harmful thoughts of Evagrius and the struggles of Antony with his demons, so colorfully described by Athanasius. We may also say that there is a link here with the non-Christian East's awareness of the dangers of dualism. The Ego-self makes a determined effort to establish a separate identity, so a nondualism can only be effected when the ego-centeredness of the self is removed. Is nondualism part of the Christian tradition? Surely it is, and the task can only be complete when, with Jesus, the practitioner can say, "The Father and I are one," or with St. Paul, "It is no longer I who live but Christ who lives within me." Clearly the call to solitude is a call to give consent to divine action within us and to actively cooperate with the transforming of our innermost being.

So, if the refining process of solitude is so essential wherein lie the dangers? I think we can see how easy it would be in a very perverse way for this ego- or I-maker to take over the whole project. The enterprise is flawed from the beginning because the venture into solitude becomes nothing more than an ego-trip. The ego remains firmly in control, and whether the solitude lasts for a matter of minutes carved out of a busy day or in the monastic cell or in a hermitage, the false self is fully yet deceptively in charge. T. S. Eliot gives us commentary on this in the poem "East Coker":

> I said to my soul, be still, and wait without hope
> For hope would be hope for the wrong thing; wait without love
> For love would be love of the wrong thing; there is yet faith
> But the faith and the love and the hope are all in the waiting.
> Wait without thought, for you are not ready for thought:
> So the darkness shall be the light, and the stillness the dancing.[2]

When the ego still reigns supreme even if the call to the solitary life is authentically from God, then the danger begins in a rugged in-

2. T. S. Eliot, "East Coker," *T. S. Eliot: The Complete Poems and Plays, 1909–1950* (London: Harcourt Brace Jovanovich, 1971) 126.

dividualism that so marks our culture. It is true that there can be no contemplation without asceticism, but in this case the asceticism is a self-controlled discipline rather than a self-surrender to the refining power of God.

The dangers that caused concern for Merton's censors, I think, lie in this area of control. Merton's article challenged their own addictive attachment to power and control. Merton, in Asia during the last weeks of his life, remarks that the time has come for us all to stand on our own two feet. He points out that we can no longer rely on the institutions to do that which we need to do ourselves. We have to take responsibility for our own lives. Now the danger is that the ego-centered self usurps control, in which case little or no progress has been made. Of course, the other side is that those who have the control in the institution become very threatened when their power is taken away. It seems to me that there is a sense in which we all have to stand alone, we have to be responsible for our own lives as creatures surrendered to the creator God. Again, in words of T. S. Eliot:

> Descend lower, descend only
> Into the world of perpetual solitude,
> World not world, but that which is not world,
> Internal darkness, deprivation
> And destitution of all property,
> Desiccation of the world of sense,
> Evacuation of the world of fancy.[3]

The dynamic of this movement toward personal responsibility is, we are told, part of the process of human maturation. We move on our life's journey from a reliance on the institution or society to give us our identity to an acceptance of who we are as created by God. Someone recently remarked that they thought one could make an analogy between the Church as the body of Christ and an individual human person's development, with each hundred years of the Church being one year in a human life. So the Church's development in human terms is that of a twenty year old. A somewhat speculative thought maybe, but as part of the body we have the responsibility not only for the fruits of genuine solitude to be effected in our own lives but in the life of all creation. There is the danger that the desire for solitude is nothing

---

3. Eliot, "Burnt Notion," *The Complete Poems and Plays,* 120.

more than a flight from our place within society. False contemplation, false solitude, is an avoidance of others, whereas a genuine contemplation or solitude leads us to a deeper solidarity with others. As Merton remarks in the introduction to the Japanese edition of *The Seven Storey Mountain*, "the monastery [we could put solitude here] is not an escape from the world. On the contrary, by being in the monastery I take my true part in all the struggles and sufferings of the world."[4] In other words, it is an immersion into the concerns of creation at a different level, away from the illusions of those solutions that really only serve to bring an even deeper alienation from God.

So what of this for us? The solitude expressed in the word "monk" is not for a select few, but the monk, as Raimundo Panikkar points out, is a universal archetype. Whatever the inherent dangers, we cannot avoid facing them because the dangers are not to be avoided—nor can they be avoided. The dangers as I have suggested them are an integral part of the whole process of our engagement with the paschal mystery that will bring about union with God.

And it is the purity of the intention that counts. We are all called to solitude in one way or another, and we have to face it at our death whether we like it or not. Against our ego-self we must remember that it is not a matter of our achievement of a hoped-for end. As Eliot writes in "East Coker":

> And do not think of the fruit of the action . . .
> For us there is only the trying.
> The rest is not our business.

When we allow it to be something other than a self-seeking achievement or lifestyle, then the inevitable and essential dangers become the very stuff that God uses in that process of inner transformation that takes place beyond our human knowing or striving.

4. Thomas Merton, *Introductions East & West: The Foreign Prefaces of Thomas Merton*, ed. Robert E. Daggy (Greensboro: Unicorn, 1981) 45.

Czeslaw Milosz's Influence on Thomas Merton's "Notes for a Philosophy of Solitude"

David Belcastro

Preceding and coinciding with his work on "Notes for a Philosophy of Solitude," Thomas Merton focused much of his attention on issues raised for him by Czeslaw Milosz. Consequently, I believe it is within the context of this relationship that we may best understand the ideas presented in this work, in particular, Merton's ideas with regard to the dangers of solitude. After a brief review of those ideas and William Shannon's recent organization of those ideas, I will suggest a way in which we can further our understanding of Merton's philosophy of solitude.

Near the beginning of the article, Merton lists some of the dangers related to the life of solitude:

> Nor do I promise to cheer anybody up with optimistic answers to all the sordid difficulties and uncertainties which attend the life of interior solitude. Perhaps in the course of these reflections, some of the difficulties will be mentioned. The first of them has to be taken note of from the very start: the disconcerting task of facing and accepting one's own absurdity. The anguish of realizing that underneath the apparently logical pattern of a more or less "well organized" and rational life, there lies an abyss of irrationality, confusion, pointlessness, and indeed apparent chaos. This is what immediately impresses itself upon the man who has renounced diversion. It cannot be otherwise: for in renouncing diversion, he renounces the seemingly harmless pleasure of building a tight, self-contained illusion about himself and about his little world. He

accepts the difficulty of facing the million things in his life which are incomprehensible, instead of simply ignoring them. Incidentally it is only when the apparent absurdity of life is faced in all truth that faith really becomes possible. Otherwise, faith tends to be a kind of diversion, a spiritual amusement, in which one gathers up accepted, conventional formulas and arranges them in the approved mental patterns, without bothering to investigate their meaning, or asking if they have any practical consequences in one's life.[1]

While Merton specifically notes the first danger, he also mentions a second without designating it as such. The first is "the disconcerting task of facing and accepting one's own absurdity." The second is making faith "a kind of diversion, a spiritual amusement."

The third danger is noted several sections later:

The true solitary is not one who simply withdraws from society. Mere withdrawal, regressions, leads to a sick solitude, without meaning and without fruit.[2]

This "sick solitude" is characterized by Merton as "the substitution of idols and illusions of his own choosing for those chosen by society."[3] Consequently, it is not solitude in the truest sense of the word. This is the danger noted in section two under the title, "In the Sea of Perils."

There is no need to say that the call of solitude (even though only interior) is perilous. Everyone who knows what solitude means is aware of this. The essence of the solitary vocation is precisely the anguish of an almost infinite risk. Only the false solitary sees no danger in solitude. But his solitude is imaginary, that is to say built around an image. It is merely a social image stripped of its explicitly social elements. The false solitary is one who is able to imagine himself without companions while in reality he remains just as dependent on society as before—if not more dependent. He needs society as a ventriloquist needs a dummy. He projects his own voice to the group and it comes back to him admiring, approving, opposing or at least adverting to his own separateness.

1. Thomas Merton, "Notes for a Philosophy of Solitude," in *Disputed Questions* (New York: Farrar, Straus, and Cudahy, 1960) 179–80.
2. Ibid., 181–82.
3. Ibid., 184.

Even if society seems to condemn him, this pleases and diverts him for it is nothing but the sound of his own voice, reminding him of his separateness, which is his own chosen diversion.[4]

The fourth danger is another subtle form of diversion:

The solitary condition also has its jargon and its conventions: these too are pitiful. There is no point in consoling one who has awakened to his solitude by teaching him to defile his emptiness with rationalizations. Solitude must not become a diversion to itself by too much self-justification.[5]

The fifth and final danger is present in the relation between the solitary vocation and social protests:

And if there is an element of protest in the solitary vocation, that element must be a matter of rigorous spirituality. It must be deep and interior, and intimately personal, so that the solitary is one who is critical, first of all, of himself. Otherwise he will divert himself with a fiction worse than that of all the others, becoming a more insane and self-opinionated liar than the worst of them, cheating no one more than himself.[6]

Briefly restated, there are five dangers noted by Merton: facing and accepting one's own absurdity; making faith into an amusing diversion; withdrawing into illusions of one's individuality; justifying one's solitude with rationalizations; and rebelling against society from the false position of self-righteousness. It should be noted that two, three, four, and five are all diversions from the first. We will recall this point later.

Shannon found this second section of Merton's article on the dangers of solitude "a mixed bag—with plenty of wonderfully quotable sentences, but at the same time somewhat wandering and repetitious."[7] He sorts out this "mixed bag" by gathering the dangers into one of three categories; three different yet related categories he appears to believe to be the substance of this section.

4. Ibid., 185–86.
5. Ibid., 189–90.
6. Ibid., 194.
7. William H. Shannon, "Reflections on Thomas Merton's Article: 'Notes for a Philosophy of Solitude,' " paper presented at the International Thomas Merton Society's Third General Meeting, Colorado College, June 11, 1993.

First, he compares and contrasts, as Merton does, true and false solitude. True solitude, unlike false solitude, does not renounce anything that is basic and human, separating oneself from society, but rather seeks solidarity with humanity at a deeper level. Then, he considers true solitude as the occasion for "taking responsibility for one's own inner life as a way into the mystery of God." That is to say, it is in solitude that one refuses to substitute the words, slogans, and concepts offered by Church and society for one's authentic experience. Last, he explains Merton's understanding of solitude as a form of social witnessing. The "hermit" has an important function to perform in society. He/she is a solitary witness to the primacy of the spiritual and mystical dimension of life, society, and the Church.

Seen in this way, the dangers of solitude listed here are understood essentially as those things that may lead the solitary person away from solidarity with humankind, an authentic religious experience of his or her own, and the responsibility of bearing witness to spiritual dimension. Any of these "movements away" will result in solitude that is an illusion and, consequently, destructive.

While I find Shannon's organization of Merton's "mixed bag of wonderfully quotable sentences" to be reasonable, accurate, and insightful, I believe there is a deeper dimension of this work yet to be explored and articulated. The way to that dimension is found in Merton's correspondence with Milosz.

On December 6, 1958, Merton, in a letter to Milosz, wrote:

> It seems to me that, as you pointed out, and as others like yourself say or imply (Camus, Koestler, etc.) there has to be a third position, a position of integrity, which refuses subjection to the pressures of two massive groups ranged against each other in the world. It is quite simply obvious that the future, in plain dialectical terms, rests with those of us who risk our heads and necks and everything in the difficult, fantastic job of finding out the new position, the ever changing and moving "line" that is no line at all because it cannot be traced out by political dogmatists. And that is the difficulty, and the challenge.[8]

This letter begins a correspondence between Merton and Milosz that extended from 1958 to 1968 and consisted of twenty-six letters; eight-

8. Thomas Merton, *The Courage for Truth: Letters to Writers,* ed. Christine M. Bochen (New York: Farrar, Straus, and Giroux, 1993) 54.

een from Milosz and eight from Merton. Michael Mott believes this correspondence was the "most vital exchange" of the early sixties, pointing out that each correspondent had acknowledged the importance of the exchange and the seriousness of the tasks to which they had committed themselves.[9]

The correspondence was initiated by Merton's reading of Milosz's book *The Captive Mind*. Written during 1951/52 in Paris when French intellectuals were seriously looking at Stalin's communist Russia as a vision of the new world order, Milosz focused his attention on the vulnerability of the twentieth-century mind to seduction by socio-political doctrines and its readiness to accept totalitarian terror for the sake of a hypothetical future.[10] The book explores the cause of this vulnerability and finds it in the modern world's longing for any, even the most illusory, certainty. This longing for certainty is understood in the context of a world torn by a great dispute; a world where people have come to believe that they must conform to one or the other of the systems advocated by the participants in the debate; systems that were equally, though differently, totalitarian. Milosz's book is a search for the third position, a position of integrity for the individual who longs for a place to stand in the modern world. Writing about this search in another publication, *Native Realm*, Milosz makes a statement quite similar to one we will later consider by Merton from *Conjectures of a Guilty Bystander*:

> Nothing could stifle my inner certainty that a shining point exists where all lines intersect. If I negated it I would lose my ability to concentrate, and things as well as aspirations would turn to dust. This certainty also involved my relationship to that point. I felt very strongly that nothing depended on my will, that anything I might accomplish in life would not be won by my own efforts but given as a gift. Time opened out before me like a fog. If I was worthy enough I would penetrate it, and then I would understand.[11]

Merton responded to *The Captive Mind* with enthusiasm. His first letter to Milosz stated his intention to join with the Polish writer and

9. Michael Mott, *The Seven Mountains of Thomas Merton* (Boston: Houghton Mifflin, 1984) 354.

10. Czeslaw Milosz, *The Captive Mind* (New York: Vintage Books, 1981) v.

11. Czeslaw Milosz, *Native Realm: A Search for Self-Definition* (Berkeley and Los Angeles: University of California Press, 1981) 87.

others in the difficult and challenging task of finding the new position, "risking heads and necks and everything" in doing so. We see
the commitment to the third position articulated by Merton over and
over again. For example, in a letter to Filberto Guala dated March 20,
1968:

> My intention was to bear witness to a common ground—a kind
> of existential searching which is implicit in the "experience" of
> struggle in which all modern men, believers included, must "ex-
> amine" the integrity of their own motives for believing (as opposed
> to the apologetic and reasonable conscious motives). Is our "faith"
> really in "good faith" or is it an evasion, a falsification of ex-
> perience?[12]

This search for the third position contributed significantly to the shaping of Merton's understanding of his vocation. With time, we see the
merging of the solitary life with the third position and political protest. For example, in his preface to the 1963 Japanese edition of *The
Seven Storey Mountain,* we read:

> It is my intention to make my entire life a rejection of, a protest
> against the crimes and injustices of war and political tyranny which
> threaten to destroy the whole race of man and the world with him.
> By my monastic life and vows I am saying NO to all the concen-
> tration camps. . . . I make monastic silence a protest against the
> lies of politicians, propagandists and agitators, and when I speak
> it is to deny that my faith and my Church can ever seriously be
> aligned with these forces of injustice and destruction.[13]

This statement is of interest because it not only indicates the coming
together of the solitary life with the third position and political protest
but also is a reminder of one of the dangers of solitude noted by Merton
in his essay:

> And if there is an element of protest in the solitary vocation, that
> element must be a matter of rigorous spirituality. It must be deep
> and interior, and intimately personal, so that the solitary is one
> who is critical, first of all, of himself. Otherwise he will divert him-

12. Thomas Merton, *The School of Charity: Letters,* ed. Patrick Hart (New York:
Farrar, Straus, and Giroux, 1990) 372.
13. Thomas Merton, *Introductions East & West: The Foreign Prefaces of Thomas
Merton,* ed. Robert Daggy (Greensboro: Unicorn, 1981) 45–46.

self with a fiction worse than that of all the others, becoming a more insane and self-opinionated liar than the worst of them, cheating no one more than himself. Solitude is not for rebels like this, and it promptly rejects them. The desert is for those who have felt a salutary despair of conventional and fictitious values, in order to hope in mercy and to be themselves merciful men to whom that mercy is promised. Such solitaries know the evils that are in other men because they experience these evils first of all in themselves.[14]

I believe that Milosz played an important role in shaping Merton's awareness and understanding of the danger of political protest to one's interior life. In the third chapter of *The Captive Mind*, Milosz described a particular kind of intellectual emerging in Eastern Europe:

In short, Ketman means self-realization against something. He who practices Ketman suffers because of the obstacles he meets; but if these obstacles were suddenly to be removed, he would find himself in a void which might perhaps prove much more painful. Internal revolt is sometimes essential to spiritual health, and can create a particular form of happiness. . . . For most people the necessity of living in constant tension and watchfulness is a torture, but many intellectuals accept this necessity with masochistic pleasure.[15]

And, in a letter to Merton, Milosz questions Merton's involvement in political activities:

Yet I asked myself why you feel such an itch for activity? Is that so that you are unsatisfied with your having plunged too deep in contemplation and now wish to compensate through growing another wing, so to say? And peace provides you with the only link with American young intellectuals outside? Yet activity to which you are called is perhaps different. Should you become a belated rebel, out of solidarity with rebels without cause?[16]

Through his book and their correspondence, Milosz became Merton's guide in the search for the third position. Because Milosz saw the Church as the last stronghold of opposition against totalitarianism

14. Merton, "Notes for a Philosophy of Solitude," 194.
15. Milosz, *Captive Mind*, 80.
16. Czeslaw Milosz, Poland, to Thomas Merton, Gethsemani, March 14, 1962, Thomas Merton Archive, Bellarmine College, Louisville, Kentucky.

and looked to the outer fringes of the Church to lead the resistance, he accepted the opportunity to work with Merton, believing that Merton's books could have some influence. But he was of the opinion that Merton would have to change a few things. His advice for Merton was threefold: address the problem of evil (he thought Merton's writings had seriously neglected the harsh realities of this world and, consequently, appeared naive and innocent); write literary essays; and read Camus.

Milosz's advice is understandable with regard to reading Camus. Camus had established himself as the "conscience of his generation." His essay "Neither Victims nor Executioners," published in 1946, placed him at the forefront of writers working on finding a third position:

> Thus we all know, without the shadow of doubt, that the new order
> we are seeking cannot be merely national or even confidential, and
> especially not Western or Eastern. It must be universal.[17]

Merton did exactly as advised. His work on the third position consisted of reading Camus, writing essays on Camus' literary work, and addressing in those essays the difficult issues of the modern world.

Beginning in 1958 and continuing for the next ten years, there are numerous references to Camus in Merton's letters, journals, and notebooks. During this period of time Merton came to the conclusion that Camus was "the greatest writer of our times."[18] Furthermore, even though Camus was clearly a secular critic of religion in general and the Church in particular, Merton recognized in him the development of an asceticism and contemplative life that was very much in line with monastic tradition—so much so that he included Camus in his hermitage library, referring to him as an "Algerian cenobite."[19] More important to our present interest is a statement made by Merton during the summer of 1966 in *A Midsummer Diary* regarding his experience of reading Camus:

> I am reading Camus on absurdity and suicide: *The Myth of Sisyphus.*
> I had tried it before and was not ready for it because of the de-

17. Albert Camus, *Neither Victims nor Executioners*, trans. Dwight MacDonald (Philadelphia: New Society, 1986) 42.

18. Mott, *Seven Mountains of Thomas Merton*, 430.

19. Thomas Merton, "Day of a Stranger," *The Hudson Review* XX.2 (Summer 1967) 212.

structive forces in myself. Now I can read it, because I no longer
fear them, as I no longer fear the ardent and loving forces in
myself.[20]

Here is a record of Merton's encounter with the absurd: the metaphysical void we experience when we become aware of ourselves as strangers
in our own universe—strangers without origin, destiny, or meaning.
This is, as you may recall, the first danger of the solitary life mentioned
in "Notes for a Philosophy of Solitude." It is also the primary concern of Camus' thought and writings. It is Milosz via Camus who
brought Merton to this place. And it is from this place that Merton
sets out in his literary essays on Camus to discover the third position.

It was not until August of 1966 that Merton wrote his first essay
on Camus. His last essay would be completed nineteen months later.
During the interim months he would write five more essays. In these
essays we find issues, all related, directly and indirectly, to the search
for the third position. Furthermore, there is a pattern in all of the essays
that is characteristic of Merton's response to Camus. And I believe it
is this pattern that reflects a movement from the absurd to the third
position.

First, there is an indication of respect for Camus as a person and
writer. Commenting on *The Plague* Merton writes, "It is a precise, well-
built, inexorable piece of reflection."[21] Second, there is acceptance of
Camus' message in general and approval of his ideas in particular. So
he writes, "I can accept Camus' ideas of nobility and certainly agree
with him. . . ."[22] This acceptance, however, is seldom without reservation. Consequently there is a third part to the pattern, the critical
part where Merton indicates that in his opinion Camus is fine as far
as he goes but he needs to go further. Commenting on Meursault in
Camus' *The Stranger*, Merton asked whether Meursault's choice justified him, that is, whether his acceptance of poverty was a spiritual
enrichment, his admission of absurdity a final somersault into sense,
and his refusal to justify himself in some sense a justification. While
Merton indicated that he was aware that the cliché interpretation of

---

20. Thomas Merton, "A Midsummer Diary," 2: quoted in Mott, *Seven Mountains of Thomas Merton*, 451.
21. Thomas Merton, *A Vow of Conversation: Journals, 1964–1965*, ed. Naomi
Burton Stone (New York: Farrar, Straus, and Giroux, 1988) 71.
22. Ibid.

The Stranger assumed that it did, he was of the opinion that Meursault remained in his poverty, unable to integrate himself completely by compassion and solidarity with others who, like himself, were poor.[23] Merton inevitably comes to this place in his essays on Camus. Accepting Camus as far as Camus goes, that is, the absurd, Merton then goes on to mention another place, a place beyond the absurd where one's solitude becomes solidarity with humankind.

As we have seen, Merton, from 1958 through 1968, was interested in finding a third position, and this search was greatly influenced by Milosz and Camus. I believe that this third position is the solitary life described by Merton in "Notes for a Philosophy of Solitude." This becomes apparent when the two are compared. For example, in Merton's summary statement of the solitary life in "Notes for a Philosophy of Solitude" we find:

> I do not pretend, in these pages to establish a clear formula for discerning solitary vocations. But this much needs to be said: that one who is called to solitude is not called merely to imagine himself solitary, to live as if he were solitary, to cultivate the illusion that he is different, withdrawn and elevated. He is called to emptiness. And in this emptiness he does not find points upon which to base a contrast between himself and others. On the contrary, he realizes, though perhaps confusedly, that he has entered into a solitude that is really shared by everyone. It is not that he is solitary while everybody else is social: but that everyone is solitary, in a solitude masked by that symbolism which they use to cheat and counteract their solitariness. What the solitary renounces is not his union with other men, but rather the deceptive fictions and inadequate symbols which tend to take the place of genuine social unity—to produce a facade of apparent unity without really uniting men on a deep level. . . . Even though he may be physically alone the solitary remains united to others and lives in profound solidarity with them, but on a deeper and mystical level.[24]

Compare this with the letter to Milosz quoted earlier:

> It seems to me that, as you pointed out . . . there *has to be* a third position, a position of integrity, which refuses subjection to the

23. Thomas Merton, *The Literary Essays*, ed. Patrick Hart (New York: New Directions, 1981) 292–301.
24. Merton, "Notes for a Philosophy of Solitude," 187–88.

pressures of two massive groups ranged against each other in the world. It is quite simply obvious that the future, in plain dialectical terms, rests with those of us who risk our heads and necks and everything in the difficult, fantastic job of finding out the new position, the ever changing and moving "line" that is no line at all because it cannot be traced out by political dogmatists.[25]

The important connection between these two selected readings is found in Merton's reference in the first to solitude as a call to "emptiness" and his reference in the second to the "ever changing and moving 'line' that is no line at all." This connection becomes clearer when we look at it in light of Merton's reflections on this "religious experience" at the corner of Fourth and Walnut in Louisville:

Again, that expression, *le point vierge*, (I cannot translate it) comes in here. At the center of our being is a point of nothingness which is untouched by sin and illusion, a point of pure truth, a point or spark which belongs entirely to God, which is never at our disposal, from which God disposes of our lives, which is inaccessible to the fantasies of our own mind or the brutalities of our own will. This little point of nothingness and of *absolute poverty* is the pure glory of God in us. It is so to speak His name written in us, as our poverty, as our indigence, as our dependence, as our sonship. It is like a pure diamond, blazing with the invisible light of heaven. It is in everybody, and if we could see it we would see billions of points of light coming together in the face and blaze of a sun that would make all the darkness and cruelty of life vanish completely.[26]

If Merton's search for the third position and his vocation to a life of solitude are one and the same, then I believe that the dangers of solitude noted by Merton in his "Notes for a Philosophy of Solitude" are best understood in light of his work with Milosz and Camus on the third position.

The first danger, "facing and accepting one's absurdity," is the reality Milosz encouraged Merton to face and Camus assisted him in accepting. The remaining dangers (making faith a spiritual amusement, withdrawing from society, becoming preoccupied with one's

25. Merton, *Courage for Truth*, 54.
26. Thomas Merton, *Conjectures of a Guilty Bystander* (Garden City, N.Y.: Doubleday, 1966) 142.

own justification, and attacking the world from a position of self-righteousness) are flights from the absurd into illusions of the solitary life, which are more destructive than the diversions offered by society.

In ''Notes for a Philosophy of Solitude'' Merton faces and accepts the absurd, identifies and avoids the illusions, and proceeds to describe the solitary life as the third position, a common ground for all humanity, the hidden Ground of Love. And it is at this place, the place that lies on the other side of the absurd, that Merton has moved beyond Camus and to what Milosz was certain existed.

Thomas Merton as Modernist Critic: The Influence of T. S. Eliot

Elsie F. Mayer

Writing in *The Seven Storey Mountain,* Thomas Merton recalls his introduction to T. S. Eliot: "I heard about T. S. Eliot from the English Master at Oakham who had just come down from Cambridge and read me aloud 'The Hollow Men.' "[1] The year was 1928, and the English master was Frank C. Doherty. In 1931, Merton mentions reading Eliot while a student at Columbia. Although Merton later sold his personal copies of Eliot's works to a Columbia bookstore as a sign of protest against what he called "artiness," his interest in Eliot persists. In 1948 as a monk at Gethsemani Abbey, he notes reading "East Coker" and appreciating Eliot: "This time I like him a lot" (ibid., 170). In his lectures to the monks, he refers to Eliot as a difficult writer. Michael Mott calls our attention to the similarities between Eliot's "What the Thunder Said" and Merton's poem, "Elias—Variations on a Theme," written in 1957.[2] Mott's observation suggests that Merton's interest in Eliot in this instance has become indebtedness. Moreover, it should be noted that since Eliot's poetry and criticism dominated the literary scene from 1920 through 1950, it would have been difficult for Merton, a man of letters concerned with contemporary literature, to remain unaware of him.

Throughout Merton's correspondence of the 1960s his interest in Eliot is evident. In 1964, Merton remarks to Dame Marcella Van

1. Thomas Merton, *The Seven Storey Mountain* (New York: Harcourt, 1948) 80.
2. Michael Mott, *The Seven Mountains of Thomas Merton* (Boston: Houghton, 1984) 303.

Bruyn his plan to read "Little Gidding" on his fiftieth birthday.[3] The following year he refers to *Murder in the Cathedral* in a letter to Father Charles Dumond.[4] When in 1967 Nancy Fly Bredenberg, a Vassar student, writes to Merton inquiring about the influences on his writing, Eliot is included in the gallery of writers Merton cites.[5] It is evident that Eliot's presence in one form or another continued to reassert itself throughout Merton's life.

Other modernists influenced Merton. There was the literary environment at Columbia, where modernist theory, better known as the New Criticism, flourished at the time Merton was a student there. Undoubtedly the English program had a lasting effect on Merton, for his later commentary on the Joycean critics, "News of the Joyce Industry," reveals a deep understanding of modernist methodology. There was also the influence of John Crowe Ransom, whose book *The World's Body* Merton reviewed. Ransom's work demonstrated for Merton the application of modernist theory to individual works. These, to name a few, contributed to Merton's understanding of modernist theory. However, it is on Eliot's influence that I wish to focus here. Examination of Merton's essays and commentaries establishes Eliot's influence in shaping Merton's critical approach to literature. To understand this influence, let us consider their views on the following: (1) the nature and function of poetry and (2) the relationship between literature and religion. (When discussing the latter subject, Eliot and Merton prefer the more inclusive term "literature" to "poetry," thereby encompassing all works of the creative imagination. Throughout this paper I shall attempt to follow their practice.)

It should be noted at the outset that neither Eliot nor Merton left a formal theory of literary criticism. There is no single document containing a set of critical principles. Instead, their theory emerged over approximately forty years, evolving from the study of individual writers. Eliot chose to publish many of his essays in several volumes during his lifetime. Patrick Hart's edition of Merton's literary essays remains the best available collection at this time. Both Eliot and Merton acknowledge the tenuous nature of literary criticism. As writers themselves they recognize the danger lurking in criticism, namely, that

3. Thomas Merton, *The Road to Joy: The Letters of Thomas Merton to New and Old Friends*, ed. Robert E. Daggy (New York: Farrar, 1989) 205.
    4. Ibid., 293.
    5. Ibid., 361.

it can be self-serving. Critics in their rush to justify their work can advocate a theory that reflects their own practices. Moreover, both Eliot's and Merton's sensibility is experiential, emerging not from absolute standards but evolving as their humanistic, moral, and religious views evolve. Their sensibility and the criticism it informs is subject to the vagaries of human experience, among which are vagueness, attitudinal changes, and even inconsistencies. For this reason it is important to identify when possible the dates of individual statements, a practice Eliot indicated is necessary and one I observe throughout this paper. In the case of Merton these circumstances eventuate not a coherent whole but random critical fragments connected by an informed and developing mind. One wishing to understand his theory must construct it piece by piece. This task when pursued yields a theory of literary criticism whose underpinnings establish Eliot as one of Merton's mentors. Thereafter, Merton, guided by his unique experience as a man of letters and a monk, builds upon Eliot's ideas, eventually formulating his own theory in the same way one architect might elaborate upon another's basic structure.

Eliot struggled with the nature of poetry before accepting a poem or any literary work as an autonomous entity. In "Tradition and Individual Talent," first published in 1917 and included in the *Selected Essays, 1917–1932*, he perceives the poet's mind as a receptacle where thoughts and feelings coalesce before emerging in a poem as images and phrases. At this time Eliot defines a poem as a fusion of elements, inexplicable because their relationship is unclear. In 1920, disputing a theory of poetry expounded by a popular critic, Eliot argues against the notion that "poetry is the most highly organized form of intellectual activity."[6] Through a series of denials, Eliot insists that poetry is not pure idea, for it expresses feelings; but to agree with Wordsworth's claim that poetry is "emotion recollected in tranquility" is to undermine the imprint of the poet's thought in favor of feeling. Further, to claim that poetry is "the most highly organized activity" is to ignore science with its dependence on induction, a form of strict linear thinking. Eliot's dismissal of poetry as philosophy comes easily for him because philosophy clearly deals with the abstract and poetry with the concrete.[7]

6. T. S. Eliot, *The Sacred Wood: Essays on Poetry and Criticism* (New York: Barnes, 1950) 1.
7. Ibid.

There is also at this time emphasis on the intricacy of poetic elements. Eliot perceives poetry as "purely personal." Emotion is "fused" with "suggestions" and "experience." Eventually it sheds the stamp of personality and assumes a new entity as "a work of art."[8] Gradually the uniqueness of poetry comes into focus for him as evident in the preface to the 1928 edition of *The Sacred Wood:*

> We can only say that a poem has its own life; that its parts form something quite different from a body of neatly ordered biographical data; that the feeling, or emotion, or vision, resulting from the poem is something different from the feeling or emotion or vision in the mind of the poet.[9]

The satisfaction of this discovery, however, is short-lived. In Eliot's thinking at this time there exists what amounts to a denial of the possibility of definition, reinforced no doubt by his reading of Levy-Bruhl, who writes of "a pre-logical mentality" persisting in civilized man and manifesting itself through the poet. By 1933 Eliot is turning his attention to the qualities of poetry with the conclusion that rhythm is its only single essential quality.

Eliot also addresses the effects of poetry and the role of language in eventuating these effects. The audience he faced held that the function of language is communication, and in the case of poetry language is expected to convey the poet's thoughts and feelings. In order to break this notion, Eliot argues for the imprecision of language in recreating poetic experience. Moreover, he rejects communication as the sole end of poetry: "We can say that in poetry there is communication from writer to reader, but should not proceed from this to think of the poetry as being primarily the vehicle of communication."[10] Having dismissed communication as the end of poetry, Eliot advocates the theory of the "objective correlative." Since a poet cannot tell what his/her poem means, the reader should not first and foremost expect meaning but an aesthetic experience. When a poem is successful, the reader's response approximates the feeling invested in the language. The poet should avoid evoking more feeling than the poem's subject and lan-

8. Ibid., 7.

9. Ibid., x.

10. T. S. Eliot, *The Use of Poetry and the Use of Criticism* (New York: Barnes, 1933) 115.

guage warrant. Other effects such as amusement or celebration are possible but accidental. What we see here is Eliot's admission that language, the very fiber of poetry, is elusive and resistant to the poet.

Thus it can be said that Eliot's thinking evolved to a position in which a poem's genesis is incomprehensible and its effects are impractical, unlike those of most prose works. Neither the writer's impulse to communicate nor the impulse to express feeling can explain a poem. It is an object with its own ontological status, a verbal construct with its own life. Archibald Macleish in his poem "Ars Poetica" illustrates this concept of poetry in the familiar lines: "A poem should not mean / But be."

Merton's view of the nature and function of poetry echoes Eliot's in its fundamental aspects. In "Poetry, Symbolism, and Typology," a chapter of *Bread in the Wilderness*, dated 1953 and reprinted in *The Literary Essays*, Merton comments on poetry in a passage I believe is seminal to understanding Merton's thinking on the subject:

> He [the poet] seeks above all to put words together in such a way that they exercise a mysterious and vital reactivity among themselves, and so release their secret content of association to produce in the reader an experience that enriches the depths of his spirit in a manner quite unique. A good poem induces an experience that could not be produced by any other combination of words. It is therefore an entity that stands by itself, graced with an individuality that marks it off from every other work of art.[11]

We are struck by the similarities in Merton's and Eliot's views. Here Merton identifies the essential qualities of poetry. Unlike a prose work, a poem is a unique verbal entity. The creative process remains a mystery; it is, nevertheless, a living act that replicates itself in the poem. The dynamism in the poem, resulting from the play among poetic elements, is internal, further reinforcing its autonomy. Merton's claim that the reader who allows the poem its autonomy and uniqueness will be rewarded with an experience approximating the life of the poem might well reflect a poem in which Eliot's theory of the objective correlative is successfully executed. The phrase "in a manner quite unique" brings to mind Eliot's response to the question once asked

---

11. Thomas Merton, "Poetry, Symbolism, and Topology," in *The Literary Essays of Thomas Merton*, ed. Patrick Hart (New York: New Directions, 1985) 327.

him: What kind of pleasure does poetry give? His answer: ''The kind of pleasure that poetry gives.''[12]

Merton's comments on the subject reveal a mind in agreement with modernist theory as articulated by Eliot. In a paper read at a meeting of Latin American poets in Mexico City in 1964, Merton reiterates the uniqueness of the creative process and poetry: ''We who are poets know that the reason for a poem is not discovered until the poem itself exists. The reason for a living act is realized only in the act itself.''[13] Poetry is both artifact and a process leading to insight. As such, it pulsates with life. Moreover, it owes no obligation to political, mercantile, or academic life. The expectation of poetry is that it be ''rooted in fidelity to life.''[14] Free from allegiance to institutions, the poet confronts life directly; his/her goal is to express the truth of reality. Poetry for Merton and Eliot alike requires no practical application. Both critics follow their Victorian predecessors in establishing poetry's utility, but their view on the nature of poetry more closely resembles the Romantic poets, for whom the basis of its utility is extrarational.

Despite the echoes from Eliot's theory of poetry in Merton's thinking, Merton did more than emulate his mentor. Departing from Eliot, he charts an independent course as evidenced in two essays entitled ''Poetry and Contemplation,'' both published in *Commonweal;* the first in 1947, the revision in 1958. As William Shannon indicates, the changes in the revision reflect Merton's evolving attitude toward contemplation. In the later essay the binary division between contemplation and poetry, so troublesome for Merton in the first essay, ceases to be problematic. This change no doubt results from changes in Merton's own life ten years after the publication of the first essay.[15] What I wish to note here is the distinction Merton makes between poetry and contemplation and the role he assigns poetry in the revised essay. According to Merton, contemplation is ''the intuitive perception of life at its Source.''[16] Moreover, contemplation is of two kinds: (1) ''the

12. Eliot, *The Use of Poetry,* 6.

13. Merton, ''Message to Poets,'' in *Literary Essays,* 371.

14. Ibid., 372.

15. William H. Shannon, *Silent Lamp: The Thomas Merton Story* (New York: Crossroad, 1992) 136.

16. Merton, ''Poetry and Contemplation: A Reappraisal,'' in *Literary Essays,* 340. See also Merton, ''The True Legendary Sound: The Poetry and Criticism of Edwin Muir,'' in *Literary Essays,* 29.

religious intuition of the artist, the lover, or the worshiper'' and (2) that which ''transcends all 'objects,' all 'things,' and goes beyond all speculation, all creative fervor, all charitable action, and 'rests' in the inexpressible.''[17] For Merton there is no conflict between poetry and contemplation in the first sense. Speaking primarily of the Christian poet, he argues that the poet draws from the contemplative experience; as an artist in the Aristotelian sense of maker, the poet possesses the skills to transform vision into images. Although the poet's form of contemplation is less perfect than contemplation in the second sense because the goal of the poet returns him/her to the natural order, the poet touches God in the creative process. To a supernatural experience he/she applies natural talent. One can argue that without the monastic life Merton may not have arrived at this position. Such a claim is defensible. It is also likely, however, that without his participation in the contemporary debate over the redefinition of poetry, Merton may not have understood the complexity of poetry. The relationship between poetry and contemplation he perceives is grounded in the study and writing of poetry.

While it is apparent that both Eliot and Merton assign poetry a privileged status, neither is a pure formalist satisfied with textual analysis for critical judgment. Literary standards based on such analysis may determine the quiddity of a poem, but textual analysis alone falls short of identifying a great poem. Both men recognize that poetry does not exist in a vacuum. Moreover, both men fear the menace of secularism in the modern age, a secularism so widespread that it threatens to banish belief in the supernatural to exile. With religious faith replaced by devotion to Mammon, Eliot and Merton seek in poetry a role beyond the aesthetic in order to combat the threat posed by modern secularism to the human spirit. The solution rests in placing poetry in a context larger than the purely aesthetic. With this purpose in mind Eliot turns to tradition; Merton, to human experience itself. Since poetry encompasses the totality of human experience, Merton believes it capable of commenting on various perspectives of that experience, be they psychological, metaphysical, or theological. Merton clings to this position. As late as 1966, in a letter to James Laughlin, he notes his agreement with Jacques Maritain ''that perhaps the most living way to approach theological and philosophical problems in our day is in

17. Ibid., 341.

the form of 'creative writing and literary criticism.' '[18] It is significant to observe that the context Merton creates for poetry is more inclusive than Eliot's.

Eliot's pursuit of a context for poetry was long and arduous. I shall limit my comments here to his view of tradition. Tradition for Eliot encompasses the historical past and an awareness of the past living in the present. A poet writes "not merely with his own generation in his bones" but with the feeling that literary predecessors and contemporaries write through him/her. This view combines the temporal and the timeless. The poet adds a new vision to his/her predecessors', a vision relevant for contemporary society. The poet is also linked to contemporaries writing in the same genre. Within this context, the poem emerges not as a clone but as a mutation that combines the new and the old. Thus Eliot expands the criteria for judging poetry beyond textual analysis. The poem must stand the scrutiny of comparison to similar entities past and present, and the critic is positioned to judge poets not only on their specific works but also on their success in embodying the tradition of the genre.

But Eliot's advocacy of poetry as a voice speaking to the present via the past only partially solves the challenge of establishing a place for poetry in a secular society. The problem becomes crucial when Eliot converts to Anglo-Catholicism. In the early 1920s before his conversion he is already acknowledging a relationship between poetry and religion. Although at the time this relationship remains unclear and although he fears the danger of wandering from the narrower practice of literary criticism by viewing poetry in a religious context, the recognition of the relationship provides a starting point for Eliot's investigation. His later admission that "a man's theory of the place of poetry is not independent of his view of life in general"[19] is further evidence that his personal faith infuses his literary principles. When eventually his notion of tradition focuses on the Christian, there follows the need for a theory that addresses the moral conflict in poetry as well as a moral tradition from a Christian perspective.

In his essay "Religion and Literature" dated 1935, Eliot writes the following: "Literary criticism should be completed by criticism from a definite ethical and theological standpoint."[20] According to Eliot, if

18. Hart, from introduction to *The Literary Essays of Thomas Merton*, xv.
19. Eliot, *The Use of Poetry*, 119.
20. T. S. Eliot, *Selected Essays* (New York: Harcourt, 1950) 343.

an age holds a common ethical and theological position the critic's task is to draw it out from a work; insofar as an age holds no common position the critic is still bound to judge a work by a particular perspective. Because Eliot believes literature influences human behavior, the critic's task becomes a moral imperative. In this same essay he distinguishes between readers' preferences and the ideal, what they ought to prefer. It is the critic's responsibility to assist in holding up the ideal for his/her readers. The Christian critic has the added responsibility to apply criteria of judgment that may be ignored by others. We are familiar with Eliot's description of himself as a critic: "classicist in literature, royalist in politics, and anglo-catholic in religion."[21] Eliot later objects to those who remove the statement from its context. (He spoke these lines in 1927 over dinner with Irving Babbitt, his teacher at Harvard and lifetime friend, to inform him of his conversion.) But it is evident that Eliot's stance on literature and religion—if not literature and politics—informs his criticism. Dante remains a favorite of Eliot's not only because the structure, lines, and imagery of *The Divine Comedy* reach new heights in his hand but because Dante's work is situated in Christianity, the dominant tradition of his time. Modern writers failing to reflect Eliot's position are dismissed as limited. For Eliot, D. H. Lawrence displays heresy in "The Shadow in the Rose Garden," and James Joyce, who demonstrates an awareness of Christian principles, approaches moral significance in a work like "The Dead." And how can one who advocated such principles write "The Hollow Men" and *The Waste Land*? The answer is simply that Eliot's goal in these works is to illustrate the consequences of secularism on modern society. A writer like Graham Greene once defined himself as a writer who happened to be a Catholic, but Eliot considered himself a Catholic writer-critic for whom the works of the imagination, literary criticism, and personal religious faith were inextricably related.

Merton, like Eliot, recognizes the necessity of situating literature in a tradition lest its merit be limited to the aesthetic. Furthermore, a tradition is necessary in order to ensure its relevance for the present. In his essay on Edwin Muir, a poet Merton admired, he agrees with Muir's claim that ignorance of the past is a tragic loss for contemporary society. Without a connection between present and past, we forfeit understanding ourselves and risk alienation because our heri-

---

21. T. S. Eliot, *To Criticize the Critic* (New York: Farrar, 1965) 15.

tage is left to atrophy.[22] Like Eliot's view of tradition, Merton's assumes a Christian character as a result of his personal faith. In their efforts to clarify Christian tradition, Eliot distinguishes between devotional poetry and religious poetry. Merton distances himself from the orthodox "Catholic poet," that is, one who writes devotional verse.[23] He believes in the need to liberate religion from specific forms of piety and narrowly focused commitments. In his essay on William Faulkner, "Baptism in the Forest," dated 1967, we have a glimpse of where Merton's thinking is leading him: "The idea of religion today is mixed up with confessionalism, with belonging to this or that religious institution, with making and advertising a particular kind of religious commitment,"[24] Clearly Merton's view of religion extends beyond the common practices of particular institutions and denominations; it is best understood as catholic in the universal sense of the word.

For Merton, questions of human origin, the human condition, and human destiny replace piety and various forms of devotion as religious concerns worthy of investigation. Hence his claim that the works of Sophocles, Faulkner, and Camus are religious, for they deal with the fundamental questions of life despite the differences in the writers' perspectives. Merton, while agreeing with Eliot about the synergistic relationship between literature and religion, crosses the threshold of orthodoxy in order to define this relationship independently. The religious poet or creative writer must tap into the "ontological sources of life" that are accessed through the imagination.[25] For Merton, the imagination is "power by which we apprehend living beings and living creatures in their individuality as they live and move not in their ideas and categories. The power of the poet's imaginative vision . . . is that it directs our eyes to beings in such a way as to *'feel the full weight and uniqueness of their lives.'* "[26] Abstractions alone are inadequate; the poet must convey the concreteness of human experience.

Eliot considers major religious literature to possess "general awareness." Merton's counterpart is *sapientia*. The latter he defines

22. Merton, "The True Legendary Sound," in *Literary Essays*, 34–35.
23. Merton, *The Road to Joy*, ed. Robert E. Daggy, 362.
24. Merton, " 'Baptism in the Forest': Wisdom and Initiation in William Faulkner," in *Literary Essays*, 97.
25. Merton, "The True Legendary Sound," in *Literary Essays*, 30.
26. Ibid., 34.

as "the highest level of cognition," lying beyond "*scientia*, which is systematic knowledge [and] beyond *intellectus*, which is intuitive understanding."[27] *Sapientia*, or wisdom, grasps ultimate truths and ultimate values.[28] Merton, who laments the lack of *sapientia* in modern society, argues that because it relies for its expression on myth and symbols, the common language of both literature and religion, the imaginative writer and the critic through interpretation are empowered to convey it.

For Eliot the methodology of modern criticism rests on analysis and comparison, the critic's literary and philosophical background, and his/her objective reading of the text. The organization of elements—linguistic and structural, their arrangement to create an effect on the reader—determines the aesthetic merit of a text. Furthermore, how the work compares to similar types also contributes to its merit. Critics who failed to embody these requisites in their totality, such as Coleridge, Swinburne, and Symons, Eliot considers flawed. It is to Samuel Johnson that Eliot awards the laurel for critical excellence, specifically for his *Life of Cowley*. Eliot approves of Johnson's criticism because he has distinguished between contemporary and traditional ideals. Moreover, Johnson judges Cowley's work not only in its immediate context but also within the context of the past. When criticism follows this model, it approximates, according to Eliot, "a voyage of discovery."

As earlier noted, Merton's review of John Crowe Ransom's work *The World's Body* confirms his understanding of the method and lexicon of modernist criticism. At the time Ransom's work appeared in 1938, his critical stance was considered in opposition to the pervasive biographical and historical criticism of the time. For the young Merton, Ransom's work provided an important step toward an understanding of literature as a special form of cognition. From Mark Van Doren he learned that left alone without the imposition of an ideology, a text will reveal its own truth. Merton tests this approach in his master's essay on Blake. His explanation of Blake's use of contraries in the latter part of the essay illustrates his reliance on textual analysis. Throughout his instruction on literature, he draws attention to syntactic structure, images, symbols, archetypes, rhythmic patterns of language, plot, and voice. For Merton all the elements are vital insofar as they assist the reader in experiencing a literary work. Those who employ

27. Merton, " 'Baptism in the Forest,' " in *Literary Essays*, 98.
28. Ibid., 99.

the New Critical methods to excess, however, lose favor with Merton. He has little tolerance for Joycean scholars who cavil over one part or another of *Ulysses* in their zeal to validate a particular theory. Merton recognizes that criticism can be damaging when it smothers a text in order to display a critic's brilliance.

If Merton's views appear derivative of Eliot's regarding the nature and function of literature, his critical writing attests to an independent voice. Clearly his interpretation of tradition, especially as it impacts on religion, extends beyond the boundaries Eliot establishes. His inclusiveness represents a departure from those modernists whose focus was limited to textual analysis. In seeking to identify the function of poetry, Merton belongs to a long lineage including Plato, Sidney, Dryden, Johnson, Shelley, Arnold, and Eliot. Arnold is credited with introducing religion into the discussion of literature in the nineteenth century. Eliot clarifies the discussion for modern society. The New Critics hold that a literary work is apolitical and ahistorical. Moreover, literature overtly religious in content is of second rank. But Merton, following Eliot's lead, voices a dissenting view. Great literature is rooted in religion because the latter constitutes an integral part of the past and because both draw upon a common use of language. Merton advances the argument beyond Eliot's. For him the value of literature is also determined by its success in framing the imponderable questions of life. That Eliot served Merton as a trusted companion throughout this process of exploration and discovery is evident.

There were many streams of influence that converged in Merton's mind. Among them, Eliot's critical theory is significant because it helps us understand the principles that inform Merton's literary judgment. Acknowledging Eliot's preeminence as both poet and critic, Merton pays him the highest compliment. Eliot's work, he remarks, embodies "wisdom for the modern world." Unwittingly perhaps, with this statement Merton voiced a debt of gratitude to one whose ideas served him well as a springboard to further exploration of the role of literature in contemporary society.

The Fire Watch Epilogue and
Life and Holiness: Opposing Rhetorics
in the Writings of Thomas Merton

Mary Murray

The rich and enigmatic prose of Thomas Merton does not lend itself readily to a traditional rhetorical analysis. Aspects of written communication that are isolated and studied evaporate when we look for them. The concern for audience, for instance, evaporates when we consider that Merton did not typically address a particular audience. Credibility, or the trust we put in an author, is frequently discarded by Merton when he declares his thoughts to be his own and not commonly shared by all monks. Logic, the staple of good rhetoric, is certainly present, but the spiritual realities Merton uncovers are so refined that the logic is merely scaffolding to look at art treasures more closely. The effect of setting, or the time and culture of a work, also evaporate, as so much of Merton's spiritual writings seem timeless.

Yet if there is one thing we know, it is that Merton's prose is powerful in its effect. It has the ability to shape one's inmost parts, to map spiritual terrain crossed unwittingly, and to open up vistas of the spiritual life. How then, rhetorically speaking, can a text achieve such effects barring standard rhetorical features?

The answer lies not in traditional rhetoric but in our ignorance of another *kind* of rhetoric of which Merton was a master. If traditional rhetoric focuses on the power of a text, its ability to influence, there is a lesser-known but equally important kind of rhetoric, a rhetoric that is a search for knowledge; it is this rhetoric that Merton used. Oddly enough, his desire to search for knowledge in language, through writing, has a powerful effect, even though this type of rhetoric does not aim at that. The effect comes, I think, through our resonance with Merton's struggles: the knowledge that he finds is equally true for us. Let us then examine the two sorts of rhetoric in Merton for the purpose of understanding this lesser-known rhetoric in order to use it ourselves and to unlock one of the most powerful passages in Merton's corpus, the Fire Watch passage in *The Sign of Jonas.*

A Lesser-Known Rhetoric

The use of language or writing in order to create knowledge is little known today among people outside the field of rhetoric and composition. Their understanding of rhetoric is the manipulative, deceitful use of language to persuade. The term itself is synonymous with lies. Yet rhetoric was a premiere art form for the ancients, one that encompassed both the aim of persuasion and the necessity of inventing one's arguments. They saw it as a civilizing force that addressed the whole person.

We do not know of this secondary type of rhetoric because rhetoric itself as an art form was lost to scholars in the 1600s, when French scholar Pierre de la Ramee split forever rhetoric and logic.[1] Rhetoric became equated with eloquence or style, and logic (what ancient rhetors knew as the invention of argument) was assigned to philosophers. Thus, to this day, school children and college students alike find themselves focusing on style and grammar in writing courses, not on invention of arguments.

That is, until fairly recently. Scholars of rhetoric in the 1960s rediscovered classical rhetoric, reintegrating the lost canon of invention to the writing classroom. The stylistically elegant but meaningless essays of students of the 1960s were an affront at the time of so much cultural change. A voice of protest and the need for powerful writing and

1. See Walter J. Ong, *Ramus, Method, and the Decay of Dialogue* (Cambridge, Mass.: Harvard University Press, 1958). The following is from "Voice and Opening Closed Systems" in *Interfaces of Word* (Ithaca, New York: Cornell University Press) 331: "Perhaps the most tight-fisted pre-Cartesian proponent of the closed system . . . was the French philosopher and educational reformer Pierre de la Ramee or Petrus Ramus. . . . Ramus' closed-field thinking is absolute and imperious, welling out of unconscious drives for completeness and security. . . . It is unencumbered by any profound philosophical speculation, and yet it is supposed to apply to every field of knowledge. Insofar as a strong stress on closed-system thinking marks the beginning of the modern era, Ramus, rather than Descartes, stands at the beginning."

compelling arguments necessitated a return to this powerful art form. It is only recently that historians of rhetoric have traced the meager threads of the use of language for discovery over the centuries.

One such historian is William A. Covino, who wrote *The Art of Wondering: A Revisionist Return to the History of Rhetoric.*[2] Rare, he writes, were those voices supporting the use of rhetoric for exploration and discovery. He names French essayist Michel de Montaigne, Italian scholar Giambattista Vico, and English philosopher David Hume as proponents of knowledge as exploration. They are notably of "renegade significance," having continued the "spirit of questing and ambiguity" in the face of the great amount of attention focused on certitude throughout the years between the 1600s and today. As Covino notes:

> The views of Montaigne, Vico, and Hume maintain the equivalence of rhetoric and intellectual free play through the centuries when rhetoric became a mechanized ornament of thought and critical thinking became schematized. Muffled by the rationalist voice of mainstream technical rhetoric, these thinkers have been dissociated from the rhetorical tradition, although, as I will propose, they continue the Ancient emphasis on rhetoric as philosophy, and look toward the postmodern alliance of language, literacy, and open speculation.[3]

It is this open speculation and risk of questioning and ambiguity that Merton radiates in the Fire Watch passage.

When rhetoric as exploration or discovery was suppressed by the attention to style or eloquence, it was also dealt a severe blow in the nineteenth century, in particular when facts alone or a logical argument alone was sufficient (claimed rhetor Richard Whately) to persuade an audience.[4] When today we try to reason with only the facts or only logic, we echo this understanding of rhetoric from the previous century. The problem with such a concept of rhetoric is that it only addresses the rational side of the audience, leaving appeals to emotion and values and appeals concerning the credibility of the speaker

2. William A. Covino, *The Art of Wondering: A Revisionist Return to the History of Rhetoric* (Portsmouth, N.H.: Boynton/Cook, 1988) 45.

3. Ibid., 46–47.

4. See James J. Golden, Goodwin F. Bergquist, and William E. Coleman, *The Rhetoric of Western Thought,* 4th ed. (Dubuque, Ia.: Kendall/Hunt, 1989) 204.

(to name the other important aspects of traditional rhetoric) completely untaught and not addressed, meaning that today we are frequently either bored or not moved by such speech, or worse, that those rhetors skilled at the ignored aspects of rhetoric have even *greater* power because we are completely unaware that we are being persuaded.

In the passages that follow, we will examine Merton using both types of rhetoric: the trap of logical rhetoric from the previous century and the rhetoric that has as its goal the search for new knowledge.

Convincing by Logic Alone: The Rhetoric of *Life and Holiness*

In *Life and Holiness* (1963) Merton reveals that he will not take his usual stance. He discards all his experience as a writer of the contemplative experience when he says, "Nothing is here said of such subjects as 'contemplation' or even 'mental prayer.' "[5] He says it is an "elementary treatment of a few basic ideas in Christian spirituality," most notably the action of grace in the life of the active Christian.[6] At once we know, in the introduction, that this is not typical of Merton's spiritual writings, for it concerns the active, not the contemplative life, and it is basic, not sophisticated.

These considerations lend themselves to a logic- or fact-driven text. We hear it in the first sentence of the book: "Every baptized Christian is obliged by his baptismal promises to renounce sin and to give himself completely without compromise, to Christ, in order that he may fulfill his vocation, save his soul, enter into the mystery of God, and there find himself perfectly 'in the light of Christ.' "[7] But let us choose for analyses longer passages that allow more room for interpretation. The two that follow concern faith:

> The faith by which we are united to Christ and receive supernatural life by the Gift of his Spirit, is not mere emotional or affective self-commitment. It is not a matter of blind will. Christ is not only our life, he is also our way and our truth (John 14:6). Faith is an intellectual light by which we "know" the Father in the Incarnate Word (John 14:7-14). Yet faith is at the same time a

5. Thomas Merton, *Life and Holiness* (New York: Image, 1963) 7.
6. Ibid.
7. Ibid., 12.

mysterious and obscure knowledge. It knows, as the medieval mystics said, by "unknowing." To believe is to know without seeing, to know without intrinsic evidence (2 Cor 5:7). Or rather, while faith truly "sees," it sees *per speculum, in aenigmatre* (1 Cor 13:12), in a manner that is dark, mysterious, beyond explanation. The "vision" or intellectual illumination of faith is produced not by the natural activity of our intelligence working on sensible evidence, but by a direct supernatural action of the Spirit of God. Hence, though it is for that very reason beyond the normal grasp of the unaided intelligence, it offers a greater certitude than natural scientific knowledge. But this greater certitude, though it remains a matter of personal conviction, is not susceptible of rational proof to anyone who does not himself accept the premises of faith. "No man can come to me," said Jesus Christ, "unless he be drawn by the Father who sent me" (John 6:44; cf. 6:65).[8]

Here is a second passage:

> Consequently it is necessary to dispose our hearts for faith in various ways, above all by inquiry, by reading, and by prayer. If we want to know what faith is, and what Christians believe, we must inquire of the Church. If we want to know what God has revealed to the believer, we must read the Scriptures, we must study those who have explained the Scriptures, and we must acquaint ourselves with the basic truths of philosophy and theology. But since faith is a gift, prayer is perhaps the most important of all the ways of seeking it from God.
>
> After all, it is not always easy to find a Christian capable of explaining his faith, and even the clergy may not be able to translate technical knowledge into terms that everyone can grasp. The Bible, too, is not always easy to understand. Subjective interpretation of Scripture may lead to disastrous error. As for theology and philosophy: where will a man without religious education begin to find out about them? Prayer is then the first and most important step. All through the life of faith one must resort constantly to prayer, because faith is not simply a gift which we receive once and for all in our first act of belief. Every new development of faith, every new increment of supernatural light, even though we may be earnestly working to acquire it, remains a pure gift of God. Prayer is therefore the very heart of the life of faith.[9]

8. Ibid., 80.
9. Ibid., 81.

Logic and facts drive these passages. There is no appeal to emotions or values here; instead Merton issues directives, reasoning that if a person wishes faith, then he or she must pursue certain paths, even though ultimately, faith is a gift. The emphasis on logic or facts alone leads Merton to write of faith in such a way that he can refer to faith as mysterious, but never acknowledge the array of human responses to the mystery of faith and its pursuit. A logic- or fact-driven text presents to the audience that which the audience should do or think, without touching the values or emotions.

Merton uses Scripture quotes as non-negotiable facts or proofs of his points. Chaim Perelman and Lynn Olbrechts-Tytecha, authors of *The New Rhetoric* (1969), would criticize Merton's use of Scripture as a way of detaching the audience from the subject: one "way of lessening the strength of arguments is to emphasize their routine, easily foreseeable character."[10] These quotes are not even integrated into the text; they exist as separate proofs that require the reader to stop and integrate them. Such reading is difficult and is the product of the belief that if the facts are present, the reader will be persuaded; nevertheless, the impact of such a text is not persuasion so much as a solely intellectual treatment of the topic.

Many twentieth-century writers fall into this rhetorical trap of believing that facts and reason alone make for persuasion. While such texts remain informative, they do not have a strong persuasive effect. Merton is at his best when he writes for himself, explores questions, and allows us to follow along. His forays into writing "persuasively" for a lay audience caused him to write in a markedly different, alien style that weakens instead of raises the power of his text.

The Fire Watch Passage as Rhetoric of Exploration

One of Merton's most famous and brilliant passages, the Fire Watch epilogue, remains mysterious, elusive, and profound. On the first or the twenty-first reading this text seems to defy any explanation; the symbolism and reflections in it can be honored as Merton's own, although they are strangely poignant. The text seems impenetrable because traditional rhetorical analysis finds nothing to analyze.

10. Chaim Perelman and Lynn Olbrechts-Tytecha, *The New Rhetoric* (Notre Dame, Ind.: Notre Dame University Press, 1969) 468.

No audience, no credibility (Merton is at a loss himself here), all setting, and God speaking at the end of the text! Appreciation seems the only fitting response, and yet the effect on readers is still profound.

Can there be an explanation for a text that meanders so? The authors cited by Covino have definite explanations. Each of these scholars agrees on three key aspects of this kind of discourse: the confrontation of darkness and asking of genuine questions; wandering or aimless discourse; and associational thinking for synthesis and discovery. In short, the writer who wishes to pursue knowledge must walk out into the unknown and abandon commonly known ways of solving the issues at hand.

Raising Questions in the Dark

Vico believed that thought began in chaos and in the dark. He also believed that the rhetor must ask questions rather than organize data. He believed knowledge is what humans make rather than what they find; he also advised that students be trained in common sense along with the traditional analytical methods because their education would be useless if they could not deal with the probable and apply what they learned to current situations. Rhetoric for Vico meant "an activity in which the mind constructs knowledge of itself."[11] Montaigne agrees that knowledge is of the self: "I would rather be an authority on myself than on Cicero."[12] He too denounces formal logical rhetorical proofs in favor of the uncertainty of writing without absolutes.

Modern rhetorician James Kinneavy classifies this type of writing as exploratory discourse.[13] He and a number of modern rhetoricians draw on psychologist Leon Festinger's term "cognitive dissonance" to explain the beginnings of the rhetoric of discovery.[14] Wonder, dis-

11. Covino, *The Art of Wondering,* 58.

12. Michael de Montaigne, *The Complete Works of Montaigne,* ed. and trans. Donald Frame (Stanford: Stanford University Press, 1967) 3:13, 822.

13. James Kinneavy, *A Theory of Discourse* (New York: Norton, 1970).

14. See also Peter Elbow, *Embracing Contraries: Exploration in Teaching and Learning* (New York: Oxford, 1986).

Janice Lauer and others, *Four Worlds of Writing,* 3rd ed. (New York: Harper Collins, 1991).

Richard Young, Alton Becker, and Kenneth Pike, *Rhetoric, Discovery, and Change* (New York: Harcourt Brace Jovanovich, 1970).

comfort, and instability prefigure writing of this type. The imagination, central to the explanations of Montaigne and Vico, searches for
truth beyond standard or current dogma, frequently calling into question aspects of the dogma itself that do not resolve the dissonance.

The Fire Watch passage is rich in question raising. Once Merton
tells us his ostensible task of being on the fire watch, he declares the
deeper intent or dissonance:

> It is when you hit the novitiate that the fire watch begins in ear-
> nest. Alone, silent, wandering on your appointed rounds through
> the corridors of a huge, sleeping monastery, you come around the
> corner and find yourself face to face with your monastic past and
> with the mystery of your vocation. The fire watch is an examina-
> tion of conscience in which your task as watchman suddenly ap-
> pears in its true light: a pretext devised by God to isolate you, and
> to search your soul with lamps and questions, in the heart of dark-
> ness.[15]

Mirroring what rhetoricians Vico, Montaigne, and Kinneavy hold about
the necessity of wondering and questioning, this text advances beyond
what they would describe because God too is asking questions of
Merton. We later hear this in the following quote: "While I am asking
questions which You do not answer, You ask me a question which
is so simple that I cannot answer. I do not even understand the question."[16] When Merton indicates that "This night, and every night, it
is the same question,"[17] the magnitude, or the weight, of these questions is felt. The dissonance Merton feels is profound and prolonged,
and it is instigated not only by his own mind and heart but by God
as well.

He wonders whether he should even ask these questions. He
writes:

> On all sides I am confronted by questions that I cannot answer,
> because the time for answering them has not yet come. Between
> the silence of God and the silence of my own soul, stands the
> silence of the souls entrusted to me. Immersed in these three
> silences, I realize that the questions I ask myself about them are

15. Thomas Merton, *The Sign of Jonas* (San Diego: Harcourt Brace Jovanovich,
1953) 352.

16. Ibid., 353.

17. Ibid.

perhaps no more than a surmise. And perhaps the most urgent
and practical renunciation is the renunciation of all questions.[18]

The density and difficulty of the questions Merton faces are apparent
here—more poignant because of the context. Not only do these deep
questions concern his own vocation but those of others as well. And
like most of us facing painful or disturbing questions, Merton wonders
whether it is better to ignore them all. Even so, it is the question of
his own vocation that seems to concern God and Merton most at this
time.

As the journey through the monastery takes place, the emptiness of the upper floors of the old guest wing takes him aback: "The
very silence is a reproach. The emptiness itself is my most terrible question."[19] At this point Merton has reached the heart of the dissonance.
"With my feet on the floor I waxed when I was a postulant, I ask these
useless questions. With my hand on the key by the door to the trib-
une, where I first heard the monks chanting the psalms, I do not wait
for an answer, because I have begun to realize You never answer when
I expect."[20] He does not release the dissonance, but he does surrender
to God's mysterious time and ways of answering.

A key to our own journeys is to ask such questions in the dark
as well. We too must risk the pain of confronting important questions,
enduring the time it takes to answer them. To move toward the resolution of these questions, we must turn to the next set of qualities rhetoricians say mark the use of language or writing for discovery.

Aimless Discourse

Another feature of the rhetoric of discovery is that it is aimless.
The text seems to ramble or wander instead of following a set or certain or expected route. Covino claims that the essays of Montaigne
demonstrate of themselves Montaigne's belief that knowledge is exploration, not information. The order of the essays should follow from
a great intellect, not from a set plan, according to Montaigne. Covino
explains Vico's accord on this point:

18. Ibid., 354.
19. Ibid., 357.
20. Ibid., 358.

Vico refuses to preestablish some "end" for learning and associates both learning and writing—his own discourse—with a journey that is regular and regulated but "aimless." The progress of
study is compared to a recursive rather than a linear process,
whose aims emerge during that process itself. Here we detect
Vico's trust in ingenuity, in the natural tendency to arrive at points
of clarity, of acute consciousness. Vico implicitly associates learning with discovery.[21]

Kinneavy too considers this kind of discourse a "wandering in some
area."[22] Because the text goes against current dogma, it cannot have
a current organizational plan.

The reader follows Merton along his travels sensing that something will happen but without knowing quite what. Even though the
route is prescribed, the effect of the text is a journey because the thinking is not following a set route. Juxtaposed are tremendously detailed
descriptions of parts of the monastery and his own ruminations. Like
on any aimless journey, we are more likely to discover treasure because we have time to look.

The key to using this aspect of composing is to let ourselves be
aimless in the pursuit of dissonances. This can feel uncomfortable and
like wasting time. Once we begin to do so, we can employ the next
strategy—associational thinking.

Synthesis through Associational Thinking

Each of the above rhetoricians believe that associational thinking is what drives discovery once a writer is committed to asking important questions but to being aimless in searching for answers.
Montaigne advised the pairing of opposites (or antithesis) as the most
appropriate way of expressing conflicts. Covino explains that Vico
paired associational thinking with civilization:

Civilization stops when we cease to think metaphorically and
associatively, cease to ponder one thing in terms of others, cease
to see each human life as a tangle of relationships to divinity and
history and the common sense. In other words, civilization stops
when we trade philosophical imagination for intellectual purity,

21. Covino, *The Art of Wondering*, 65.
22. Kinneavy, *A Theory of Discourse*, 102.

when we trade the unstable world of human affairs for the deep solitude of certainty.[23]

He also believed that "ingenuity 'calls up' or 'discovers' a connection between terms; it is the power of associative thinking."[24] Kinneavy and a number of modern rhetoricians echo these concerns when they advise students to engage in varied levels of associational thinking in order to explore the questions they pose.

The entire text of the Fire Watch passage is associational. Everything Merton sees reminds him of something past, present, or future. Everything from his next dentist appointment to the history of the monastery is included. As one instance, the following quote shows how much depth is implicit in such associational thinking:

> And here, now, by night, with this huge clock ticking on my right hip and the flashlight in my hand and sneakers on my feet, I feel as if everything had been unreal. It is as if the past had never existed. The things I thought were so important—because of the effort I put into them—have turned out to be of small value. And the things I never thought about, the things I was never able either to measure or to expect, were the things that mattered.
>
> (There used to be a man who walked down the back road singing, on summer mornings, right in the middle of the novices' thanksgiving after Communion: singing his own private song, every day the same. It was the sort of song you would expect to hear out in the country, in the Knobs of Kentucky.)[25]

The association of what really matters with the scene he describes is suggestive. One can imagine how silent and fervent the young monks were after Communion, only to have a joyful unknown man like themselves singing his own song every day during this time of "thanksgiving." In the same manner that God questions Merton about his vocation, this scene can imply that God lightly illustrated what really matters to the young monks regarding their Communion reflection.

Associational thinking in the epilogue does not discriminate: rich (and even silly) sensual detail accompanies philosophical ponderings and frustrations. Like every good poet, he links the mundane and the abstract and even inverts them. Everything from "the sneakers on my

23. Ibid., 58.
24. Ibid., 65.
25. Merton, *The Sign of Jonas*, 353.

feet'' to ''sweat running down our ribs'' to a mention of the different color of each of the kitchen walls is given his notice. Not only was Merton fully alive and present to his reality, but one can sense that the writer/poet in him raced back to compose this text conscious of every detail so as to capture the drama of the discovery next to the mundane task during which it was found.

The most famous passage where Merton sees the ''chorus of living beings'' dramatically exemplifies associational thinking, synthesis, and new knowledge. The last pages of the Fire Watch epilogue hold the culmination of Merton's search for new knowledge.

In order to understand these last pages where so much new knowledge is given, we must first contrast it to Merton's initial status. Two objects are in question: the enigmatic questions God keeps asking Merton and the implicit questioning of Merton's monastic vocation. Most important, Merton has chosen the *via negativa* of monasticism marked by extreme asceticism, isolation, silence, and unknowing. This dark way is a kind of interior death (or search) for God in God's absence because therein God reveals a more mysterious presence.

In an attempt to highlight and focus on the knowledge Merton gained (instead of the richness and beauty of the text itself), at least five insights can be specified:

- The *via negativa* is filled with life.
- The mysterious God is compassionate and merciful.
- Communion with God is the way to know God.
- God's vision integrates the vile and cruel into mercy.
- The world and all people are united in God.

When contrasted to Merton's previous state of confusion or dissonance, the knowledge that erupts from his exploratory venture in both the physical experience and in his recounting the experience in writing is profound. The certitude and joyful attitude at the end of the text signal Merton's discoveries. The risk of engaging in exploratory discourse are the dead ends, the confusion that the earlier parts of the text present. The end of the text also presents images of freedom that contrast to earlier darkness: the white dove flies into the dawn. His July Fourth has become a liberation from darkness, confusion, and a false sense of isolation.

Merton's search for knowledge can be readily described by theories proposed by Montaigne, Vico, Kinneavy, and other modern rhetoricians. The risks of false starts and further confusion are part of the journey, but the end results so profound that they look of little consequence in comparison. We should be encouraged, then, to ask (and be asked) the hard questions, to wander aimlessly in text, and to engage in associational thinking. The impact of Merton's prose in the Fire Watch epilogue comes not from a direct address, as in traditional persuasive strategies, but from the resonance with our own too quiet journeys.[26]

26. The author would like to thank Brother Augie Jackson, Charles Murach, and Paul Weingartner for their helpful comments.

Thomas Merton's
Late Metaphors of the Self

John S. Porter

Thomas Merton's Cartesian formula in the early years was not only "I write, therefore, I am," but "I write about the self, therefore, I must have one."[1] Autobiography, which John Berger characterizes as an "orphan" form, is Merton's most frequently used literary genre, whether in poetry or journal.[2] Each of his works may be considered as a new "Book of the Self" in which Merton tries to find new metaphoric mirrors for his fluid and changing personality. Merton, the monk who lives without family, close relatives, possessions, and even social status—the total orphan who to a large measure invents himself out of language—chooses an "orphan" form for his fullest and richest literary expression.

In a 1939 journal entry he writes: "Anything I create is only a symbol for some completely interior preoccupation of my own." He realizes quite early in his writing vocation that the talent of the novelist, that of being able to inhabit and make real another person and identity, escapes him. Merton performs best when he is writing about himself and the things he loves: "ideas, places, certain persons—all very definite, individual, identifiable objects of love."[3] And yet the

1. Ivan Illich, in his illuminating study co-authored with Barry Sanders, *ABC: The Alphabetization of the Popular Mind* (New York: Vintage Books, 1989), reminds readers that "the idea of a self . . . cannot exist without the text. Where there is no alphabet, there can neither be a memory . . . nor the 'I' as its appointed watchman" 72.

2. John Berger, *Keeping a Rendezvous* (New York: Pantheon Books, 1991) 47.

3. William H. Shannon, *Silent Lamp: The Thomas Merton Story* (New York: Crossroads, 1992) 19.

mystery of Merton has always been, in sketching his own self-portrait, that he draws the faces of others who see themselves in his face. Personal statement evolves into communal statement. Readers are witnesses to a life, voyeurs of the tics and turns of a personal history, and privy to the unveiling of a self that, in its doubts and criticisms, resembles so many other questers for authenticity.

The philosopher Charles Taylor makes the point that the self develops "in relation to certain interlocutors." The self exists within what he calls "webs of interlocution."[4] Merton's interlocutors were missing. To compensate for the lack of early and significant interlocutors—later in life he certainly does not lack correspondent-interlocutors—he carries on a lifelong conversation with himself about himself. He tells and retells his own inner story, for he has a strong need to hear it. He has few significant others to whom to tell his story, and the early memories he does have of significant others are charged with ambivalence: the memory of a critical mother and the memory of a father more interested at times in his art and girlfriend than in him.[5] Merton is forced to work very hard at being the architect of his own identity; through writing he strives to project, in metaphor, the images of selfhood that are not reflected to him by his family, images that would otherwise be unaffirmed.[6]

One of the intriguing facts of Merton's life, however, is that he has no sooner achieved his hard-won sense of self than he is willing to abandon it. He no sooner finds himself as a writer when he wants to lose himself as a hermit; he is willing to return to spiritual orphan-hood as a needy man rather than maintain the self-image of an important writer, a respected monk, and an ebullient *bon vivant*. In a lecture to fellow monks while master of novices, Merton disposes of his false images or idols with a recurrent metaphor: fire. "If I want my idols to go into the fire, I myself must go into the fire."[7] Fire in this context

---

4. Charles Taylor, *Sources of the Self: The Making of the Modern Identity* (Cambridge: Harvard University Press, 1989) 36.

5. I am indebted to Dr. R. E. Daggy for this point.

6. Elena Malits' *The Solitary Explorer* (San Francisco: Harper & Row, 1980) undergirds my own metaphoric investigations. She has mapped Merton's mental geography so thoroughly that anyone writing on Mertonian metaphors owes her an immense debt.

7. AA2267, "The True and False Self," *The Merton Tapes* (Kansas City: Credence Cassettes, 1990).

suggests cleansing, purification, perhaps even remodeling. But as Merton often reminded his readers, to lose the ego-self in the fire implies having one to lose. The ego-self has to be strong at first in order to be burned off later. In his final address in Bangkok, Merton advances the idea of having a strong self and then losing it in transformation from "self-centered love into an outgoing, other-centered love."[8]

One would expect Thomas Merton to construct interesting metaphors for the self simply because he had so much practice. But there are other reasons for his striking metaphor generation. He has two-eyed vision: the vision of a monk and the vision of a poet, the monk's meditative seriousness and the poet's ease with words. Who but a monk and a poet could define himself as neither "white-collared" nor "blue-collared" nor "Roman-collared," but rather a "Man without a Collar"?[9]

Merton also read voraciously. Vast reading deepened and broadened his sense of self. He is, after all, one of the great readers of the century, somewhat akin to Carl Jung in his subject range, from existentialism to psychoanalysis to Sufism, from poetry to Buddhism to theology. The poet, essayist, and storyteller Guy Davenport colorfully spells out Merton's uniqueness as a writer and reader: "When he wrote about the Shakers, he was a Shaker. He read with perfect empathy: he was Rilke for hours, Camus, Faulkner. . . . I wonder whether there has ever been as protean an imagination as Thomas Merton's."[10]

The number of works read, quoted, and commented on, for example in *The Asian Journal* alone, is simply staggering. In the thousands of volumes he read in his lifetime it would not be an exaggeration to say that he would have read hundreds that in some way or other commented on the self. At Columbia University where he studied the poet-priest Gerard Manley Hopkins, about whom he planned to pursue a doctorate, he doubtless would have come upon the words "A self then will consist of a centre and a surrounding area or circumference, of a point of reference and a belonging field. . . ."[11]

8. Thomas Merton, *The Asian Journal of Thomas Merton*, ed. Naomi Burton Stone, Patrick Hart, and James Laughlin (New York: New Directions, 1973) 334.

9. Thomas Merton, *The Collected Poems* (New York: New Directions, 1977) 808.

10. Ralph Eugene Meatyard, *Father Louie: Photographs of Thomas Merton*, ed. Barry Magrid (New York: Timken, 1991) 34.

11. John Pick, ed., *A Hopkins Reader* (Garden City, N.Y.: Image Books, 1966) 402.

In studying his final years one may be tempted also to single out his ongoing dialogue with D. T. Suzuki's Zen essays and his encounter with the Sufi psychotherapist A. Reza Arasteh's *Final Integration in the Adult Personality* as enriching his understanding of the self. Important works on spirituality about the Indians of the Americas, reviewed in his *Ishi Means Man*, additionally played their part in his growth. In Native American thought Merton discovered "a conception of identity which is quite different from our subjective and psychological one, centered on the empirical ego regarded as distinct and separate from the rest of reality." In Native American thought "one's identity was the intersection of cords where one 'belonged.' "[12] One was simply a branch on a tree with its roots in the ancestors and guardian spirits and its trunk connected to the family and tribe. The self, as Hopkins hinted, was always surrounded by something larger than itself.

T.R.V. Murti's *The Central Philosophy of Buddhism*, read on his Asian journey, proved to be a rich catalyst for Merton's final thoughts on the self. He frequently copies quotations into his notebooks, such as "to accept a permanent substantial self is for Buddhism the root of all attachment,"[13] though Merton is also quick to record ". . . the Madhyamika does not deny the real; he only denies *doctrines* about the real. For him, the real as transcendent to thought can be reached only by the denial of the determinations which systems of philosophy ascribe to it."[14] In the Buddhist dialectic the person presumably may be a part of what is real, but what we understand to be the self, as a permanently fixed identity, is an illusion. In the same way that there is no abiding "milkness," in Buddha's own analogy, since milk can become curds or cheese or ice cream, so there is no abiding self other than self-concepts that attempt to freeze it.[15]

Merton's readings, then, freshly define and explore the self. Arasteh's book, for example, which he reviewed in detail in his essay "Final Integration: 'Toward a Monastic Therapy,' " inspired him to write one of his most comprehensive summing-up statements of the transcultural self in general and his own transcultural self in particu-

---

12. Thomas Merton, *Ishi Means Man: Essays on Native Americans* (Greensboro, N.C.: Unicorn, 1976) 58.

13. Merton, *The Asian Journal*, 275.

14. Ibid., 140.

15. Michael Carrithers, *The Buddha* (Oxford: Oxford University Press, 1983) 45.

lar: "He has a unified vision and experience of one truth shining out in all its various manifestations. . . . He does not set these partial views up in opposition to each other, but unifies them in a dialectic or an insight of complementarity. . . ."[16] Arasteh also gave Merton the confidence that he could pass through the tunnel of neurosis, despair, and personal crisis and come out the other side, stronger, healthier, and more integrated. His afflictions could be spurs, not inhibitors, to growth.

In his journey through metaphor making and metaphor reading, Merton does not so much invent new metaphors of the self as reshape old metaphors. He comes to know who he is and what he might be through his metaphor mirrors. And these metaphor mirrors—mountains, fire, seeds—remain remarkably consistent. Mountains, for example, figure prominently in his work from beginning to end, a fact his official biographer, Michael Mott, was quick to take advantage of in calling his biography *The Seven Mountains of Thomas Merton*. Merton wrote about mountains, and if one grants mountain-status to knolls, or knobs, he lived near them for most of his life.

In that haunting first sentence of *The Seven Storey Mountain* Merton lays claim to being "in the shadow of some French mountains on the borders of Spain," and in the very title of the book he sketches his first famous metaphor of the self in pilgrimage.[17] The metaphor suggests an ongoing climb to new stations of awareness and realization. In the Western tradition, the mountain embodies one of the principal metaphors of verticality and hierarchy, presupposing a base, a summit, and frequently, a climber. The mountain in Merton's context is an aggressive metaphor; the mountain is something to be climbed, to be overcome, scaled, surmounted; each storey is to be left behind for a higher and better one until one reaches the top, which for Merton at the time was to be a monk in the Cistercian order. *The Seven Storey Mountain* is an aggressive book. Not only does Merton's young soul reach for new heights of spirituality, but he is willing to abandon those on lesser slopes—Protestants, Marxists, hedonists, and non-believers.[18]

16. Thomas Merton, "Final Integration: 'Toward A Monastic Therapy,'" *Contemplation in a World of Action* (New York: Doubleday, 1973) 117.
17. Thomas Merton, *The Seven Storey Mountain* (New York: Harcourt Brace & Jovanovich, reprinted 1978) 3.
18. Professor Jacques Goulet develops this point with great clarity in his paper

Twenty years later in his Asian journey Merton has dramatically shifted metaphors. He no longer defines himself exclusively by what he is not, but inclusively by the breadth of his emotional and intellectual embrace. He is no longer the questing pilgrim, the aggressive climber; he is the marginal man, for the monk is "a marginal person who withdraws deliberately to the margin of society with a view to deepening fundamental human experience."[19] He has replaced a vertical metaphor with a horizontal one. His new metaphor of the self is not concerned with up or down, high or low, but with the concept of the circle. Far from conceiving himself as one triumphantly atop a mountain, Merton now sees himself as someone at the margins, occupying the furthest point from the center of the circle.

When he engages the mountain metaphorically at all in *The Asian Journal*, it is with the mountain disengaged from a conquering verticality. His mountain now is "the side that has never been photographed and turned into post cards"; the mountain with "another side," not susceptible to climbing or photography.[20] The many-sidedness of the mountain grips Merton's attention, but he again chooses to identify himself with the "margins"—the side of the mountain that is not seen, that cannot be seen.

In *The Asian Journal* Merton follows his brief meditation on the mountain with a meditation on doors, the three doors that are one door: "the door of emptiness," "which cannot be entered by a self"; "the door without sign," which is "without information"; and "the door without wish," which "does not respond to a key." These doors are "without a number" and have "no threshold, no step, no advance, no recession, no entry, no nonentry."[21] As with the metaphor of the mountain, Merton starts with the familiar (a door) and proceeds to deconstruct the metaphor until it is strange and foreign; he denudes the metaphor of its usual connections and connotations. The door, which usually symbolizes a passageway to a new stage or beginning, in Merton's context, is freed from transformative successions and is simply something there without sign or wish. Merton, who so effortlessly slips from Buddhist metaphors—the mountain that is no-

"Thomas Merton's Journey toward World Religious Ecumenism" in *The Merton Annual* 4 (New York: AMS Press, 1992) 113–29.

19. Merton, *The Asian Journal*, 305.
20. Ibid., 152–53.
21. Ibid., 154.

mountain, the door that is no-door—to Christian metaphors, closes the meditation with the thought that Christ is the "nailed door" (the crucifixion) and the no-door (the resurrection), which is "the door of light, the Light itself."[22]

Merton's door, like his new mountain, is not something to be dominated or controlled or even sought. "When sought it fades. Recedes. Diminishes. Is nothing."[23] The door "cannot be entered by a self" or opened by a key. Merton has come a long way, from aggressive Western metaphors of the self to more flexible Eastern metaphors in which the ego-self or false self must be abandoned in order for the true self to emerge. In both the biblical and Buddhist traditions freedom from the ego-self is a necessary stage in human growth. As Merton informs novice monks in his lecture "The True and False Self," true freedom consists of "freedom from idolatry" in which sometimes "the real idol is me."[24] While the Bible associates sin with self-idolatry, Buddhism also encourages detachment from the illusory self, the self as object. Both traditions compel adherents to shed the "everyday conception of ourselves as potential subjects for special and unique experiences or as candidates for realization, attainment and fulfillment."[25]

What happens to Merton in the intervening years between his first major autobiographical work (1948) and his last autobiographical notebook (1968) is a deepening experience of "selfhood" and a deepening understanding of Zen as a technique to lift the false veils covering one's true face. In *Mystics and Zen Masters* (1967) Merton defines Zen as "the ontological awareness of pure being beyond subject and object, an immediate grasp of being in its 'suchness' and 'thusness.' "[26] Zen, as he was to say repeatedly, formed neither a doctrine nor a body of knowledge nor a religion but provided a means whereby one might awaken and see. Zen's great metaphors have to do with wakefulness and sight. To see, in a Zen context, implies that one is blind and to awaken implies that one is asleep.

22. Ibid., 154–55.
23. Ibid., 154.
24. "The True and False Self," *The Merton Tapes*. See note 7 above.
25. Thomas Merton, *Zen and the Birds of Appetite* (New York: New Directions, 1968) 76–77.
26. Thomas Merton, *Mystics and the Birds of Appetite,* (New York: New Directions, 1968) 14.

Zen seeks to awaken the somnolent person and to liberate him or her from the narcotic of self-ego. The master jars or shocks or disorients the novice by a koan or a kind of theater of the absurd, hence the crack of bamboo on one's head or the spilling of tea in one's lap, to unlock the ego-prison. As early as *The Seven Storey Mountain* Merton recognizes himself as a "prisoner of [his] own violence and [his] own selfishness."[27] Throughout his writings, and by means of his writings, he seeks "the awakening of the unknown 'I' that is beyond observation and reflection and is incapable of commenting upon itself."[28] This "Zen" way of looking at the self is perhaps best expressed in the journals of the early sixties, published in 1965 as *Conjectures of a Guilty Bystander:*

> The taste for Zen in the West is in part a healthy reaction of people exasperated with the heritage of four centuries of Cartesianism: the reification of concepts, idolization of the reflexive consciousness, flight from being into verbalism, mathematics, and rationalization. Descartes made a fetish out of the mirror in which the self finds itself. Zen shatters it.[29]

The metaphors at work in Merton's psyche in the last years of his life are often drawn from Zen or Zen-like sources. The sixties ferment his consciousness, but not so much from new seeds—another favorite Merton metaphor—but from the harvesting of old seeds planted in his Columbia years. In the late 1930s, for example, his exposure to Aldous Huxley's *Ends and Means* had already propelled him toward Eastern philosophies. In his Columbia master's thesis of 1939 on William Blake he prophetically quotes Chuang Tzu, the Chinese sage whose poems he will later reconstruct, and in his notes for the thesis he makes reference to D. T. Suzuki, the Zen authority with whom he will later spend a "rap" weekend in New York. In a letter to Aldous Huxley dated November 27, 1958, he pointedly writes: "May I add that I am interested in yoga and above all in Zen, which I find to be the finest example of a technique leading to the highest natural perfection of man's contemplative liberty."[30]

27. Merton, *The Seven Storey Mountain,* 3.
28. Thomas Merton, *New Seeds of Contemplation* (New York: New Directions, 1961) 7.
29. Thomas Merton, *Conjectures of a Guilty Bystander* (New York: Doubleday, 1966) 285.
30. Thomas Merton, *The Hidden Ground of Love: Letters on Religious Experience*

In his 1963 *Emblems of a Season of Fury* in poems such as "The Fall," "Song for Nobody," "Love Winter When the Plant Says Nothing," and in "Night-Flowering Cactus" one begins to see the influence of Zen reshaping his ways of seeing and understanding the self. In "The Fall," for example, he writes:

> There is no where in you a paradise that is no place
>   and there
> You do not enter except without a story.
>
> To enter there is to become unnameable.
>
> Whoever is there is homeless for he has no door and
>   no identity with which to go out and to come in.

The poem, in part, seems to prefigure what Merton will say in his meditation on doors in *The Asian Journal*. There Merton makes the point that no one "with a self can enter," and here, five years earlier, he asserts that "he who has an address is lost."[31]

In *The Way of Chuang Tzu* (1965) Merton continues with what I have chosen to call Zen metaphors, though one might as correctly say Taoist, or even Eastern, metaphors. In "The Man of Tao" he writes:

> "No-Self"
> Is "True-Self"
> And the greatest man
> Is Nobody.[32]

In another poem in the same work, "The Empty Boat," Merton, through the mask of Chuang Tzu, says that the "perfect" man goes through life "like Life itself / With no name and no home. . . . His boat is empty."[33]

One of the remarkable aspects of Merton's late metaphor generation is his tendency to take words to the limits of sense and to the ends of language. In his Zen metaphors, or perhaps more accurately his Zen paradoxes, visible in his poetry and in his Asian works, Mer-

---

and Social Concern, ed. William H. Shannon (New York: Farrar, Straus & Giroux, 1985) 439.

31. Merton, *The Collected Poems,* 334.

32. Thomas Merton, *The Way of Chuang Tzu* (New York: New Directions, 1965) 92.

33. Ibid., 115.

ton speaks of the self as "nobody" found "nowhere" in "nothing." The meaning of these words eclipses their presence: they are and are not; they self-destruct. The self, for late Merton, is without name and address, even without attribute. It has no particular face and needs no concrete metaphor mirrors such as mountains or seeds in order to see itself. The self then sees the sham of separateness and specialness and comes to an appreciation of its own nakedness, aloneness, and utter dependency on the love of others. Notably, Merton's great epiphanies, early and late, from Our Lady of Cobre to Polonnaruwa, are epiphanies of love and solidarity. In such visions the mystery of the self is ceremonially honored, and the gap between the self and the other is successfully bridged.

The picture of the self Merton finally draws is akin to Kafka's K in its being without name and address, but the self in Merton differs from Kafka's K in being neither alienated nor isolated; rather, the self throws itself at Mercy and propels itself toward Love. As Merton himself puts it in his last notebook, "Our real journey in life is interior: it is a matter of growth, deepening, and of an ever greater surrender to the creative action of love and grace in our hearts."[34] The self in such a journey is "merely a locus in which the dance of the universe is aware of itself. . . . Gladly. Praising, giving thanks, with all beings. Christ light—spirit—grace—gift. . . ."[35]

34. Merton, *The Asian Journal*, 296.
35. Ibid., 68.

Thomas Merton and the
Vocation of the Cultural Critic:
Prophetic and Poetic Imagination

Robert F. Morneau

Introduction

The question of vocation is one of the most haunting and vex-
ing challenges of life. The literary giant Dante states boldly: "Not many
come in answer to this call,"[1] that adventuresome descent into hell
and the search for the beloved Beatrice. The seventeenth-century Angli-
can poet/divine George Herbert summarizes his vocation:

I live to show his power, who once did bring
My joys to weep, and now my griefs to sing.[2]

Frederick Buechner presents the vocational question in these terms:
"A man's life is full of all sorts of voices calling him in all sorts of directions. Some of them are voices from inside and some of them are voices
from outside. The more alive and alert we are, the more clamorous
our lives are. Which do we listen to? What kind of voice do we listen
for?"[3]

Before having Thomas Merton comment directly on his own
unique vocation, I cite one last person, much admired by Merton, who
knew that in his own life many voices clamored for attention. I refer
to the poet Rainer Maria Rilke:

1. Dante Alighieri, *The Divine Comedy*, trans. Lawrence Grant White (New
York: Pantheon, 1948) 58.
2. George Herbert, "Joseph's Coat," in *George Herbert: The Country Parson,
the Temple*, edited, with an introduction by John N. Wall, Jr. (New York: Paulist,
1981) 284.
3. Frederick Buechner, *The Hungering Dark* (New York: Seabury, 1981) 27.

My life is not this steeply sloping hour,
in which you see me hurrying.
Much stands behind me; I stand before it like a tree;
I am only one of my many mouths,
and at that, the one that will be still the soonest.

I am the rest between two notes;
which are somehow always in discord
because Death's note wants to climb over—
but in the dark interval, reconciled,
they stay there trembling.
    And the song goes on, beautiful.[4]

The song of Thomas Merton goes on, beautiful. Though he has been dead twenty-five years, Merton continues to touch the minds and hearts of individuals and nations. Major biographies have attempted to track his mysterious life, four volumes of his letters have now been published, his books and tapes continue to sell, workshops, seminars, classes, and conferences are available on an annual basis. People are interested in knowing who this man was, what voices he heard, how he responded to life and love in the twentieth century. We are all desirous of mentors and models. Thomas Merton has been a teacher and guide for many of us.

Was Thomas Merton's vocation one of being a cultural critic? Beyond doubt he played that role, since he boldly challenged the values of our national and international ethos. Merton knew the values of the gospel, and he understood, theoretically and experientially, the values of the world. He felt within his bones the discrepancies of his own heart and of the culture, the distance between the ideal and real, the goal of integrity and the facticity of brokenness. As a critic he was not afraid to speak out and shout words of confrontation, especially against the foolishness of war and the insanity of mass armament.

To be called to the vocation of cultural critic was one of many callings and certainly not the deepest for Merton. In the end, Merton saw his vocation to be a writer. Six years before his death he reflects:

If the monastic life is a life of hardship and sacrifice, I would say that for me most of the hardship has come in connection with writing. It is possible to doubt whether I have become a monk (a doubt

4. Rainer Maria Rilke, "My life is not this steeply sloping hour," *Selected Poems of Rainer Maria Rilke*, trans. Robert Bly (New York: Harper & Row, 1981) 31.

I have to live with), but it is not possible to doubt that I am a writer, that I was born one and will most probably die as one. Disconcerting, disedifying as it is, this seems to be my lot and my vocation. It is what God has given me in order that I might give it back to Him.[5]

And what does one write about? Great authors record their experience of life, inner and outer. Merton wrote about his hunger for God, about his own strange journey in and out of light and darkness, about the political forces that shaped the century, about the cultural movements that influenced individual and national destinies, about the inner landscapes of his often tormented and confused soul. What he felt and thought had to find its incarnation in words to take on full reality. Writing for Merton was a vocation verging on an addiction. But then, can the two be separated?

Rilke's poem talks about one of many mouths. Merton expressed his self-identity in other terms than that of a writer. Here are just a few examples that must be mentioned before venturing into the poetic and prophetic imagination that empowered Merton to do his work as a cultural critic:

For it had become evident to me that I was a great rebel. I fancied that I had suddenly risen above all the errors and stupidities and mistakes of modern society—there are enough of them to rise above, I admit—and that I had taken my place in the ranks of those who held up their heads and squared their shoulders and marched on into the future. In the modern world, people are always holding up their heads and marching into the future, although they haven't the slightest idea what they think the "future" is or could possibly mean. The only future we seem to walk into, in actual fact, is full of bigger and more terrible wars, wars well calculated to knock our upraised heads off those squared shoulders.[6]

. . . I am not only not a Saint but just a weak, proud, self-centered little guy, interested in writing, who wants to belong to God. Intercede for me, a stuffed shirt in a place of stuffed shirts and a big dumb phony Tramp as I am.[7]

5. Thomas Merton, *A Thomas Merton Reader*, ed. Thomas P. McDonnell, revised edition (New York: Doubleday/Image, 1974) 16. First published in 1962.
6. Thomas Merton, *The Seven Storey Mountain* (New York: Harcourt Brace Jovanovich, 1948) 93.
7. Thomas Merton, *The Hidden Ground of Love: The Letters of Thomas Merton*

My outlook is not purely American and I feel sometimes disturbed by the lack of balance in the power civilization of this country. It is technologically very strong, spiritually superficial and weak. There is much good in the people, who are very simple and kind, but there is much potential evil in the irresponsibility of the society that leaves all to the interplay of human appetites, assuming that everything will adjust itself automatically for the good of all. This unfortunately is fatal and may lead to the explosion that will destroy half the world, of which there is serious danger. I entered the monastery twenty years ago, and am novice master here. I believe my vocation is essentially that of a pilgrim and an exile in life, that I have no proper place in this world but that for that reason I am in some sense to be the friend and brother of people everywhere, especially those who are exiles and pilgrims like myself. . . . My life is in many ways simple, but it is also a mystery which I do not attempt to really understand, as though I were led by the hand in a night where I see nothing, but can fully depend on the Love and Protection of Him Who guides me.[8]

Merton's complex personality is evident in this self-portrait. Also in evidence is his marvelous capacity to name reality, the bright and the dark side of life. There is an honesty, and therefore humility, that is very appealing in someone who refuses to romanticize or idealize the mystery of life, which is permeated with comedy and tragedy, faith and doubt, love and much hatred.

Thomas Merton was essentially a writer but one who did not heed the line in Nikos Kazantzakis' *The Last Temptation of Christ:* ''I keep my nose out of God's business.'' Merton put his nose under the divine canvas and was concerned with God's business, that is, people, creation, salvation. As a writer he had to be a cultural critic as well as a poet and contemplative. Through the instrumentality of the written word, Merton was bonded in a rich solidarity with the twentieth century and all it stood for. The famous scene in Louisville is embedded in many of our imaginations:

In Louisville, at the corner of Fourth and Walnut in the center of the shopping district, I was suddenly overwhelmed with the reali-

---

on Religious Experience and Social Concerns, selected and edited by William H. Shannon (New York: Farrar, Straus, Giroux, 1985) 9, 137, 147.

8. Ibid., 51–52.

zation that I loved all those people, that they were mine and I theirs, that we could not be alien to one another even though we were total strangers. . . . This sense of liberation from the illusory difference was such a relief and such a joy to me that I almost laughed out loud. . . . Thank God, thank God that I am like other men, that I am only a man among others.[9]

The Gift of Imagination

Biography must deal with imagination. To know the story of another is to come to an appreciation of the deep psychic images and symbols that govern and guide one's attitudes and behavior. Imagination is many things: the capacity to dream, the power to discern possibilities and fresh alternatives, the faculty of flexibility that makes us forever restless, "a nest of wires" (Mary Oliver) impossible to unravel. Amos Wilder warns us: "When imagination fails doctrines become ossified, witness and proclamation wooden, doxologies and litanies empty, consolations hollow, and ethics legalistic."[10]

The culture of any given era, and by culture I understand the influences of art and politics, economics and song, education and theater, on the consciousness and lifestyle of a given people, is grounded on certain large operative metaphors, indeed on a dominant imagination. The critic comes along with a different set of images and symbols that challenge and sometimes contradict the reigning culture. This person is sometimes called a prophet, sometimes a critic, quite often a rebel. The critic has a different set of eyes (metaphysics), a different way of knowing (epistemology), and therefore a different lifestyle (ethics, morality). It is difficult to overestimate the significance of symbols and images. Avery Dulles gives us a clue to the influences of symbols and thus the importance of the imagination:

Symbols transform the horizons of man's life, integrate his perception of reality, alter his scales of values, reorient his loyalties,

9. Thomas Merton, *Conjectures of a Guilty Bystander* (New York: Doubleday/Image, 1968) 156–57.
10. Amos Niven Wilder, *Theopoetic* (Philadelphia: Fortress, 1976) 2.

attachments and aspirations in a manner far exceeding the powers of abstract conceptual thought.[11]

What about Merton's poetic imagination? Poetry has to do with experience and words. The poet is skilled in making words do extraordinary things in creating new and significant experiences for the reader. When the poetic imagination is activated, our experiences of life are deepened and broadened, our contact with reality is sharpened and enriched, our sense of life takes on greater fullness and intensity. Merton was a poet. He felt life deeply, he wrote about it in extraordinary ways using images and verse to communicate what he felt and saw.

The poet Merton demonstrates his skill in capturing the human struggle through the poetic medium:

This afternoon, let me
Be a sad person. Am I not
Permitted (like other men)
To be sick of myself?

Am I not allowed to be hollow,
Or fall in the hole
Or break my bones (within me)
In the trap set by my own
Lie to myself? O my friend,
I too must sin and sin.

I too must hurt other people and
(Since I am no exception)
I must be hated by them.

Do not forbid me, therefore,
To taste the same bitter poison,
And drink the gall that love
(Love most of all) so easily becomes.

Do not forbid me (once again) to be
Angry, bitter, disillusioned,
Wishing I could die.

While life and death
Are killing one another in my flesh,
Leave me in peace. I can enjoy,
Even as other men, this agony.

11. Avery Dulles, *Models of the Church* (New York: Image Books, 1974) 24.

Only (whoever you may be)
Pray for my soul. Speak my name
To Him, for in my bitterness
I hardly speak to Him: and He
While He is busy killing me
Refuses to listen.[12]

Merton insists on "being like the rest of men." Being allowed this privilege/burden arose out of his deep sense of solidarity with people (and with all creation) and an awareness of the human condition. As he used images and symbols to understand and critique himself, he also relied on imaginative language to do his work as a cultural critic.

In a letter to Pope John XXIII dated November 10, 1958, Merton uses the imagery of the cloister, contemplation, solitude, to describe his sense of vocation and mission to the larger world. The monastic life must not be limited to prayer and penance. Merton felt an obligation, if not a compulsion, to be connected with the major movements going on in the world, and to be connected in sympathetic ways. His poetic sensitivity demanded that contact be made and sustained despite the cloister walls. He writes:

It seems to me that, as a contemplative, I do not need to lock myself into solitude and lose all contact with the rest of the world; rather this poor world has a right to a place in my solitude. It is not enough for me to think of the apostolic value of prayer and penance; I also have to think in terms of a contemplative grasp of the political, intellectual, artistic and social movements in this world—by which I mean a sympathy for the honest aspirations of so many intellectuals everywhere in the world and the terrible problems they have to face. I have had the experience of seeing that this kind of understanding and friendly sympathy, on the part of a monk who really understands them, has produced striking effects among artists, writers, publishers, poets, etc., who have become my friends without my having to leave the cloister.[13]

Merton's rich and fertile imagination was grounded in three disciplined and extraordinary capacities: the capacity to notice, the

12. Thomas Merton, *The Strange Islands* (New York: New Directions, 1957) 25–26.
13. Merton, *Hidden Ground*, 482.

capacity to speak, the capacity to care.[14] Noticing, the ability to pay attention to reality, is an art that was well developed in the life of Thomas Merton. Nor was this skill merely one of a keen sensitivity. Rather, Merton's noticing cut to the quick of reality and led him, often painfully, into the truth of things. As a cultural critic he simply ''saw'' what others were blind to: he saw the stupidity of war, he saw the insanity of the arms race, he saw the evils of racism. Dialectically, he also was attuned to beauty and goodness, praising God and people in appropriate ways.

Merton's skills in naming were extensive. What helped him was his broad education: schooling in France and England, studies in New York, his teaching experience, and perhaps most of all, the breadth of his reading. What came in was given out. His letters, books, poetry, and lectures were all means for Merton of putting in ordered fashion the vast store of knowledge he had accumulated. Part of his speech was sharp and biting, speech directed to acts and institutions of inhumanity. Merton condemned evil, in society and in the Church. He spoke, as we have seen, sharp words about himself: tramp, rebel, big dumb phony, stuffed shirt. Different noticing demands different words. Not all people who notice are able to speak with eloquence. But Merton was one who did.

Poetic imagination demands the capacity to notice, the capacity to use language well. But not all poets are gifted with the capacity to care. Merton knew that the key to a Christian existence lay in the heart, a heart grounded and centered on faith: ''Men without deep faith live as it were with no center, and no heart, and consequently one can only expect violence, injustice, confusion and chaos.''[15]

There were four things that deepened Merton's faith and fostered his capacity to care: prayer, penance, poverty, and solitude. His structured Trappist life helped to make these means both accessible and, through mutual witness, believable. In prayer, God's word pointed the way to radical concerns for others; in penance, freedom from the false self assisted in breaking down the walls of self-protectiveness; in poverty, space was made for the other, the room of hospitality remained uncluttered; in solitude, an authentic listening allowed the cry

14. See Walter Brueggeman's *Finally Comes the Poet* (Minneapolis: Fortress, 1989).

15. Merton, *Hidden Ground*, 67.

of the poor and lonely to be heard. Yet even here Merton knew of dark dangers:

> The crises of the age are so enormous and the mystery of evil so unfathomable: the action of well-meaning men is so absurd and tends so much to contribute to the very evil it tries to overcome: all these things should show us that the real way is prayer, and penance, and closeness to God in poverty and solitude. Yet there is no question that sometimes this too is also preached as an evasion of responsibility.[16]

Our images of God, of self, and of life are determinative. Robert Jay Lifton begins his book *The Broken Connection* in this fashion:

> We live on images. As human beings we know our bodies and our minds only through what can be imagined. To grasp our humanity we need to structure these images into metaphors and models. Writers, artists, and visionaries have always known this— as have philosophers and scientists in other ways. Depth psychologists, however, take on the special and perhaps impossible task of bringing order to this dazzling array of images and the equally impressive range of feelings with them.[17]

Merton understood intuitively Boulding's principle: "Behavior depends on image." Two images were embedded in Merton's imagination as they are in our own: August 6, 1945, the mushroom cloud of an atomic bomb; August 7, 1959, the haunting photograph of the earthrise from outer space. Merton's poetic imagination was used to speaking about war and peace, war that mutilates human bodies and human spirits, peace that reflects the kingdom of God. War and peace is the subtitle that underlies Merton's poetic critique of our times.

Prophetic Imagination

The formation of one's imagination can take different tacks. So much depends upon environment, genes, where one is born, and the historical circumstances of one's times. Poetic imagination is not necessarily prophetic. In fact, many poets isolate themselves from political

16. Ibid., 20.
17. Robert J. Lifton, *The Broken Connection* (New York: Basic Books, 1979) 3.

and economic realities in an attempt to protect their solitude so as to avoid dissipating limited energies. But Merton's personality could not bear such restrictions. He was a monk universal, concerned about everything. His poetic imagination necessarily had to be prophetic.

The contemporary Scripture scholar Walter Bruggemann states in his work *The Prophetic Imagination* that a prophet is one who criticizes and energizes:

> It is the task of prophetic ministry to bring the claims of the tradition and the situation of enculturation into an effective interface. That is, the prophet is called to be a child of the tradition, one who has taken it seriously in the shaping of his or her own field of perception and system of language, who is so at home in that memory that the points of contact and incongruity with the situation of the church in culture can be discerned and articulated with proper urgency.[18]

Merton fits well this description: his studies grounded him in the tradition, his curiosity and sense of solidarity attuned him to cultural realities, his faith pushed him with urgency into speaking the truth achieved through prayer and study. His imagination was deeply prophetic.

Today the prophet sees much of the world as dysfunctional. Merton's analysis sees our sickness as one of disordered love:

> Our times manifest in us a basic distortion, a deep-rooted moral disharmony against which laws, sermons, philosophies, authority, inspiration, creativity, and apparently even love itself would seem to have no power. On the contrary, if man turns in desperate hope to all these things, they seem to leave him more empty, more frustrated, and more anguished than before. Our sickness is the sickness of disordered love, of the self-love that realizes itself simultaneously to be self-hate and instantly becomes a source of universal, indiscriminate destructiveness. This is the other side of the coin that was current in the nineteenth century: the belief in indefinite progress, in the supreme goodness of man and of all his appetites. What passes for optimism, even Christian optimism, is the indefectible hope that eighteenth- and nineteenth-century attitudes can continue valid, can be *kept* valid, just by the determi-

---

18. Walter Brueggeman, *The Prophetic Imagination* (Philadelphia: Fortress, 1978) 12.

nation to smile, even though the whole world may fall to pieces. Our smiles are symptoms of the sickness.[19]

Besides this disordered love, Merton's prophetic stance takes on the emancipation and autonomy of the technological mind. This attitude claims unlimited possibilities, holds that science can do everything—that science is "infallible and impeccable," that it is responsible to no power and has its own "ethic of expediency and efficiency." Merton writes: "If technology remained in the service of what is higher than itself—reason, man, God—it might indeed fulfill some of the functions that are now mythically attributed to it. But becoming autonomous, existing only for itself, it imposes upon man its own irrational demands, and threatens to destroy him. Let us hope it is not too late for man to regain control."[20]

Half prophets are neither nice to be around nor are they terribly helpful. Their criticism may be accurate, but unless alternatives are offered we should not expect an improvement of the common good. Merton, during one of his stays in the hospital, where he had access to newspapers and the events of the world, suggests that we have the following needs: "First, we need to recover the belief that order is possible, and that it rests with us to preserve it. Then we need the desire to do it." He goes on to say that we have to believe in the good potentialities of people, however wasted or misused in the past. The key is that the order must come from the inside. "Finally, all this requires the hope that independent and personal initiative will not be entirely useless: we need to recover the belief that it is worthwhile and possible to break through the state of massive inertia and delusion created by the repetition of statements and slogans without meaning and without any effect in concrete action. In a word, the arbitrary, fictitious, and absurd mentality of our society—reflected in its advertising and entertainment particularly—must be recognized as an affront to man's personal dignity."[21]

A social analysis done in 1993, twenty-five years after Merton's death, presents us with a number of crises: alienation and loneliness; the gap between the have's and have-not's; the inability of the community to care; the "forgetting of Being"; the disintegration of our

19. Merton, *Conjectures of a Guilty Bystander*, 67–68.
20. Ibid., 75–77.
21. Ibid., 255.

stories (images, symbols, metaphors); the civil strife we call violence; the blatant consumerism that dehumanizes people and society. The writings of Thomas Merton the prophet assist us in once again focusing on values that point us toward a "civilization of love." Without this critique and others like it, we may not avoid the vicious vortex of twentieth-century muddleness.

Conclusion

As I think of Thomas Merton in his role as a cultural critic, three books come to mind: *Blessed Simplicity, The Seven Habits of Highly Effective People*, and *Care of the Soul*.

Raimundo Panikkar, in *Blessed Simplicity*, subtitled *The Monk as Universal Archetype*, maintains that "[t]here are four sociological groups of capital importance in society: (1) church or religious groups; (2) academia, or teaching and research institutions; (3) government and military; (4) industry and commerce."[22] He goes on to say that the monk, in the strict sense, is not priest, intellectual, public officer, producer; the monk does not fit into any of these four sociological groups. A fifth state exists in which a person has abandoned the world and has renounced the ordinary human enterprises. Panikkar then mentions a sixth group, namely, the guerrillas who are dissidents and revolutionaries.

These categories may be too clean for some, but they do provide a way of identifying lifestyles and value systems. Regarding the function of the monk in society, he is, Panikkar writes,

> the person who has abandoned the world, the monk, the *samnya-sin*, the renouncer, the one who has forsaken all the rules of the game of human intercourse, who has leapt over the wall and yet remains as a symbol to the majority of mortals of the provisionality of all human enterprise. In his own eyes the monk is one segregated, set apart, but in people's consciousness he is holy and thus by no means a marginal or peripheral being. The monk resides in the very center of society, and when they are faced by what appears to be technically insoluble problems the people approach their saints, their monks, hermits, and ascetics.[23]

22. Raimundo Panikkar, *Blessed Simplicity: The Monk as Universal Archetype* (New York: Seabury, 1982) 86–87.
23. Ibid.

I wonder whether the Western world holds the monk in such esteem. I do not wonder nor do I doubt that one monk, Thomas Merton, has articulated many insights that will help us deal with our near-insoluble problems.

The second book: Stephen R. Covey's *The Seven Habits of Highly Effective People*. A friend of mine suggested that this book and others like it are the spiritual manuals of our day, replacing official texts. Covey and his cohorts speak about values and mission statements, principles of communication and relationship, the art of dialogue and achieving one's goals. From Covey's first principle of "Be Proactive" to the seventh guideline of "Sharpen the Saw," we hear the basic dynamic of growth toward full human potential.

Merton's critique of such works would probably center on the self-reliance emphasis and the short-changing of grace. But Merton would appreciate the desire that is arising in various management fields to deal with the whole person, to live by a set of principles, to take seriously and responsibly the human journey.

On the best seller list of the *New York Times Book Review* magazine is Thomas Moore's *Care of the Soul*. The thesis of this text is that we have lost our soulfulness, we are no longer connected to what is deepest and most human and divine within us. *Care of the Soul* simply affirms much of what Merton stood for. Merton's voice cried out in the wasteland, cried out that we must care for the inner life. His stress on tending the inner life so that our outer lives might be authentic and human remains a great service to our time.

Two of Merton's seven mountains were poetry and prophecy. He climbed those roughed slopes and reported back to us his find. For that report, I am grateful.

Merton, Friend of God and Prophet

Response to
"Thomas Merton: Prophetic and Poetic Imagination"
by
Robert F. Morneau

Sandra M. Schneiders, I.H.M.

Introduction

Let me begin by thanking Bishop Robert Morneau for his thought-provoking paper on Thomas Merton as cultural critic. His conclusion, that Merton was indeed a cultural critic but that that was not his primary or defining vocation, is one with which I would agree. I also agree that somehow Merton's true vocation had more to do with imagination than with analysis, with writing itself as a creative process and the evocator of creativity than with its use as an informational tool. I think that Bishop Morneau has identified something important about Merton's distinctive mode of cultural criticism in pointing out that it was rooted in a prophetic capacity for imagining an alternative reality that was itself deeply rooted in his contemplative vocation and best expressed in his writing, perhaps at least as effectively in his poetry as in his prose.

My task, to stimulate further discussion, was made a little more challenging by the fact that I did not find myself in sharp disagreement with anything in Bishop Morneau's paper. That being the case, I decided to pursue one point he made but did not develop, which I think bears further reflection and which might find its way into our discussion.

The Question

At the beginning of his paper Bishop Morneau applied to Merton a poem of Rilke that ends ''And the song goes on, beautiful.'' The question I would like to pursue is *why* does Merton's song go on? What is the secret of his ongoing attractiveness to all kinds of people? Why have serious thinkers speculated that Merton may be the most important spiritual voice of our times? Bishop Morneau made two suggestions toward an answer, both of which are undoubtedly true: that Merton is a mentor and model for many of our contemporaries and that his humility and truthfulness, not only about the world but about himself, make him especially attractive. My question is this: *why* do many find Merton a mentor and model? And does his truthfulness about himself have anything to do with it? If so, what?

A Suggestion

The thesis, perhaps somewhat naive, I would like to suggest is that the secret of Merton's attractiveness is that he was holy. Frankly, important and interesting as most of Merton's writings are in terms of their content, I doubt that he would have the influence he does, evoke the kind of interest that he evokes, if he were not, as a person, somehow fascinating to his contemporaries. Merton receives the kind of scrutiny, generates the kind of curiosity and devotion in people, that we humans tend to reserve for the very good and the very evil. Obviously, if the theory is valid in regard to Merton, he belongs to the category of the very good, of what we in the Christian community have historically called saints.

If this is true, that the secret of Merton's attractiveness is his holiness, we certainly have to think again about holiness. It is probably a measure of how operative certain stereotypical notions of holiness are, despite our loud disclaimers, that the term is seldom used in regard to Merton, even though he certainly defined his life project in terms of the quest for sanctity. Merton is often referred to as a writer, a poet, a monk, a social critic, a mediator between East and West, a major figure in spirituality—but not usually as a saint.

Merton certainly does not fit the classical picture of the saint. In many ways, especially in his early monastic years, Merton was self-absorbed, arrogant, priggish, clerical, self-important—indeed, as he says himself in a passage quoted by Bishop Morneau, he was at times a stuffed shirt and a phony. He got over a lot of that as his experience of himself deepened, as he experienced both in prayer and through his numerous contacts with others his real solidarity with the rest of the human race, and as he came to the almost bitter realization that monastic life not only did not make people superior to others but that the form of life itself was not intrinsically superior even in principle and certainly not in fact. Nevertheless, Merton remained to a large extent a restless monk torn between his vocation to write and his call to hiddenness, often rebellious toward his superiors, given to sensual excess when he had the chance. Close to the end of his life he carried on a brief sexual affair not only in violation of his vow of chastity and behind his superior's back, but perhaps even more shockingly, he even kept up his work of preaching to the monastic community while violating both the vows and the discipline of the life itself. And one could go on. The point is that Merton's failings were real and serious, not the charming peccadillos of the saint who is kept humble by occasional harmless slips. Merton raises the question of what is sanctity in a particularly acute way, precisely because of the real failings that were part of his life virtually to the very end.

In recent conversations with friends and colleagues about this question of holiness I have picked up two interesting and important pieces of wisdom, which I think are intrinsically related to each other and illuminating in regard to Merton. One friend, with whom I co-taught a doctoral seminar on saints and holiness, made the accurate observation that there is virtually no trait associated with holiness that some recognized saint has not lacked or violated. Whether we select kindness, prayerfulness, discretion, meekness, faith, joy, hope, zeal, or any other trait, we will find some saint who was rather singularly lacking in it, at least as far as human observation permits us to judge. And no saint had them all. My colleague's conclusion was that all that the saints really have in common, all that can be considered universally characteristic of saints, is that they are friends of God.

Another friend made a very helpful and important distinction between holiness and perfection. Some people are actually quite perfect. They are quiet, respectful, judicious, kind, dutiful, patient, obedient, prayerful, hard-working, self-effacing, humble, and so on. And they might well be, indeed probably are, actually holy. But there are others, especially complex, gifted, and multiply-involved people, who

usually have many ineradicable imperfections that are quite real and
even sinful. Such traits as anger, arrogance, self-centeredness, ambi-
tion, attachment, competitiveness, intolerance, and so on are likely to
be part and parcel of their personalities and seemingly not finally
amenable, or at least not totally so, even to deep prayer and serious
ascetical effort. These traits seem to be the flip side, the shadow, of
the very traits that enable such people to do great things for God and
humanity—traits like imagination, courage, drive, magnanimity, self-
confidence, breadth of vision, adventuresomeness, zeal, inability to
accept the mediocre in themselves, institutions, or others, intolerance
of compromise. One has only to think of saints like Moses, Jeremiah,
Jerome, Teresa of Avila, or Catherine of Siena, or those who have not
made the rolls like Origen, Meister Eckhart, Margery Kempe, or Dorothy Day, to realize that there is a major distinction between sanctity
and perfection.

It seems to me that both of these observations throw some light
on Merton's appeal. First, Merton was clearly not perfect, not even
at the end of his life. He was a complex personality—so complex he
made a sometimes tiresome cottage industry out of figuring himself
out in public. The breadth of his interests and concerns, his passion
for integrity, his lust for life, his genius for friendship, his leadership
capacity, his sheer energy, his thirst for knowledge, his burning compassion for his contemporaries, had their shadow side in the very
flaws, imperfections, and sins he relentlessly revealed to his readers
with that truthfulness, that existential humility which Bishop Morneau
pointed out.

But, Merton was, first and foremost, a friend of God. He was,
we might say, terminally obsessed with God. Whether he was in the
depths of prayer or the depths of sin and self-loathing, the compass
needle of his life always pointed due North—toward the mysterious
God hidden in the wasteland of contemplative nothingness and whom
Merton tenaciously believed would be finally revealed as love. Sometimes that compass needle marked his path as true; sometimes it
showed him how badly off course he was; sometimes the instrument
itself seemed to get lost in the rubble. But the only thing that made
anything in his life or his world interesting enough for him to reflect
on it, write about it, fight over it, or even sin for it was its relationship
to God. A friend is not someone who is perfect; a friend is someone
who cares, passionately and always, and includes the beloved friend

totally in his or her life, even and perhaps especially when that life is particularly unadmirable. Whatever else Merton was, he was a friend of God. When holy Wisdom enters into human souls, Scripture tells us, she makes them friends of God and prophets. Merton is heard by his contemporaries as someone who was both wise and prophetic.

Conclusion

My tentative conclusion about the attractiveness of Merton is that he responds to a feature of our culture that is rarely overt but that is very deep, namely, a kind of agonized obsession with transcendence. It has often been remarked that the absence of God is a striking feature of our cultural experience, but it is a felt absence, like the cavity of a just-pulled tooth. The meaninglessness of our sated culture, the numbing terror of living too long on the brink of ultimate disaster, the intractable and overwhelming complexity of our problems, the opening on an alternative reality provided to many by drugs, and the encounter with the great mystical traditions of the East are among the features of twentieth-century culture that keep the God issue alive, as an ache if not as an articulated question. Merton thematized the search so many of our contemporaries are on, whether or not they can or choose to name it. Is it not strange that so many people have said about Merton, who had such a profound, even exaggerated, sense of his own uniqueness and specialness, that they are fascinated by Merton because "his story is my story." What makes him so interesting is his single-minded perseverance in the quest that, whether we can name it or not, is ours.

What Merton said with his person as well as in his writing was that our true identity (what every modern is finally looking for) lies in God and that it makes sense to pursue that identity, even with the whole of one's one and only life. It is possible to pursue it, Merton said, no matter who you are or where you are or how imperfect you are by the standards of the world or your own standards or the standards of the institutions of religion. Merton's experience says to his contemporaries that you can pursue it through work you love (like writing) or work you hate (like making cheese), through the people you love (even in the wrong circumstances) and the people you admire (like Suzuki) and the people who drive you crazy (like the abbot), through sin and loneliness and the oppression of others, through succeeding and failing, through silence and conversation, through involvement and solitude, in the thought-world of your own time and through the classics of the tradition, in your own culture or by crossing over into the culture of others, in labor and leisure and contemplation and teaching and watching for fires, in the monastery or a hermitage or a hospital bed or on an airplane or on the street corner, through your own tenacious weakness and evil and that of others, in the beautiful and the plain and even the ugly.

By his compulsion to record, with the ruthless honesty and humility Bishop Morneau mentioned, details of his everyday life as if every moment he lived had some kind of cosmic significance, Merton makes us all aware that the banalities and the ordinariness as well as the occasional soaring heights of our lives are indeed of cosmic significance, but only insofar as they are related to God, as they relate us to God. Happy is the person who becomes conscious of this, says Merton, not as an abstract idea or even an intellectual conviction but as the very air one breathes. Perhaps Merton is so fascinating, so loved by so many, because he has made us conscious, in the idiom of the twentieth century, not only that our hearts are restless for the Beauty ever ancient, ever new, but that if we can learn, however late or early, to love that restlessness, it will make our lives not less conflictual or confusing, because in the end that does not really matter, but it will give them depth and intensity and significance, and that matters a great deal. The ultimate adventure, Merton says convincingly to a generation that has gone to the moon, is the journey into the vastness of God.

Eight Freedom Songs:
Merton's Sequence of Liberation

Patrick F. O'Connell

Thomas Merton's "Eight Freedom Songs," written in the spring of 1964, have probably been more read about than actually read themselves. Moreover, the account in William Shannon's biography of Merton[1] as well as Merton's own extensive correspondence with Robert Williams, the young black tenor who had originally asked Merton to compose the songs,[2] focuses on the complicated, at times tragicomic, circumstances attending their composition, setting, and eventual performance (at a memorial service for Martin Luther King in August 1968)[3] rather than on the structure and themes of the poems themselves. The relative obscurity of the poems is due in part to the fact that they are not printed as a group in the *Collected Poems*, but are scattered among the alphabetically arranged "Uncollected Poems" in that volume.[4] But

1. William H. Shannon, *Silent Lamp: The Thomas Merton Story* (New York: Crossroad, 1992) 234–38.

2. Thomas Merton, *The Hidden Ground of Love: Letters on Religious Experience and Social Concerns*, ed. William H. Shannon (New York: Farrar, Straus, Giroux, 1985) 587–607.

3. Four of the songs, "Sundown," "All the Way Down," "The Lord is Good," and "Earthquake," were set to music by composer Alexander Peloquin and first performed at the 1968 Liturgical Conference in Washington, D.C., at which King had originally been scheduled to speak. See the headnote to Merton's letters to June Yungblut in *The Hidden Ground of Love*, 635, and Merton's letters to Yungblut, pp. 645–48; see also Thérèse Lentfoehr's note to her article, "Social Concern in the Poetry of Thomas Merton," in Gerald Twomey, ed., *Thomas Merton: Prophet in the Belly of a Paradox* (New York: Paulist, 1978) 136.

4. *The Collected Poems of Thomas Merton* (New York: New Directions, 1977); the Freedom Songs are found on pp. 669–70, 692–93, 701–3, 711–12, 714–15, 756–

even readers who make the effort to read the songs in their proper order may initially find themselves rather unimpressed. Like traditional black spirituals,[5] the Freedom Songs are adaptations of biblical texts (in this case taken either from the Psalms or the Prophets of the Old Testament) reworked to highlight their pertinence for contemporary experience, specifically the pursuit of racial justice and equality. The poems are definitely songlike in form, with a great deal of verbal repetition, including frequent refrains; like hymns and songs generally they may appear to be "thin" in comparison with other types of poetry, particularly when considered apart from their music. But to dismiss these poems too hastily as minor achievements, or as less significant in themselves than as an occasion for observing Merton's sensitivity and concern in a sometimes exasperating situation, would fail to do justice to a series of poems that, within the accepted limitations of their genre, can be considered both artistically successful and spiritually challenging. Read as a coherent sequence, the Freedom Songs trace a pattern of personal and social transformation in which the nonviolent struggle for civil and human rights serves as a paradigm for the fundamental Christian journey to full redemption, a liberation from both outer and inner oppression due to human sinfulness.

I

The opening poem, "Sundown," begins the sequence by directing attention to the structural injustice in which even religious institutions are implicated and provides a good example of the apparent

---

57, 775–76, 779–80; a note on p. 668, at the beginning of the "Uncollected Poems" section, does provide a list of the eight poems in the proper order, though here and after the individual poems the date of composition is given as 1966, the year in which they were privately published by Williams as a fund-raising effort (see Shannon, *Silent Lamp,* 235).

5. Merton himself makes this connection with regard to an appropriate musical setting in his first letter to Williams, on March 31, 1964 (*The Hidden Ground of Love,* 588). See also his comments on spirituals and "Freedom Songs" as "prophetic" in *Seeds of Destruction* (New York: Farrar, Straus & Giroux, 1964) 72–74. The songs may also owe something to Merton's familiarity with Ernesto Cardenal's contemporary versions of the Psalms, which Merton had read as early as September 1961: see his letter of September 16 to Pablo Antonio Cuadra in *The Courage for Truth: Letters to Writers,* ed. Christine M. Bochen (New York: Farrar, Straus, Giroux, 1993) 189.

simplicity and actual subtlety of Merton's technique in the poems. Based upon the denunciation of false prophets in chapter 3 of Micah, this poem is particularly dependent on the refrain with which it opens and closes and which recurs three other times between the successive stanzas:

> O sundown, sundown
> Like blood on Sion! (ll. 1–2).

The basis of the comparison initially seems to be twofold, a reference both to the color of the sunset reflecting on the walls of Jerusalem and to ritual sacrifice, the blood shed on the altar of the Temple, located on Mount Sion; thus, at the outset and without any further context the relation between sundown and blood might appear to be based simply on empirical observation. But with each successive repetition the connotations of the simile will grow more ominous.

In the first stanza, the approach of night becomes an image of the failure of prophetic vision:

> The sun goes down
> Upon the prophets;
> Night is falling
> And there is no answer (ll. 3–6).

The physical darkness into which the prophets are drawn implies a lack of spiritual enlightenment. Here Merton condenses verses 6–7 of the original biblical text: "Therefore you shall have night, not vision, darkness, not divination; the sun shall go down upon the prophets, and the day shall be dark for them. Then shall the seers be put to shame, and the diviners confounded; they shall cover their lips, all of them, because there is no answer from God."[6] In the poem, no reason for the prophets' failure is yet apparent, but after the negative interpretation given to the sundown in this stanza, the comparison to blood in the refrain that follows is less likely to be read now as based only on color or sacrificial practices; indeed, as the first stanza functioned as a commentary on the first line of the refrain, so the second stanza does the same for the second line:

6. The translation cited is that of the Confraternity version of the Old Testament, which would have been the approved Catholic text at the time Merton was writing; it is identical in all cited Old Testament passages to the text of the New American Bible; names of the prophetic books are given their more familiar spelling.

> For men build Sion
> Out of blood;
> They build Jerusalem
> With wrong (ll. 9–12).[7]

Here a cause-effect relationship between the two parts of the refrain is implied: it is because there is "blood on Sion," because there was bloodshed and injustice in building the city, that the sun goes down upon the prophets, who are left in darkness with no word from the Lord. Religious figures and institutions are compromised by their collaboration with, or at least failure to denounce, the forces of oppression. This idea is reinforced in the following stanza, in which the Temple is directly mentioned and the imagery becomes more explicit:

> They build the temple
> With dead men's bones;
> They build Jerusalem
> With wrong (ll. 15–18).[8]

The implication is that religion countenances not merely animal sacrifices but the sacrifice of human beings: the Temple is not a house of life but a charnel house, a shrine built on and dedicated to death; worship in such a place is not only meaningless but blasphemous. Thus the stanza sharpens the attack on a sterile religious formalism divorced from concern for justice.

The final stanza appears to be truncated, with the refrain incorporated as the last two lines of the quatrain:

> Night has fallen
> Is there still no answer?
> O sundown, sundown
> Like blood on Sion! (ll. 21–24).

7. See Micah 3:10: ". . . who build up Sion with bloodshed, and Jerusalem with wickedness!"

8. The reference to bones is found in Micah 3:2-3: "You who tear their skin from them, and their flesh from their bones! They eat the flesh of my people, and flay their skin from them and break their bones. . . ." There may also be a reminiscence of the opening lines of Robert Lowell's poem, "Children of Light": "Our Fathers wrung their bread from stocks and stones / And fenced their gardens with the Redman's bones" from *Lord Weary's Castle*, a volume Merton praised highly when it first appeared in 1947 (see *The Sign of Jonas* [New York: Harcourt, Brace, 1953] 81–82, and Robert Lowell, *Lord Weary's Castle and the Mills of the Kavanaughs* [Cleveland: World Publishing, 1961] 28).

The alteration of the pattern here is highly significant. The first two lines rephrase lines 5–6 as a question; the inclusion of the refrain suggests that for those with ears to hear there is an answer, has been an answer all along, though unrecognized by the false prophets and their followers: the refrain is the authentic prophecy. The final stanza implicitly reflects the contrast in the biblical source between the false prophets, who have no answer, and Micah, whose prophecy is a prediction of the downfall of the oppressors: "But as for me, I am filled with power, with the spirit of the Lord, with authority and with might; to declare to Jacob his crimes and to Israel his sins. . . . Therefore, because of you, Sion shall be plowed like a field, and Jerusalem reduced to rubble, and the mount of the temple to a forest ridge" (Mic 3:8, 12). The refrain in its final appearance looks not only to the past but to the future: the blood of past injustice becomes a portent of the blood of future retribution; the end of daylight foreshadows the end of Sion, the downfall of the old order, the coming day of the Lord as a *"dies irae,"* a time of darkness, defeat, judgment.

Thus by linking together two images present but not related in Micah, the sunset of verse 6 and the blood of verse 10, and gradually allowing the full implications of their relationship to unfold for the perceptive reader, Merton has created a powerful introduction for his sequence. The poem challenges the complacent assumptions of the social and political establishment that the foundations of its power remain secure. Though analogies remain implicit with the American situation, in which the "city on a hill" was built on the enslavement of human beings, those with ears to hear will recognize the contemporary application of the scriptural word, which is simultaneously a warning to the powerful and a promise to the poor and oppressed.

II

The title of the second poem in the series, "Evening Prayer," suggests an immediate point of comparison with "Sundown," since both are set at the same time of day, but the coming of darkness here is an occasion for a reaffirmation of trust in God, even when faced with threats and dangers from precisely the sort of people who "build Jerusalem / With wrong" in the preceding poem. The speaker's fidelity under trial provides a counter-example to the spiritual emptiness of the pseudoprophets and the hypocrisy of conventional worshipers. This poem depicts the struggles of the just person of the Psalms (Pss 140 and 141 are the sources cited)[9] while continuing to probe the causes, manifestations, and consequences of injustice.

The opening verse-paragraph presents a model of authentic worship and suggests what the rest of the poem will explore in detail, the cost of being a sign of contradiction to a faithless society:

> Lord, receive my prayer
> Sweet as incense smoke
> Rising from my heart
> Full of care
> I lift up my hands
> In evening sacrifice
> Lord receive my prayer (ll. 1-7).

The most immediately noteworthy aspect of these lines is probably their symmetry: not only does the final line repeat the first but the image of incense smoke (l. 2), associated with sacrificial offerings, corresponds to the explicit mention of sacrifice in line 6; and "Rising from my heart" (l. 3) closely parallels "I lift up my hands" (l. 5). Not only does this balanced pattern suggest that the speaker is characterized by a calm and ordered perspective but it draws attention to the central line, "Full of care," which seems all the more anomalous in this context. At least three related questions arise from reflection on the form and content of this remarkable passage: What is the cause of the speaker's care? How can he remain so evidently at peace yet be "full of care"? How can his prayer be described as "sweet" though arising from a care-filled heart? (It is worth noting that neither the care nor the sweetness is found in the scriptural source, Psalm 140:1-2).[10] Answers to these questions will become evident as the prayer continues, even as the act of praying will have on the speaker a transforming effect, which becomes its own unanticipated yet fully satisfying answer, incorporating and transcending the others.

---

9. The Vulgate numbering of the Psalms is retained in conformity with Merton's usage.

10. "O Lord, to you I call, hasten to me: hearken to my voice when I call upon you. Let my prayer come like incense before you; the lifting up of my hands, like the evening sacrifice."

The lines that follow make clear the reasons for the speaker's care, in the context of the basic image of the journey that will continue throughout the sequence:

> When I meet the man
> On my way
> When he starts to curse
> And threatens me,
> Lord, guard my lips
> I will not reply
> Guide my steps in the night
> As I go my way (ll. 8–15).

This verse-paragraph consists of two balanced halves, the first part focused on the danger the speaker faces, the second a prayer for a proper response. His adversary, "the man," a term generic enough to have broad application but having a special resonance for those in the civil-rights movement, both curses and threatens, and the two petitions the speaker makes address these two forms of hostility. It is significant that he prays first not for protection but for faithfulness, the strength not to reply in kind to the enemy's curses; his words recall the attitude of the Suffering Servant, who remained silent under abuse, a stance embodied perfectly by Christ before his tormentors.[11] Even the second petition, a plea for guidance through the darkness,[12] indicates the speaker's determination to remain steadfast on "my way" rather than taking the way of "the man," returning curse for curse and threat for threat. It is really a prayer for nonviolence, for remaining at peace even when provoked, and it suggests that his prayer is sweet to the Lord because it is an offering not just of words but of self.

11. See Isaiah 53:7; Matthew 26:63, 27:12 and parallels; John 19:9; the silence motif in Psalm 140 itself is oriented more toward not becoming one with evildoers: "O Lord, set a watch before my mouth, a guard at the door of my lips. Let not my heart incline to the evil of engaging in deeds of wickedness with men who are evildoers" (140:3-4).

12. Here too the figure of the Isaian Servant seems to be the source. See Isaiah 50:10: "Who among you fears the Lord, heeds his servant's voice, and walks in darkness without any light, trusting in the name of the Lord and relying on his God?" Psalm 24:8-9 also seems to be a source here: "Good and upright is the Lord; thus he shows sinners the way. He guides the humble to justice, he teaches the humble his way"; the opening words may also have influenced the reference to the "other Lord / Who is not so wise and good" in the following verse-paragraph.

The third verse-paragraph attributes the very different attitude of his enemy to his devotion to another god:

> Maybe he belongs
> To some other Lord
> Who is not so wise and good
> Maybe that is why those bones
> Lie scattered on his road (ll. 16–20).

The contrast between "his road" and "my way" is central here: because he is in the power of "some other Lord," of a god of death, not of life (though he may well claim that he follows the "real" Lord), his way is covered with bones. It is not made clear whether the bones are those of his victims or whether they belong to those who have chosen this path and found death along it themselves.[13] Ultimately both interpretations would apply, as those who take the path of violence for whatever reason are on the road to destruction.

While the poem thus far has presented the traditional pattern of the "Two Ways,"[14] the three lines that follow briefly focus on those who think they can remain on the sidelines, taking neither road:

> When I look to right and left
> No one cares to know
> Who I am, where I go (ll. 21–23).[15]

The use of the word "cares" here is a particularly effective indicator of the speaker's isolation: no one cares to know him because to care about him would be to make a costly commitment, to take his cares, his burdens, upon oneself; easier to remain an "innocent bystander," who does not want to get involved. But to choose safety over compas-

13. The interpretation of Psalm 140:7, the source of the reference to the bones, is a notorious crux; the Confraternity version reads, "[T]heir bones are strewn by the edge of the nether world," referring to unjust judges, but the Vulgate makes the bones those of the oppressed victims: "dissipata sunt ossa nostra secus infernum."

14. The first psalm is the best-known presentation of this contrast; Merton discusses the Two Ways in connection with the *Didache*, a classic source, on the second side of "Life and Prayer: Journey in Christ," *The Merton Tapes* 2 (Chappaqua, New York: Electronic Paperbacks, 1972).

15. The source here is Psalm 141:5: "I look to the right to see, but there is no one who pays me heed. I have lost all means of escape; there is no one who cares for my life."

sion is literally to miss the opportunity of a lifetime, because by pay-
ing no attention to ''where I go'' the bystanders fail to recognize that
his is the true path, the way to life, and so they are themselves left
without direction. By situating this short section on the uncommitted
at the center of the poem, Merton presents an implicit challenge to
those who think they do not need to take sides in the contemporary
freedom struggle and suggests that their response is crucial for their
own salvation.

The consequence of this failure of human solidarity is the
speaker's realization that he can rely on the Lord alone, since the Lord
alone cares:

> Hear my prayer
> I will trust in you
> If they set their traps
> On my way
> If they aim their guns at me
> You will guide my steps
> I will pass them by
> In the dark
> They will never see (ll. 24–32).

The focus now centers on the speaker's security. Here again the form
conveys a sense of balance as the pair of threats is matched by a corresponding set of protections: in response to the danger of traps, ''You
will guide my steps'' (note the link of the slant rhyme here); an ambush with guns (a contemporary addition to the scriptural source, of
course)[16] will be eluded by ''pass[ing] them by / In the dark.'' (The
interweaving is even more balanced as the two lines of the first ''if''
clause have a one-line main clause, while the single line of the second
''if'' clause has a two- [or three-] line main clause.) The final line here
can be read to refer not only to their failure to see the speaker and
so to harm him, but to a failure of vision in a wider sense (signaled
by the word ''never''): they remain ''In the dark'' (a phrase that may
be read either with the preceding or the following line, with different
connotations), unable to recognize and respond to the truth just as
surely as the prophets of ''Sundown'' were unable to hear the divine

---

16. The reference to traps is found both in Psalm 140:8 (''Keep me from the
trap they have set for me, and from the snares of evildoers'') and in Psalm 141:4
(''In the way along which I walk they have hid a trap for me'').

Word. (Note also that this section which began with the word "Hear," addressed to the Lord, ends with the word "see," which they will never be able to do.)

The blindness of his persecutors contrasts with the speaker's ability to see the Lord, see the truth, even in the midst of the darkness:

> Lord to you I raise
> Wide and bright
> Faith-filled eyes
> In the night
> You are my protection
> Bring me home (ll. 33–38).

These lines are filled with a sense of serenity conveyed by the simple rhymes of the first four lines and the movement from petition to direct statement in the fifth. The reference to raising the eyes to God here seems to draw not only on Psalm 140:8 ("For toward you, O God, my Lord, my eyes are turned"), but on the even closer parallels in the Songs of Ascents, the pilgrimage hymns of those on the way to Jerusalem: "I lift up my eyes toward the mountains; whence shall help come to me? My help is from the Lord, who made heaven and earth" (Ps 120:1-2); "To you I lift up my eyes who are enthroned in heaven . . . so are our eyes on the Lord, till he have pity on us" (Ps 122:1-2). Like those psalms, the song here now envisions a goal, an arrival "home," where the Lord is.[17] Though the speaker has not yet arrived there, he is confident that he will, so that this word brings the movement of the poem, if not of the journey, to a close.

The final four lines repeat the opening four lines, again emphasizing the sense of order and balance,[18] with one crucial difference:

> And receive my prayer
> Sweet as incense smoke
> Rising from my heart
> Free of care (ll. 39–41).

17. There is, however, a similar passage in Psalm 141:6: "I say, 'You are my refuge, my portion in the land of the living.'"

18. The balance may extend to the previous verse-paragraph as well, as the reference to raising eyes in the night would relate chiastically to the lifting up of hands in evening sacrifice in the final lines of the opening segment of the poem.

By casting his cares upon the Lord, who alone "cares to know / Who I am, where I go," he has been relieved of them. Yet what has remained the same is perhaps as remarkable as what has changed: both states, both stages, have provided a sweet offering to God. It is not the presence or absence of care that makes the prayer sweet or bitter but how the care is dealt with, the attitude one takes toward one's trials. The speaker's fidelity under persecution is just as sweet, as acceptable to God, as the deepened confidence in God's prior faithfulness, a confidence that grows out of that fidelity and that leads the speaker to feel "Free of care," though the objective conditions to be faced may have changed little. The song is thus an encouragement to the freedom movement not to allow bitterness at opposition and persecution to corrode the purity of its commitment, and a promise that to bear the burden of one's cares as an offering to God is paradoxically to be freed of them.

III

Merton is quite aware, of course, that discouragement, even apparent despair, is unavoidable in any genuine struggle for justice, or even for authentic personhood: to come face to face with evil is to risk being overwhelmed by it, above all perhaps when one becomes aware that the same capacity for evil can be found in oneself. But to avoid the encounter is to cling to an illusion about the world and about oneself, to prefer superficial optimism to radical hope. The third poem of the sequence, "All the Way Down," loosely based on the psalm sung by the prophet Jonah in the belly of the great fish, is another variation on the theme of confronting the darkness (though the word itself is not used). Here the "dark night" experience is psychological and spiritual, as the speaker is plunged into the depths of desolation, apparently forsaken by the God to whom he had prayed with such confidence in the previous song. But the paradigm of Jonah—and of Jesus, to whom Jonah is traditionally likened (as Merton himself had done in *The Sign of Jonas* a decade earlier)[19]—reveals that descent is the

---

19. Lawrence S. Cunningham's discussion of the epilogue to *The Sign of Jonas* in "Thomas Merton: Firewatcher," *The Merton Seasonal* 15:2 (Spring 1990) 6–11, is very helpful in exploring the Jonah-Jesus typology.

necessary prelude to ascent, that the end of the journey is not destruction but restoration. Death to the false self makes possible a rebirth to authentic identity as one with the risen Lord: ''I have been crucified with Christ; it is no longer I who live, but Christ who lives in me'' (Gal 2:19-20). This fundamental paschal pattern structures the poem, as all inadequate sources of support are stripped away in order that the speaker's life and actions may be firmly grounded on the only sure foundation.

The opening stanza consists of four pairs of lines, each set including the word ''down,'' each intensifying what had preceded it:

> I went down
> Into the cavern
> All the way down
> To the bottom of the sea.
> I went down lower
> Than Jonas and the whale
> No one ever got so far down
> as me (ll. 1–8).

The pattern of ever-deepening descent, of sinking further and further into the depths, suggests intense feelings of abandonment, a sense of separation from God, traditionally imaged as being ''above.'' The words echo those of Jonah: ''[Y]ou cast me into the deep, into the heart of the sea'' (2:4); ''Down I went to the roots of the mountains'' (2:7). Yet the tone is quite matter-of-fact and dispassionate, not a cry of present anguish ''out of the depths''; the use of the past tense makes clear this is a retrospective description of an experience that has not ended in disaster. The reader might even suppose that the events related here preceded the trials presented in the previous song, and that this poem is included at this point in the sequence as a kind of explanation of the extraordinary peace of spirit depicted there. In any case, each of the details in the stanza can be seen as already containing the potential for a counter-movement, an ascent: the cavern suggests the cave-tomb of the crucified Jesus; the image of drowning in the sea the baptismal passage through death to new life; the reference to Jonas an allusion not only to the catastrophe that struck the prophet but to his eventual reemergence with a more adequate and committed understanding of his calling. Even the final two lines are most properly attributed to Christ, who alone touched the absolute depths, the nadir of human experience, in his kenosis, his total self-emptying: though they express subjectively the speaker's sense of his dereliction, they are objectively true only insofar as he is participating in the redemptive process of the paschal mystery.

This focus on the descent to death which also intimates a resurrection continues in the second stanza, which like the first consists in eight lines loosely linked by rhyme in the fourth and eighth lines, though here there are only two images used for comparison:

> I went down lower
> Than any diamond mine
> Deeper than the lowest hole
> In Kimberly
> All the way down
> I thought I was the devil
> He was no deeper down
> Than me (ll. 9–16).

Both halves of the stanza include the word "deeper," not found in the opening stanza, which carries different connotations than "lower" or "lowest"—a sense of getting in contact with the most fundamental realities. This notion is confirmed in each part of the stanza. The reference to the South African mine ties in with the theme of racial oppression, since the black miners in Kimberly were forced to work under terrible conditions down in "the lowest hole"; but the fact that this is a diamond mine also suggests that if one goes down deep enough, there is something precious to be recovered, and that the intense pressure by which coal is transformed into diamond might represent an analogous transformation in oneself.[20] The identification with the devil

20. See the reference to the "point vierge" as being "like a pure diamond, blazing with the invisible light of heaven" toward the conclusion of the famous "Fourth and Walnut" passage in *Conjectures of a Guilty Bystander* (1966; Garden City, New York: Doubleday Image, 1968) 158; Merton may be recalling an analogous use of the image in Hopkins' poem, "That Nature is a Heraclitean Fire and of the comfort of the Resurrection," ll. 21–24: "In a flash, at a trumpet crash, / I am all at once what Christ is, since he was what I am, and / This Jack, joke, poor potsherd, patch, matchwood, immortal diamond, / Is immortal diamond." [W. H. Gardner, ed., *Poems and Prose of Gerard Manley Hopkins* (Baltimore: Penguin, 1963) 66]. See Merton's reference to this poem, including an abbreviated quotation of these lines, in *The Behavior of Titans* (New York: New Directions, 1961) 91–92. See also *New Seeds of Contemplation* (New York: New Directions, 1961) 38:

in the second part of the stanza concretizes the sense of being abandoned by, and perhaps of abandoning, God; it may also signal the internalization of negative stereotypes with which the oppressor stigmatizes the oppressed, a demonizing of those who are different. But if the speaker thinks he is the devil "all the way down,"[21] the self-discovery made at the deepest point of his descent is that he is not. Like Dante's, this journey into hell is a recognition and rejection of sin, in oneself and in the world, in order that the true self created in the divine image may come forth from the world of the dead, "the lowest hole" of the tomb, to incarnate and radiate goodness.

Such an outcome is confirmed by the stanza that follows, in which death leads to resurrection:

> And when they thought
> That I was gone forever
> That I was all the way
> In hell
> I got right back into my body
> And came back out
> And rang my bell (ll. 17–23).

Here the point of view changes, to what "they thought"—presumably the same anonymous "they" who appeared in the role of oppressors in the two preceding poems. The implication is that they are glad to

---

"This true inner self must be drawn up like a jewel from the bottom of the sea, rescued from confusion, from indistinction, from immersion in the common, the nondescript, the trivial, the sordid, the evanescent." The conclusion of Merton's prose-poem "The Early Legend" mentions volcanic islands rising out of the sea and "the men who come up out of those fires with diamonds in their hands" (*Raids on the Unspeakable* [New York: New Directions, 1966] 137–38).

21. In what is evidently the only published critical discussion of any of the Freedom Songs ("Merton's Bells: A Clarion Call to Wholeness," *The Merton Seasonal* 18:1 [Winter 1993]), Robert G. Waldron provides a Jungian reading of this poem and interprets the devil as the shadow self that must be encountered and integrated in the process of individuation (p. 26); though a generally insightful reading, the article never mentions that the poem is part of a group of Freedom Songs and interprets it exclusively in a biographical context, as "a retrospective view of [Merton's] individuation" (p. 25), with no recognition of its relation to the other poems in the sequence, or to the civil-rights struggle. Substantially the same material is included as chapter 8 of Waldron's book *Thomas Merton in Search of His Soul: A Jungian Perspective* (Notre Dame: Ave Maria Press, 1994) 127–34.

see the speaker permanently out of the way, and that it was their judgment, not God's, that had sentenced him to hell. The reversal of expectations is all the more powerful in conjunction with the complacent
satisfactions of these enemies. Again the experience of the Servant of
the Lord in Isaiah provides an apt parallel: "Oppressed and condemned, he was taken away, and who would have thought any more
of his destiny?" (53:8); but contrary to the presumption of all, "See,
my servant shall prosper, he shall be raised high and greatly exalted"
(52:13). Thus the turning point of the poem comes in line 21, an un-
sophisticated yet effective description of the experience of resurrection. The juxtaposition of "back into" and "back out" suggests the
two dimensions of a renewed life: a restored sense of personal integrity
and identity and a rededication to encountering the world beyond
the self. Like Jonah, the speaker sees his return to life not only as a
personal gift but as a summons to mission. The bell he rings is not
a tolling of death but a victory peal, a call to others to listen to his story.[22]
He does not hide away but is prepared to proclaim what has happened,
to announce the good news he has experienced of new life triumphant
over the forces of death.

If the first half of the poem established the pattern of the journey, the second half (which also consists of two parallel stanzas, now
of seven rather than eight lines, followed by virtually the same "refrain" stanza) communicates the meaning of the experience and the
change it has brought about in the speaker:

> No matter how
> They try to harm me now
> No matter where
> They lay me in the grave
> No matter what injustices they do
> I've seen the root
> Of all that believe.

---

22. Bell imagery is pervasive throughout the canon of Merton's poetry. Somewhat helpful in this regard is Sheila M. Hempstead, "Bells in Thomas Merton's
Early Poetry, 1940–1946," *The Merton Annual* 2 (1989) 257–87, though some of her
readings might be considered less than fully persuasive. Merton's most important
prose discussion of bells, as both temporal markers and as eschatological summons, is in *Thoughts in Solitude* (New York: Farrar, Straus & Cudahy, 1958) 67 ff.

I've seen the room
Where life and death are made
And I have known
The secret forge of war
I even saw the womb
That all things come from
For I got down so far!

But when they thought
That I was gone forever
That I was all the way
In hell
I got right back into my body
And came back out
And rang my bell (ll. 24–44).

The first of these stanzas, built upon three parallel clauses ("No matter how . . . where . . . what . . ."), makes clear that the speaker
is now beyond any evil "they," his persecutors, can inflict. Their efforts
to destroy him have had the opposite effect: they can attempt to harm
him but cannot succeed in any meaningful sense; even if they kill him,
his experience has freed him from all terror of death; they can continue to do injustice but they have lost power, control over him. He
has been liberated from fear because he has come into contact with
the ground of all reality: nothing they can do to him can alter that
vision. Ironically, by trying to destroy him, by stripping him of all
ordinary defenses, they have forced him to confront the question of
what he really believes in: his suffering has brought him insight. It
has also provided a point of contact with other people: getting in touch
with the center of his own faith has brought him to "the root / Of all
that believe," so that his experience and witness are now recognized
to be applicable to others as well.

    The fifth stanza is linked to the previous one by another parallel
construction: "I've seen the root . . ." becomes "I've seen the
room. . . ." (Note also the rhyme in the fourth and seventh line of
each stanza, a pattern shared with the refrain stanza as well.) Here
the experience the speaker underwent is presented as revelatory of primal causes, both positive and negative: he has plumbed the depths
of both destructive ("forge of war") and creative ("womb / That all
things come from") impulses, and now knows these aspects of reality
personally, existentially. In these two stanzas, then, the descent has

shown itself to impart the gift of discernment, the ability to distinguish the life-giving from the death-dealing. The speaker has gone, he now realizes, not low but deep, not away from the goal but down to the source.

The effect of the repetition of the refrain stanza to conclude the poem is now not a reversal of expectations but an awareness that he has returned to bring precisely the message he has just spoken; he has become a sort of Dantesque pilgrim, back from the nether world to reveal what he has seen for his listeners' sake. Like "Sundown," this poem has a prophetic character: if the message of the former was denunciation, that the destroyers will be caught up in their own destruction, here it is annunciation: those whom the destroyers try to destroy will ultimately be victorious. The power underlying this renewal is preeminently paschal: it belongs first of all to Christ, and through Christ to "all that believe," but a privileged place, the poem suggests, is given to those who suffer persecution for justice' sake, for it is through their suffering that they are united to the one who cried out, "My God, my God, why have you forsaken me?" (Mark 15:34), and who promised, "This day you will be with me in Paradise" (Luke 23:43).

IV

In the fourth song, "I Have Called You," it is the voice of the Lord that is heard rather than that of the speaker. The words of consolation to the exiles from the first verse of Isaiah 43, "Fear not, for I have redeemed you; I have called you by name; you are mine," are the basis for the two opening stanzas, which establish a tone of spareness and simplicity that contrasts sharply with the complexity of the human voice in the previous poems:

Do not be afraid
O my people
Do not be afraid
Says the Lord:

I have called you
By your name
I am your Redeemer
You belong to me (ll. 1–8).

The stanzas are related as statement and explanation: the intimate relationship the Redeemer[23] has with those he has called and chosen is
the reason for not being afraid. The assurance given here addresses
the concerns expressed in previous poems, particularly ''Evening
Prayer.'' The detail of being called by name[24] contrasts with the lines
of that poem, ''no one cares to know / Who I am'' (ll. 22–23), and the
key line ''You belong to me,'' which will be repeated exactly or approximately three more times in the poem, recalls the earlier lines,
''Maybe he belongs / To some other Lord'' (ll. 16–17); the promise of
safety and restoration responds to the expression of trust in the earlier poem. But there is also a significant difference here: the song is
addressed to ''my people,'' not just to a single individual. The perspective begins to widen in this poem to situate the speaker in the context of ''all that believe'' (''All the Way Down'' l. 30); this awareness
that he is part of a pilgrim people, a community of faith, will become
more prominent in the second half of the sequence.

What follows serves as a kind of commentary on these opening
stanzas. The word ''call'' as used in line 5 focuses on the idea of calling as identifying, calling by name; but the poem's title, which does
not include the prepositional phrase, suggests a second meaning: to
summon, to call forth. This redemptive sense of the word, which
complements the more creative meaning indicated by naming, is already intimated by the title the Lord uses to identify himself and becomes increasingly important as the poem develops. The third stanza
already implies the idea of the people moving forward in response to
this divine call:

> When you cross the river
> I am there
> I am with you
> When your street's on fire
> Do not be afraid
> O my people
> You belong to me (ll. 9–15).[25]

23. The noun form occurs later in chapter 43: ''Thus says the Lord, your
redeemer, the Holy One of Israel: . . .'' (v. 13).
24. The exact words ''by your name,'' rather than ''by name,'' are found
in Isaiah 45:3, 4, but are spoken there in reference to Cyrus, not to Israel.
25. See Isaiah 43:2: ''When you pass through the water, I will be with you;
in the rivers you shall not drown. When you walk through fire, you shall not be
burned; the flames shall not consume you.''

These lines are marked by an exquisite balance in which the form actually conveys the meaning. The first four lines form a chiastic pattern ("When . . . I am . . . I am . . . When . . ."), which implies that the divine presence, expressed by variants of the divine name understood in an existential, relational sense,[26] is to be found hidden within the crises symbolized by water and fire,[27] just as the two inner lines are framed by the outer lines. The three final lines, which condense the opening stanzas by repeating lines 1–2 and 8, have a converse structure, in which "my people" (l. 14) are surrounded by assurance of protection in lines 13 and 15.

The impression of formal balance continues in the following stanza, which consists in two structurally similar halves:

> Bring my sons from afar
> Says the Savior
> Bring them from that dark country
> Bring them glad and free
> Says the Lord
> They belong to me (ll. 16–21).[28]

Here the redemptive call out of oppression emerges as central, though the proclamation is not addressed directly to "my people" but becomes a general command for all to assist in their liberation. The pattern established by the first half of the stanza, "Bring . . . Says . . . Bring . . .," in which the first and third lines are paralleled, each amplifying one element of the other ("my sons" [l. 16] for "them" [l. 18]; "that dark country" [l. 18] for "afar" [l. 16]), seems to be echoed in the second half, except that the last line does not appear to fit: "Bring

26. In *The Problem of God* (New Haven: Yale University Press, 1964), published the same year as these poems were written, John Courtney Murray popularized this relational interpretation of the divine name as "I will be with you" (p. 9) or "I shall be there" (p. 10), but this interpretation is already implicit in Isaiah 41:10: "Fear not, I am with you; be not dismayed; I am your God." Merton comments on this relational understanding of God in *Faith and Violence* (Notre Dame: University of Notre Dame Press, 1968) 266–67.

27. Though this line might recall scenes of urban ghettos in flame, the poem actually was written more than a year before the first major riot of the sixties, in Watts.

28. See Isaiah 43:6-7: "Bring back my sons from afar, and my daughters from the ends of the earth: everyone who is named as mine, whom I created for my glory, whom I formed and made."

. . . Says . . . They. . . ." But the pattern already set suggests that the first and third lines here should also show some sort of connection. They do, but it is a relationship not of parallelism but of paradox: the final line of the stanza repeats the refrain of lines 8 and 15 but in a new context, juxtaposed with the word "free"; "belong" now recalls connotations of enslavement, of the very oppression from which the people are to be rescued, but the implication here is that they are to be free, can be truly free, only because they belong to the Lord. Because they belong to God, they cannot and must not belong to anyone else, for to belong to the Lord is not an enslavement but a liberation, an empowerment to be the people they were created and called to be ("my people").[29]

The following stanza continues the divine proclamation, echoing and amplifying what has already been spoken but with a more intricate pattern: the six lines form two interlocking chiastic sections, each of four lines:

> Bring my sons and daughters
> From that far country
> From their house of bondage
> Set them free
> Bring them back in glory
> Home to me (ll. 22–29).

The first four lines work a set of variations on the same material from the previous stanza, expanding the reference to "my sons" to "my sons and daughters"; combining "afar" and "from that dark country" into "From that far country"; and adding a new parallel phrase, "From their house of bondage," borrowed from the traditional translation of Exodus 20:2. The two imperatives, "Bring" and "Set," form the outer frame, enclosing the two parallel prepositional phrases. The last four lines, taken together, also create a chiastic pattern, with the paired imperatives "Set" and "Bring" now forming the inner lines; here, however, the outer "frame" lines work by contrast: "house of bondage" is replaced by "home" (another point of contact with "Evening Prayer," which concludes its penultimate stanza with the petition "Bring me home" [l. 38]); and the movement "from . . .

29. See *New Seeds of Contemplation*, 110: "Paradoxically it is the acceptance of God that makes you free and delivers you from human tyranny, for when you serve Him you are no longer permitted to alienate your spirit in human servitude."

bondage'' is completed by ''to me.'' Thus the call as a summoning and the call as a naming are ultimately an identical invitation to divine intimacy, expressed once again directly in the final quatrain, which recapitulates the opening stanzas:

> Do not be afraid
> O my people
> I have called you by your name
> You belong to me (ll. 28–31).

While this final stanza adds no new lines or even new words, the arrangement is new: the direct juxtaposition of ''O my people'' and ''I have called you by your name'' suggests that ''your name'' is in fact ''my people,'' that their deepest identity is inseparably bound up with that of their Lord, and that therefore they indeed have no reason for fear. This assurance, expressed in shifting patterns of symmetry comparable to the graceful steps of a formal dance, serves as an appropriate conclusion to the first half of the cycle of Freedom Songs.

V

The poem that begins the second half of the sequence, ''Be My Defender,'' modeled on Psalm 4, might initially seem to be a regression from the serene beauty of ''I Have Called You.'' Unlike the previous poem (and the three that will follow), it does not take a communal perspective: the speaker once again appears as solitary and persecuted. In many ways the poem seems to replicate the situation described in ''Evening Prayer.'' But a careful reading reveals a definite progression on the speaker's part, which actually continues to develop during the course of the poem itself.

The opening stanza might at first appear rather shapeless and marked by redundancy, but actually it is as carefully patterned as the central stanzas of the previous poem:

> Lord, when there is no escape, be my Defender
> When they crowd around me, Lord
> Be my Defender,
> Steal me out of here,
> Have mercy Lord, show your power
> Steal me out of here,
> Be my Defender (ll. 1–7).

The stanza can be divided into two segments, lines 1–2 and 3–7, which share a common pattern. The opening lines express a feeling of enclosure, the trapped sense of being surrounded by one's enemies;[30] but the form (corresponding to the pattern *abcba*) already serves to counteract this impression: "Lord, when . . . be my Defender / When . . . Lord." At the very center of the crowd, between the two "when" clauses, is the Lord, the Defender, who is also found at beginning and end, thus "surrounding the surrounders." The same pattern, even more evident in the arrangement of the lines, structures the second part of the stanza, though the elements are rearranged: the plea "Be my Defender" now becomes the outer frame, repeated as lines 3 and 7, exchanging places with "Lord," which is now the center of the central line, flanked by a double plea for help: the Lord continues to be at the center and circumference of the scene. The repeated prayer for escape in lines 4 and 6 addresses directly the situation presented in the "when" clauses, which occupy the corresponding position in the first two lines: the verb "steal"[31] is particularly apt, with its connotations not only of surreptitious escape but of being treated by one's enemies as a possession, recalling the reference to bondage in the previous poem and the enslavement/liberation polarity in general.

But the surprising development is that the speaker's prayer is answered in a way quite different from the terms of his petition: he receives not the means of escape but the grace to remain, and in two successive stanzas he boldly confronts the foes who surround him. Whereas in "Evening Prayer" (ll. 11–17) the speaker had simply refused to respond in kind to curses and threats, he is now able to challenge his opponents' evil deeds directly. The first of these stanzas turns the two questions of Psalm 4:3, ("Men of rank, how long will you be dull of heart? Why do you love what is vain and seek after falsehood?") into four parallel "why" questions:

Man
Crowding all around

30. This image apparently comes not from the psalm itself but from the notes of the Confraternity version for this psalm: "The psalmist, surrounded by enemies, implores God's help. . . ."

31. The image here seems closer to the Vulgate "dilatasti" than to the Confraternity translation, "you who relieve me"; cf. also the Authorized Version's "thou hast enlarged me," and the Revised Standard Version's "Thou has given me room."

Why are you
  So cold, so proud
Why is your tongue so mean
  Why is your hand
So quick to harm
Why are you like
A rattlesnake
So quick to strike? (ll. 8–17).

The stanza divides into two sub-units, lines 8–12 and 13–17, each con-
sisting of two questions and unified by various sound devices. The first
is linked together by the rhyme of "crowd–" and "proud" (along with
the assonance of "around") and the consonance of "crowd–" and
"cold" as well as of "Man" and "mean," which frames the entire
section; the second part includes the alliteration of "hand" and
"harm," and particularly the slant rhyme of "quick"/"like"/"-snake"/
"quick"/"strike," in dimeter lines which likewise reflect the emphasis
on quickness. The two parts are themselves connected by the inner
parallel of "Why is your tongue . . ." and "Why is your hand" and
the common form of the outer questions, "Why are you. . . ." The
generic address to "Man," though logically inconsistent with the plural
implications of "crowding all around," recalls the reference to "the
Man" in "Evening Prayer" (l. 8) and also suggests the loss of personal
identity when one becomes merged into a crowd. Speaking the truth
forthrightly, without rancor or fear, the speaker urges his opponent
to recognize and take responsibility for his actions rather than submerg-
ing himself in a faceless mass.

This willingness to engage the enemy in dialogue continues in
stanza 3, which moves from challenge and denunciation to a call to
conversion, an appeal to the Man's better self:

Man
Crowding all around
You have children in your home
You have looked for happiness
  You have asked the Lord
  For better days
Kneel and tremble in the night
Ask my Lord to change your heart
Fear my Lord and learn the ways
Of patience, love and sacrifice (ll. 18–27).

Again the stanza contains two parts, the first (ll. 18–23) an appeal to a common humanity, a reminder of universally shared dreams of "happiness" and "better days" for oneself and one's children.[32] Such dreams, the speaker claims, can be realized only through the change of heart he prescribes in the concluding section of the stanza, a regular tetrameter quatrain of two couplets linked by slant rhyme. Asking for "better days" must yield to asking ("in the night") for a transformed heart, as the first is a consequence of the second: better days require better "ways"; happiness depends on the practice of "patience, love and sacrifice." Here the audience is no longer simply an enemy but a fellow human being in need of counsel. He is urged to seek help from "my Lord," a reminder that the oppressor in "Evening Prayer" belonged to "some other Lord" (l. 17), but also an indication that the virtues being recommended are precisely those the speaker himself is putting into practice in the very act of speaking. Taken together, the two stanzas provide a model of nonviolent response to oppression, a stance analogous to Martin Luther King's two-part strategy of denouncing injustice and appealing to the very ideals his opponents claim to profess.

The result, as evidenced by the following stanza, is a limited success at best. Whether any individual "Man" heeds the speaker's invitation is not known, but "they" as a group continue in their arrogance, though the direct threat to the speaker seems to have diminished:

> Lord, when they all go by, riding high
> Looking down on me, be my Defender
> Be my Defender, Lord
> And my secret heart will know
> A sweeter joy, Lord, a sweeter joy
> For I'll walk alone
> With only you
> I'll lie down to sleep in peace, in hope
> For though I cannot trust in Man
> I trust in you (ll. 28–37).[33]

32. See Psalm 4:5-6: "Tremble, and sin not; reflect, upon your beds, in silence. Offer just sacrifices, and trust in the Lord. Many say, 'Oh, that we might see better times!' . . .''

33. See Psalm 4:8-9: "You put gladness into my heart, more than when grain and wine abound. As soon as I lie down, I fall peacefully asleep, for you alone,

The pattern evident here seems to parallel Merton's analysis of the results of the nonviolent civil-rights movement: though external circumstances have been altered, hearts have not: the listeners have failed to take advantage of the "kairos," the time of decision.[34] Instead of finding the happiness they "looked for" in the previous stanza, they are now "looking down on me." Rather than humbling themselves before "my Lord," they are "riding high." But the stanza portrays not only their failure but the speaker's fidelity in living a transformed life. While they have looked in vain for happiness because their hearts remain unchanged, he "will know / A sweeter joy" in his "secret heart," for true joy is not a consequence of external power or public notoriety but a hidden treasure, unnoticed and disregarded by the world. While they "all go by / Riding high," he will "walk alone / With only you": because he travels along "the ways / Of patience, love and sacrifice," he is able to "lie down to sleep in peace, in hope," whereas they declined even to "Kneel and tremble in the night." While they refused to "Fear my Lord," he trusts in his Lord and so fears no Man. He is a sign of contradiction, modeling an alternative way of living that is not dependent upon or shaken by the fact that "they" refuse to reciprocate. Thus the final verse-paragraph recapitulates his commitment not to rely on the methods of the world or align himself with the mighty but to depend on God alone:

> Lord, when they all go by
> Riding high
> Looking down on me
> Be my Defender,
> Lord, be my Defender (ll. 38–42).

VI

The sixth poem, "The Lord is Good," based on Psalm 72,[35] opens with an affirmation of faith in God's provident care that could

---

O Lord, bring security to my dwelling." The phrases "in peace, in hope," are apparently taken from the Vulgate: "*In pace* in idipsum dormiam, et resquiescam; quoniam tu, Domine, singulariter *in spe* constituisti me" (Ps 4:9-10).

34. See in particular the essay "Religion and Race in the United States," in *Faith and Violence*, 130–44; see also *Seeds of Destruction*, 65–66, 76–77, 83–84.

35. The headnote to this poem in the *Collected Poems* erroneously reads "(Psalm 71)."

be read as a direct response to the protection received in the previous poem:

> O the Lord is good
> To the steady man
> He is good
> To the man of peace (ll. 1–4).[36]

The rest of the poem, however, struggles to reconcile these statements with the speaker's knowledge of the ways of the world. Each of the two parallel declarations will be put to the test: the Lord may be good to "the steady man," but the speaker is in danger of becoming unsteady, of stumbling (cf. ll. 5, 19, 38), and so of being disqualified from receiving the Lord's goodness; the cause of his stumbling is that the Lord's goodness to the "man of peace" is brought into question by the evident prosperity of the "men of war" described in the rest of the poem. The issue here is less experiential than philosophical, not a matter of personal danger as in previous poems but of intellectual doubt. This confrontation between his profession of faith and the empirical evidence he has gathered seems to suggest either that his affirmations are not in fact true or that, whether true or not, they no longer apply to him, since he is no longer "steady."

Neither of these conclusions will prove to be valid: though he stumbles the speaker will not be so unsteady as to fall, and though contrary evidence appears plausible, God's goodness is not ultimately in doubt. In fact the speaker is relating a struggle that has already been resolved, as the use of the past tense through the rest of the poem indicates. But this eventual resolution must be reached not by avoiding the fact of the apparent triumph of the wicked but by confronting it directly, as he does in the second verse-paragraph:

> But I stumbled, I stumbled in my mind
> Over those men
> I did not understand
> Rich and fat
> With big cigars and cars
> They seem to have no trouble,

36. See Psalm 72:1: "How good God is to the upright; the Lord, to those who are clean of heart!"; "the man of peace" is borrowed from Psalm 36:37; "the steady man" is Merton's own contribution.

Know no pain
I do not understand those men of war
Strong and proud
Rich and fat
The more they have
The more they hate
And hate rolls down their skin
Like drops of sweat (ll. 5–18).[37]

This stanza has two sub-units, equal in length, each posing a some-what different problem for the speaker's understanding. The first focuses on the prosperity of the nightmarish figures depicted here, who seem to be exempt from the normal difficulties of the human condi-tion; but what is simply a puzzling anomaly in the first section becomes a threat in the second, where these men are revealed to be "men of war," so filled with hate that it seems to seep out their pores. Such an attitude is even more incomprehensible to the speaker, since one might expect the have-nots to hate the rich, but not vice versa. Thus the speaker wrestles with two related issues: why the rich have what they have, and why they act as they do even though they have what they have.

The next verse-paragraph considers not just the intellectual conundrum posed by this situation but its adverse consequences for others:

I stumbled, I stumbled in my mind
Over those men of war
Full of power
Rich and fat
The more they have, the more they hate
And they jeered
At my people
Showed their power
Rolled their pile of fat
And my people

37. See Psalm 72:2-7: "But, as for me, I almost lost my balance; my feet all but slipped, because I was envious of the arrogant when I saw them prosper though they were wicked. For they are in no pain; their bodies are sound and sleek; they are free from the burdens of mortals, and are not afflicted like the rest of men. So pride adorns them as a necklace; as a robe violence enwraps them. Out of their crassness comes iniquity; their fancies overflow their hearts."

> Listened to their threat
> My people were afraid
> Of those men of war
> When hate rolled down their skin
> Like drops of sweat (ll. 19–33).[38]

The first five lines basically repeat material from the previous stanza, with one ominous addition: these men are "Full of power," so that their hatred becomes dangerous. The next unit, of six lines (framed by the chiastic "they jeered / At my people" and "my people / listened . . ."), shows the enemy in action, with an emphasis on gross, even grotesque, materiality, in which power is equated with physical bulk, and physical bulk perhaps implicitly with wealth ("Rolled their pile of fat" suggests riffling through a fat roll, or pile, of bills as well). Significantly, their actions are described as directed toward "my people": the speaker now assumes the broader communal perspective first envisioned in "I Have Called You," which will be retained throughout the rest of the sequence. The jeers and threats directed toward them parallel the curses and threats the speaker himself experienced in "Evening Prayer" (ll. 10–11). His struggles are now identified with theirs, but what he had resolved on the personal plane, the issue of unjust persecution and unmerited suffering, now reemerges in this broader context. The final four lines, summing up the people's reaction to their danger, recall, and call into question, perhaps the pivotal lines of the entire sequence, the Lord's own words in "I Have Called You": "Do not be afraid / O my people."

The final verse-paragraph brings the matter to a crisis point before it is resolved by a revelation from the Lord. The first four lines of this section sharply contrast with the confident statements of the opening quatrain:

> My heart was sore
> Seeing their success
> "Does God care?
> Has He forgotten us?" (ll. 34–37).

The "sore" heart here has lost the "sweeter joy" of the "secret heart" in the previous poem, while the questions seem to cast doubt on the

---

38. See Psalm 72:8: "They scoff and speak evil; outrage from on high they threaten."

rest of the final stanza of "I Have Called You" ("I have called you by your name / You belong to me"); the use of the word "care" recalls the lines from "Evening Prayer," "No one cares to know / Who I am, where I go" (ll. 22–23), which were not applied to the Lord then, but apparently could be now (though with reference to "us" rather than to the singular "I").

But in fact the implied answers to these questions are not the correct ones: God has not forgotten his people or ceased to care for them. The speaker makes this clear in the poem's final lines, which take the form of a prayer that both acknowledges his own weakness and presents the divine response to the issues raised:

> Lord I nearly fell
> Stumbling in my mind
> About those men of war
> It was hard to see
> Till you showed me
> How like a dream
> Those phantoms pass away (ll. 38–44).[39]

The answer provided here might not immediately seem especially cogent or satisfying: the men of war, with their obtrusive fleshly presence looming over their victims, scarcely look like "phantoms." But the solution to the speaker's dilemma lies precisely in the ironic appropriateness of this word. By investing all their resources in the world of the senses, by adopting a completely quantified perception of reality, such people have denied their own humanity. Even their distorted appearance, the exaggeration, the caricature that marks their description, is a graphic illustration of their futile efforts to create their own identity out of material possessions, resulting in an imposing, even threatening facade that can disguise only temporarily the emptiness within. Such people have deceived themselves into believing that the transitory is permanent, that the contingent is absolute, that wealth and pleasure and power are exempt from the passage of time and the process of dissolution. They enflesh, in all their massive carnality, what Merton himself calls in *New Seeds of Contemplation* "the smoke self that

39. See Psalm 72:16-17, 20: "Though I tried to understand this it seemed to me too difficult, till I entered the sanctuary of God and considered their final destiny. . . . As though they were the dream of one who had awakened, O Lord, so will you, when you arise, set at nought these phantoms."

must inevitably vanish.''[40] From this perspective, life is an unceasing contest for possessions, status, power, part of a futile attempt to fill an infinite "space," the human capacity for the divine, with finite objects, of which there can never be enough. According to Merton, such people

> imagine that they can only find themselves by asserting their own desires and ambitions and appetites in a struggle with the rest of the world. They try to become real by imposing themselves on other people, by appropriating for themselves some share of the limited supply of created goods and thus emphasizing the difference between themselves and the other men who have less than they, or nothing at all.[41]

It is no surprise, then, that "The more they have, the more they hate"; theirs is a logic of competition, of each against all: "I have what you have not. I am what you are not. I have taken what you have failed to take and I have seized what you could never get. Therefore you suffer and I am happy, you are despised and I am praised, you die and I live; you are nothing and I am something, and I am all the more something because you are nothing.''[42] Because they have equated who they are with what they have, and because what they have cannot and will not last, they themselves are ultimately doomed to disappear. Again, Merton provides his own best commentary:

> I use up my life in the desire for pleasures and the thirst for experiences, for power, honor, knowledge and love, to clothe this false self and construct its nothingness into something objectively real. . . . But there is no substance under the things with which I am clothed. I am hollow, and my structure of pleasures and ambitions has no foundation. I am objectified in them. But they are all destined by their very contingency to be destroyed. And when they are gone there will be nothing left of me but my own nakedness and emptiness and hollowness, to tell me that I am my own mistake.[43]

For such persons, there is no more apt description than the word "phantoms," for "The man who lives in division is living in death.

40. *New Seeds of Contemplation*, 38.
41. Ibid., 47.
42. Ibid., 48.
43. Ibid., 35.

He cannot find himself because he is lost; he has ceased to be a reality. The person he believes himself to be is a bad dream."[44]

In finally recognizing the delusory nature of such "success," the speaker is rescued from the danger into which he "nearly fell," a willingness to accept the standards of judgment of the powerful, the criteria of value of the rich, to look at the world and the self as they do. It is from this temptation that he is delivered when he is finally able "to see," to discern the difference between truth and illusion, appearance and substance. Thus the poem concludes with the Lord's goodness vindicated, and the speaker's identity as "the steady man . . . the man of peace" reaffirmed and strengthened.

VII

The seventh poem, "There is a Way," envisions the goal of the journey, which has been the major organizing image throughout the sequence. The pilgrims' destination is the new Jerusalem, the eschatological reign of "the Lord of peace": the threats and dangers have indeed vanished like "phantoms," and the way to the holy city lies open. Each of the three stanzas of the poem reworks one verse from the scriptural source, Isaiah 35:8-10, part of a hymn of joy and thanksgiving at Israel's return from exile.

The first stanza is mainly negative in approach, though not in tone, focusing on those who will be excluded from the "holy way":

> There is a way to glory
> Clear and straight
> But not for men of blood
> They shall not stray
> Upon my road
> Nor the unclean
> Whose hands have taken life:
> They shall not find this holy way
> To Jerusalem
> Where the Lord of peace
> Rules in glory (ll. 1–11).[45]

44. Ibid., 48.

45. See Isaiah 35:8: "A highway will be there, called the holy way; no one unclean may pass over it, nor fools go astray on it."

Connections with earlier songs in the sequence are evident here and will become even more prominent as the poem continues. The reference to "glory" in the first and last lines recalls the Lord's command in "I Have Called You," line 26: "Bring them back in glory," while "my road" echoes "my way" from "Evening Prayer" (ll. 9, 15, 27, contrasted with "his road" in l. 20); the "Lord of peace" is the same Lord who "is good / To the man of peace" in the sixth poem.

Mention of Jerusalem brings the sequence full circle in this seventh poem: the city polluted with blood and threatened with destruction in "Sundown" has been transformed into the city of shalom, into which no "unclean" persons, no "men of blood" (recalling the "men of war" from the previous poem) may enter. Though the way to Jerusalem is "clear and straight,"[46] therefore easy to travel on and presumably easy to locate, evildoers can neither "stray"[47] onto it nor will they be able to "find" it: neither by accident nor by effort can the wicked come upon this road. This assertion presents something of a puzzle: as the way is so readily accessible, why would anyone miss it?

The second stanza provides an answer to this implicit question:

> Love is this way to glory
> Truth and Mercy
> No beast of prey
> Shall be there
> No angry wolf or bear
> By my highway
> Murder shall not stain
> That way with blood
> But forgiveness everywhere
> Shall teach my people how
> To go to glory (ll. 12–22).[48]

The play on "way" as both path and method explains why the wicked are unable to walk here: if Love, Truth, and Mercy are the only "way to glory," those who have rejected these virtues have prevented themselves from taking this road; neither can they hinder others from tak-

---

46. See the Vulgate for Isaiah 35:8: "Haec erit vobis directa via."

47. The Vulgate reads, "stulti non errent per eam."

48. See Isaiah 35:9: "No lion will be there, nor beast of prey go up to be met upon it. It is for those with a journey to make, and on it the redeemed will walk."

ing it. The way here contrasts with the road covered with bones in "Evening Prayer" (ll. 19–20): the people journey in total security. But there is also an implicit warning in the further statement that forgiveness (set over against anger and murder) teaches the way to glory. The central role of forgiveness means that those who do walk the road are able to do so not by their own merits but because they themselves have been forgiven; any gnostic or manichaean division of humanity into mutually exclusive groups of good and evil is precluded here, and the possibility of conversion, of finding the road through repentance and pardon, is disclosed: by confessing the truth about oneself, one is enabled to receive the divine mercy. But the focus on forgiveness is also a caution against self-righteousness, against setting up standards more stringent than those of God. People may exclude themselves from the holy way, but may not be excluded by others. To attempt to do so would be to act as a "beast of prey" oneself. There must be an openness to reconciliation, even with former enemies, former oppressors. If only those who have been forgiven learn how to go to glory along the way of Truth, only those who forgive, those who act as God acts, learn how to go to glory along the way of Mercy.

This focus on the redeemed community, signaled by the reappearance of the term "my people" in the second stanza,[49] continues in the final stanza as the "holy people" approach the holy city:

Songs of love and joy
Echo everywhere
And the holy people
Travels there
Glad and free
Forgiving and forgiven
Riding on to Sion
Where the Lord of Peace
Their Defender, their Redeemer
Rules in glory (ll. 23–32).

49. The speaker in the poem is evidently not the Lord, who is referred to in the third person, yet the perspective of the speaker is so identified with that of God at this point in the sequence that the tone is very like that of "I Have Called You." Even the references to "my road" (l. 5) and "my highway" (l. 17) do not carry any individualistic connotations; the voice here is genuinely prophetic, "speaking for" God.

The opening lines are particularly resonant here: the echoing songs suggest that those bringing love and joy with them are met with love and joy by those within the city (see the Confraternity reading of this verse [35:10] of Isaiah, where the travelers, "crowned with everlasting joy . . . meet with joy and gladness"); "Echo everywhere" itself echoes "Forgiveness everywhere" four lines earlier, indicating that love and joy are coextensive with and indeed a consequence of forgiveness. But the mention of echoing songs in this seventh poem might also recall the series of Freedom Songs themselves. This final stanza is filled with echoes, beginning with the joy itself, renewing and extending the "sweeter joy" experienced in "Be My Defender" (l. 32); "Glad and free" (l. 27) is a direct quotation from "I Have Called You" (l. 19) and is a reminder that the work of liberation from captivity commanded there has now been accomplished.[50] The double title, "Their Defender, their Redeemer" (l. 31), identifies the "Lord of peace" with "your Redeemer" from "I Have Called You" (l. 7) and "my Defender" from "Be My Defender" (ll. 1 and passim). The image of the people of God "Riding on to Sion" (l. 29) contrasts with that of the proud who "go by / Riding high" in "Be My Defender" (ll. 28, 38–39) and recalls the king who entered Jerusalem "on an ass, on a colt, the foal of an ass. He shall banish the chariot from Ephraim, and the horse from Jerusalem; the warrior's bow shall be banished, and he shall proclaim peace to the nations" (Zech 9:9-10; cf. Matt 21:4, John 12:14).

This is surely "the Lord of peace" who "Rules in glory" over a people of peace, now described as "Forgiving and forgiven." This key line can be read in two ways: it could refer to the same group, as both active and receptive, both giving and receiving forgiveness (though the more logical order would seem to be "forgiven and forgiving," since divine forgiveness makes possible human forgiveness, this arrangement recalls the petition from the Lord's prayer, which stresses the reciprocal point that a refusal to forgive blocks God's forgiveness); but it also suggests two groups joined together in reconciliation, those who freely forgive and those who are freed by forgiveness, oppressed and oppressors united in joy and freedom—at this point, of course, the two interpretations coalesce, since the two groups have become one. Thus the vista along the way to Jerusalem opens

50. The last line of verse 9 in the Vulgate reads, "et ambulabant qui liberati fuerint."

out to include, at least potentially, those who have been sinners, "men of blood." They too can be redeemed, rescued from enslavement to their own self-will, and the message of the sequence as a whole is that such a transformation may be due in large part to the faithful witness of those who have suffered and struggled against oppression. This is of course part of the essential dynamic of nonviolence: "The only real liberation is that which *liberates both the oppressor and the oppressed* at the same time from the same tyrannical automatism of the violent process which contains in itself the curse of irreversibility."[51] It is in particular the vision of the "beloved community" animating the nonviolent freedom movement, which maintains that "the Negro . . . is really fighting not only for his own freedom, but also, in some strange way, for the freedom of whites."[52] The belief that "unearned suffering is redemptive" offers the possibility for healing even to the oppressor: "Dr. Martin Luther King . . . has based his non-violence on his belief that love can unite men, even enemies, in truth. That is to say that he has clearly spelled out the struggle for freedom not as a struggle for the Negro alone, but also for the white man. From the start, the non-violent element in the Negro struggle is oriented toward 'healing' the sin of racism and toward unity in reconciliation."[53] It is such a vision of the reign of God that concludes the seventh Freedom Song, a vision of shalom that summons and welcomes all willing to heed the good news of liberation and reconciliation.

VIII

"There is a Way" would have served as an effective conclusion to the cycle of Freedom Songs for a number of reasons: as the seventh poem, it fulfills the scriptural pattern of completion; it incorporates and weaves together images from much of the rest of the sequence; it provides a symmetry with the opening poem by its focus on Sion/Jerusalem; it brings the central journey-motif of the sequence to full realization by leading the pilgrims into the holy city.

51. Thomas Merton, *Gandhi on Non-Violence* (New York: New Directions, 1965) 14.
52. *Seeds of Destruction*, 40.
53. Ibid., 43.

But there is an ancient Christian tradition of the "eighth day,"[54] the beginning of the new creation, which is associated with the resurrection of Christ on the day following the Sabbath. It is this conception that evidently prompts the inclusion of the final poem, "Earthquake." This is the only one of the songs that does not have its title taken from the text of the poem itself, and though its headnote cites Isaiah 52 as the source, no earthquake is mentioned in that chapter.[55] The implicit background, rather, seems to be the resurrection scene in Matthew, marked by an earthquake (Matt 28:2) and followed by a commissioning of the apostles to preach the Good News, which is likewise a central aspect of the poem, in which the initial revelation of the new creation is followed by a much longer section commanding the people to become "messengers of peace."

The poem begins with a section of ten lines divided into two verse-paragraphs, establishing a formal pattern that will continue throughout:

Go tell the earth to shake
And tell the thunder
To wake the sky
And tear the clouds apart
Tell my people to come out
And wonder

Where the old world is gone
For a new world is born
And all my people
Shall be one (ll. 1–10).

As in "I Have Called You," which completed the first half of the sequence, so here also the Lord is the speaker, and directs his prophet

54. See "The Epistle of Barnabas," chapter 15: "He is saying there: 'It is not these sabbaths of the present age that I find acceptable, but the one of my own appointment: the one that, after I have set all things at rest, is to usher in the Eighth Day, the commencement of a new world.' (And we too rejoice in celebrating the eighth day; because that was when Jesus rose from the dead, and showed Himself again, and ascended into heaven.)" *Early Christian Writings: The Apostolic Fathers,* trans. Maxwell Staniforth (Baltimore: Penguin, 1968) 315; see also Merton's own reference to Sunday as "the eighth day in a seven-day week" in *Sign of Jonas,* 299.
55. The opening words of Isaiah 52 in the Vulgate, "Consurge, consurge," along with the beginning of verse 2, "Excutere de pulvere, consurge," might possibly have suggested the idea of an earthquake, but only by loose association; they are addressed not to the earth but to Sion/Jerusalem, the focus of the entire chapter.

to transmit the divine word: first to the cosmos is given a word of transformation that is also a word of revelation, symbolized by the tearing apart of the clouds to disclose the heavens; then to the people a word of revelation that is also a word of transformation, as the new world is declared to be a place of perfect unity among people. The command to "come out" signals a recognition to be developed throughout the rest of the poem, that the ingathering of the holy people into Sion must be complemented by an outgoing mission "to all the nations, beginning from Jerusalem" (Luke 24:47). While the journey in one sense has reached its goal, the kingdom of God, the holy city where "the Lord of peace / Rules in glory," this final song is a strong reminder that those who have experienced salvation, who have seen the vision of a new heaven and a new earth, are obliged to be signs and heralds of the new order. As Merton would later put it in his most significant essay on nonviolence, "Blessed Are the Meek":

> The disciple of Christ, he who has heard the good news, the announcement of the Lord's coming and of His victory, and is aware of the definitive establishment of the Kingdom, proves his faith by the gift of his whole self to the Lord in order that *all* may enter the Kingdom. . . . The great historical event, the coming of the Kingdom, is made clear and is "realized" in proportion as Christians themselves live the life of the Kingdom in the circumstances of their own place and time.[56]

It is this emphasis on the dynamic character of discipleship that becomes the major focus of the rest of the poem, which is based on the deeply evangelical words of Isaiah 52:7 (quoted by St. Paul in Rom 10:15): "How beautiful upon the mountains are the feet of him who brings glad tidings, announcing peace, bearing good news, announcing salvation . . ." This passage is reworked into a refrain stanza in which the single messenger of Isaiah has become an entire people on the march:

> So tell the earth to shake
> With marching feet
> Of messengers of peace
> Proclaim my law of love
> To every nation
> Every race (ll. 11–16).

56. *Faith and Violence*, 16.

These lines parallel in both form and content the poem's opening verse-paragraph: the earth which shook in the throes of cosmic rebirth now is shaken by the feet of the apostolic witnesses, aptly described as "marching feet," a reminder that it was the civil-rights march that characterized the nonviolent freedom movement perhaps more than any other activity, that became a sign of solidarity as well as a sign of contradiction, and that expressed the message of peace and the law of love to "Every race." Not the heavy tramp of military boots but a nonviolent army bearing the message of peace is powerful enough to shake the earth itself.

The "glad tidings, . . . good news, . . . salvation" of the scriptural source are summed up in the phrase "my law of love," a term particularly rich in association for Merton, especially in conjunction with the description of the people as "messengers of peace." It reflects Gandhi's declaration: "If love is not the law of our being the whole of my argument falls to pieces."[57] It affirms the capacity for transformation inherent in the very constitution of the human spirit, as Merton himself writes in *Conjectures of a Guilty Bystander:* "The Law of Love *is the deepest law of our nature,* not something extraneous to our nature. Our nature itself inclines us to love, and to love freely. The deepest and most fundamental exigency of the divine law in our hearts is that we should reach our fulfillment by loving."[58] Such love is not simply an obligation but an empowerment: "the most fundamental demand of the Law of Love is that we should love *freely.*"[59] It is ultimately a participation in the divine transfiguration of the world: "The Law of Love is the law that commands us to add new values to the world given us by God, through the creative power that He has placed in us—the power of joy in response, in gratitude, and in the giving of self."[60] Thus the "law of love" expresses not only the message of nonviolence but the central proclamation of the gospel, the "glad tidings" of "salvation" to be brought to "all nations . . . even unto the consummation of the world" (Matt 28:19, 20).

---

57. *Seeds of Destruction,* 234; in the Introduction to *Gandhi on Non-Violence,* the statement is quoted as "If love or non-violence be not the law of our being, the whole of my argument falls to pieces" (11; see also p. 25 for the same quotation).

58. *Conjectures of a Guilty Bystander,* 121.

59. Ibid.

60. Ibid., 123.

This refrain occurs four times in the poem, in each case followed by some variation of the message of peace to be announced, always concluding with the declaration "My people shall be one," continuing the pattern begun in lines 7-10. While that stanza simply contrasted "the old world" and "a new world" (ll. 7, 8), these stanzas will become progressively more specific as to the nature of the change. The first of these, also a quatrain, is presented as an explanation of why the marching and preaching of the refrain are now taking place:

> For the old wrongs are over
> The old days are gone
> A new world is rising
> Where my people shall be one (ll. 17-20).

The heavily stressed lines, alternating feminine and rhymed masculine line endings, create a simple but strong contrast between "old wrongs" and "old days" and the eschatological era in which the new creation itself is "rising," participating in the paschal translation from death to life. The nature of the "old wrongs" is not specified here, but will be in the next post-refrain stanza, expanded to six lines (linked by rhyme in the third and sixth lines):

> And say
> The old wrongs are over
> The old ways are done
> There shall be no more hate
> And no more war
> My people shall be one (ll. 27-32).

It is evident here that these stanzas following the refrain are to be understood as the content of the proclamation the messengers make. The "old wrongs" and "old ways" are now identified as hate and war, the antitheses of the "law of love" and reign of peace mentioned in the refrain. The pairing of hate and war also recalls the "men of war" whose "hate rolled down their skin / Like drops of sweat" in "The Lord is Good" (ll. 32-33). This reminiscence is even stronger in the next of these stanzas, which moves from an impersonal to a personal construction:

> For the old world is ended
> The old sky is torn
> Apart. A new day is born

They hate no more
They do not go to war
My people shall be one (ll. 39–44).

Here the anonymous "they," so prominent and threatening in earlier songs, are said to have given up hatred and war—whether willingly or unwillingly is not known, though there is at least an implicit hope that even "they" may finally be incorporated into "My people." While this stanza matches the preceding one (and the refrains) with its six lines, here linked by rhymed couplets in the interior lines (the first of which is created by the particularly effective enjambment of "torn / Apart" describing the "old sky"), the final lines of the poem, and thus of the sequence, return to the quatrain form, with a concluding rhymed couplet:

There shall be no more hate
And no more oppression
The old wrongs are done
My people shall be one (ll. 51–54).

The mention here of "oppression" along with "hate" as final examples of "old wrongs" is particularly appropriate in concluding a series of poems celebrating the struggle against racial oppression, as it looks forward in faith to a day when all such injustice will be permanently overcome.

This final poem is the longest in the sequence, only because it is the most repetitive. But the repetition has a functional purpose, even more evident, perhaps, when set to music. The recurrence of the refrain, followed in each case by some variations of the message to be announced, represents the successive waves of evangelization, progressively extending to encompass "every nation / Every race." It should be noted that while the non-refrain stanzas specify in some detail and some variety the elements of the old order that are to disappear, the single characteristic of the new age, repeated insistently and invariably, is unity, the fruit of peace and love. The alternating pattern formed by the last lines of successive verse-paragraphs, moving back and forth between ". . . every nation / Every race" and "My people shall be one," fosters attentiveness both to the universality of the message and to the unity it creates. The pattern reflects the twofold dynamism of the gospel, mission and communion, continually reaching out beyond the circle of the community so that the boundaries of that circle will eventually exclude no one. But it also sustains a balance between diversity and unity, suggesting the need for a mutually affirming complementarity if many nations and races are to form one people of God. This is for Merton a central lesson of the freedom movement and an integral element of authentic catholicity: "a genuinely Catholic attitude in matters of race is one which concretely accepts and fully recognizes the fact that different races and cultures are *correlative. They mutually complete one another.*"[61] It is this vision of wholeness, of integrity, in which divisions are healed, offenses are forgiven, alienation is overcome, that brings the poem and the cycle of songs to a close. In witnessing to peace and proclaiming unity, the messengers are walking in the footsteps of Christ: "For he himself is our peace, he it is who has made both one. . . . He announced the good tidings of peace to you who were afar off, and of peace to those who were near; because through him we both have access in one Spirit to the Father" (Eph 2:17-18). They are preaching a union that transcends distinctions of race, class, status, gender: "There is neither Jew nor Greek; there is neither slave nor freeman; there is neither male nor female. For you are all one in Christ Jesus" (Gal 3:28). They are prophesying the fulfillment of the high priestly prayer of Jesus: "that all may be one even as thou, Father, in me, and I in thee; that they also may be one in us, that the world may believe that thou hast sent me" (John 17:22-23). This, Merton suggests, is the deepest truth revealed by the courage and commitment of the freedom movement and a fitting conclusion to the sequence of Freedom Songs. "My people shall be one" is both a word of consolation to those who have suffered and struggled to defend the common dignity and affirm the common destiny of all persons, and a word of challenge and command to others to go and do likewise.

Merton himself was somewhat ambivalent about the worth of the Freedom Songs. In May 1964, while still working on them, he wrote to his Aunt Kit in New Zealand, "I wanted to do something in this line but I am not sure if this particular project was wise, as I do not

---

61. *Seeds of Destruction*, 61.

know if the 'songs' are turning out to be very wonderful."[62] On July 1, shortly after finishing them, he refers to them in a letter to W. H. Ferry as "some rather poor Freedom Songs I was asked to write."[63] But by November 1964 he is writing to Rabbi Zalman Schachter, "I was deeply moved at your reaction to the Freedom Songs. I like very much writing that kind of thing and maybe will do much more. Who knows? Meanwhile, back in the hole, with our faces in the dust [a reference to "All the Way Down"?]. . . ."[64] By April 9, 1968, he can write of them to June Yungblut: "The music for them is powerful and they are quite effective."[65] While by inference he gives much of the credit for the songs' effectiveness to their music, it is to be hoped that this examination of the texts of the poems provides evidence of their effectiveness not only as testimony to Merton's own passionate dedication to the cause of civil rights for African Americans, but also as a coherent, well-crafted series of poems in their own right.

62. Thomas Merton, *The Road to Joy: Letters to New and Old Friends*, ed. Robert E. Daggy (New York: Farrar, Straus, Giroux, 1989) 62.

63. *The Hidden Ground of Love*, 218.

64. Ibid., 541.

65. Ibid., 645.

"The Climate of Humor and Freedom": An Interview about Thomas Merton with Ron Seitz

Conducted by George Kilcourse
Edited by Matthew McEver

George Kilcourse: Your book *Song for Nobody: A Memory Vision of Thomas Merton* has gained a wide readership in the past year. Brother Patrick Hart complimented it with praise, saying "at last, here is the Merton I knew." What has it been like to see your interpretation of Merton in print?

Ron Seitz: The reason it took so long to get in print was that I was hesitant. I was encouraged by Brother Pat, the monks, and Sally (my wife). After publication I was, to be honest, a little embarrassed, quite self-conscious about the reception that poets such as Bob Lax or J. Laughlin would give it. And it might be inadequate or poor work. I wouldn't want to embarrass the monastery as well because, after all, I really don't have the direct experience of monasticism, the life of a monk. I suppose I'm a tourist. I say things that, many times, may be superficial. Also, I took a risk, I think, in the form that I chose in writing this book as a "memory vision." It is anecdotal, conversational, and I present much of it as a dramatic narrative, almost a fictional approach. But I had to put all of those doubts behind me and just go with who I was.

Really, the book is about a relationship between the two of us; it's not a biography of Merton. Anyone can tell that. It's a memoir; it's my response to and my portrait of Thomas Merton. In that light, it's not a question of viewing the work as "objectively accurate" or not. It has been received very positively by critics and the reading public

129

in general. In all of my years of writing (and publishing), it's the first time I've ever had people call me long distance and say enthusiastically that they have just read the last part that very minute. And there are the letters; quite a few of them, very personal letters. The book seems to be touching people in a very strange way, possibly because it is somewhat confessional. Many readers say that at times it's almost intimate to the point of blush-embarrassment that I'm saying these things. I hope the writing is not an expression of false humility.

I am appreciative that the book is being well received, as well as about what Brother Pat Hart says in the introduction. And the reviews, many more than I anticipated, have been intelligent and perceptive, that is, "positive."

Kilcourse: You talk in the book about the title of Merton's poem "Song for Nobody." Could you say more?

Seitz: The "Song for Nobody" appeals to me. It's an apophatic poem. The "Song" is a spiritual soliloquy. I see it as having no particular audience. Merton's not trying to give a person's life-identity here. The poem's "say" is not for approval, fame, or acclaim. If anything, the song is addressed to God. Or better still, you could say a spiritual soliloquy is always addressed to "nobody"—literally.

Merton had several other poems, such as "Night-Flowering Cactus," very much in that particular vein. They're minimal, concrete. And it's the anonymity that I appreciate in such writing as this—not only in the song, but in the saying.

Kilcourse: I know you have a new book out now. Tell us about the new Merton work.

Seitz: The one that will be published shortly is *Being Center: The Merton Poems.* It's a very large collection of poetry—over one hundred pages. It includes many of the poems that are in *The Gethsemani Poems* (the earlier limited edition, which is out of print) and many pieces written after that. I'm very excited about my poetry books, far more than the prose (although they're not received by as large an audience).

I'm also working on another book, not quite what you would call a sequel or follow-up to *Song for Nobody;* the tentative title is *The Road to Cold Mountain.* I don't know if you are acquainted with Han Shan's collection of Cold Mountain poems about an eccentric Chinese hermit and Zen master with his minimal, pithy sayings. They're very appealing and analogous to Merton's *The Way of Chuang Tzu* (at least at the beginning). Merton will be my "companion" along the way in my Cold Mountain book—very much like the Basho's *Narrow Road to the Deep North*. I want to flesh out some of the allusions, incidents, and conversations from *Song for Nobody*. The work will definitely be in the Eastern vein: Tao, Zen, and Vedanta—things of that sort. As I said, it will include Merton, but not so much as the first book.

Kilcourse: From other things that you've written, it is apparent that you yourself flirted with a monastic vocation as a young man. Is that accurate?

Seitz: I like your choice of words. "Flirted." That word is especially appropriate. It probably was sort of a romantic infatuation with monasticism that I picked up, possibly from reading *The Sign of Jonas,* far more than *The Seven Storey Mountain*. Many people think I came to Thomas Merton through *The Seven Storey Mountain,* but that's not the case at all. I read that later. I think there was an attraction to the asceticism, the silence and solitude. It was something that I wanted, something other than what I was at the time, the culture I was involved in.

But soon, I found out that I'm not a community person. Once you have the experience of staying in the monastery, you find that there is an element of loneliness within solitude; I didn't think I could quite handle that. I went as a spectator and a tourist and that's probably the way I approached the vocation. They didn't dismiss me outrightly, but they said I wasn't quite ready three or four times. So, yes, I did "flirt."

Kilcourse: They said that you were "not ready." Did you actually make an overture to them?

Seitz: Yes, I went down to the monastery for counseling. The monk (Father "H") I approached there and talked to several times could see my interests. Some of them were artistic or aesthetic; in my writing, for instance. In being honest and frank with him, I realized I was attracted to women and I would've had a real problem with that. And ultimately, I did marry.

I also think I would have had problems with some of the disciplines there. An obvious one was obedience. Father "H" probably saw a very arrogant young man. He probably saw my instability; I had wandered all over the country, going here and there. He may have seen that I would've been very impatient and would've been one who runs out of there very quickly. I think he had an accurate reading of who I was.

Kilcourse: When did you first visit Gethsemani? Could you describe some of your first impressions of Cistercian monastic life?

Seitz: I first visited Gethsemani when I entered Bellarmine College in 1956. I didn't hear much about Gethsemani and Merton when I was in high school at Saint Xavier, here in Louisville. I had been in the army for two years, and when I came back to Bellarmine there was talk of Gethsemani, Merton, and *The Seven Storey Mountain.* I was a sophomore in college, twenty years old, and my first impressions of Cistercian monastic life were "guest-house focused" in vision. Actually, the present guest house is quite different from the old one. That experience included narrow cells, shared bathrooms, being cold, and getting up for the (then) 2 A.M. Vigils service. There was a mystique about all of that and a sense of mystery. I had a sense of awe about the ritual, the monastic climate of silence and solitude—the, to me, almost otherworldly chanting of the monks. There was imagery all over the place. I was just overwhelmed by my first imagist impressions. As a writer, most often I'm making a collage and painting in my mind of all that.

Kilcourse: When did you first meet Merton?

Seitz: It took place in October of 1958 and I was a junior at Bellarmine College. Merton had requested (from someone?) a meeting with some of the promising young artists in Louisville. Why I was included with four painters is still a mystery to me. Anyway, the five of us waited in the front courtyard near the old monastery and we met him there. He was very accessible, earthy, laughing, and relaxed. He wasn't that Gandhian, thin, ascetic-looking, starving monk that we stereotypically imagine. He didn't look like that at all. That jarred me somewhat (not that it shattered any pious icon image, as it did for some of the others) but made me very relaxed as well. We struck up a rapport because he found out I was a writer. As I said, the other artists were painters. He himself painted and sketched some ink drawings. But we had this special connection—poetry. After that first meeting we started corresponding.

Kilcourse: One of your teachers and mentors was Dan Walsh, who also taught Merton at Columbia University. When did you first meet Dan? How was it that he came to introduce you to Merton?

Seitz: I started teaching at Bellarmine in 1962 and I knew of Dan from the description in *The Seven Storey Mountain.* In 1962 or 1963 Father John Loftus, the dean then, said, "Guess who's coming here? It's Dan Walsh . . . and we're having a reception tonight. Would you come and meet him?"

Dan had come down from retirement at Manhattanville College to be close to Merton, but his primary reason was to teach the monks at Gethsemani. While he was here, Father John and Father Alfred Horrigan, Bellarmine's president, requested him to teach a course or two at the college. He consented, and I began to take all of his classes at every opportunity during the time he was there. I felt as if I had almost a Sorbonne Ph.D. in philosophy because we went from the pre-Socratics all the way up to the Modernists.

I was also a chauffeur to Dan, driving him to his home downtown, but also back and forth to Gethsemani. He would take my mail and my writing (poems and letters) and hand deliver them to Merton. Tom would give him some things to bring back for me to read. Much of it was his own writing, and sometimes it was other writers. There was a large group of international poets who exchanged their works in manuscript copies. Tom would hand me some René Char, Raissa Maritain, Nicanor Parra, or Margaret Randall from Mexico, and many others. I was in this "underground network" of what he was reading, what people were sending him, and I got involved in exchanging my writing with all of these people.

Kilcourse: What was Dan like around Bellarmine College when he was teaching during the 1960s?

Seitz: Although I was a professor there, I immediately began taking his courses. He said that was an inspiration to my students—that one of the teachers would go to another teacher to learn something, that we never stop learning. I was there because honestly, to this day, I consider him the only true "classroom" teacher I ever had. He became what he taught.

Everyday I'd go to Dan's class and he would totally convince me of a certain philosopher's point of view and I would unconditionally embrace it, walking out of that room euphoric! The next day he would dismantle that and replace it. I was a convert daily. I was impressionable—almost hysterically so. I was seduced by philosophy and totally in love with it. It was an intellectual experience in the truest sense.

There was always a spirit of inquiry going on in Dan. As he taught, he was creative. He wasn't mouthing someone else's finished thoughts; he was *thinking* as he taught. He was philosophizing and coming to conclusions right there before your eyes because he didn't work from a prepared text. He had a few three by five cards in the palm of his hand and would say, "I want to cover this." And then he would close his eyes (a habit I picked up) and you could see that he became this person he was teaching. A smile would break across his face because (creatively) he'd realize something for the first time in his own life, something that he had never come to before. That is what I consider real teaching, when you have that enthusiasm and joy while searching yourself, and the students can witness that. It was a community of learning. It was a rarity in education and we'd never had anything like that before, or since.

Dan's my intellectual model and at that time he was even somewhat of a hero. I once told him, "What you said today was beautiful . . . my head's like a brushfire, like dry wheat." He said, "I am an instrument of truth," and laughed. I thought to myself: that was either arrogant or total humility.

Dan's life, once you got to know him, had its tragic side too. But in spite of all of that, he was being "used" by God for this special purpose. Of course, Merton had come to realize the same thing: that as a sinner, he was forgiven and blessed with the unbounded mercy of God. Both saw themselves as voice boxes of truth and beauty.

Kilcourse: Were you surprised when Dan decided to be ordained a priest for the Archdiocese of Louisville?

Seitz: No, because I said to him one time, "You know you are a priest, but not officially so. You don't have the union card or acknowledgement at the Vatican." He, of course, was into the sacramental nature of the priesthood and knew it far better than I do. It was obvious in Dan's hierarchy of spiritual values and roles that the priest was the ultimate vocation. There were certain things you could do within the faith and he aspired to the highest, that of being a priest.

He thought himself possibly unworthy for years and years. I think he was graced with humility enough to go ahead with it, though. I was privileged again to be able to take him for his instructions with Archbishop Floersh. I didn't sit in on their sessions, but we had lunch together each time with informal talks.

No, I wasn't surprised. I always thought that he should have "officially" been part of the Church.

Kilcourse: What was Merton's reaction?

Seitz: We didn't discuss it that much, except that they would often call each other "dreamers." Tom would smile at the thought, but I think privately he convinced him not to be afraid. I think, with Dan, it would be a frightful responsibility. I always thought of the awesome responsibility of being a priest. I'm sure Merton encouraged Dan to go ahead.

Kilcourse: In reading Merton's letters to writers, *The Courage for Truth,* it strikes me the way he often writes about how the poet and monk are kindred spirits. You obviously intuited the same connection.

Seitz: Initially, I probably didn't know what a monk was. I had visited the monastery and seen monks in a cloistered community. Then Merton went on to redefine a monk in a broader sense as a "marginal" person. I can't imagine these two, the monk and the poet, not being one and the same because I do see the creativity of the poet as spiritual. I'd have to redefine monk and poet to even answer this question. Paul Tillich says we have the cognitive process of wanting to know truth and the aesthetic one to express truth: both are religious activities. I began to appreciate that poetry is a solitary vocation, one which I sought as romantically as a priestly one. My poetry wasn't on the plane of Augustine's *Confessions,* but it was my way of praying or talking to God or bearing witness and testimony. So, the monk and poet are both spiritual vocations. For awhile, I thought they might be in opposition. Merton struggled back and forth with being the artist and monk at the same time. I don't think he ever reconciled this until the last five years of his life. Then it freed him from thinking he was betraying one vocation for the other. I can see the two reinforcing one another. Merton redefined the monk to include the secular one out here, and contemplative poetry as a way of responding to life. You have your own sense of vows, stability, and obedience. This may be an idealistic elevation of the role of a poet, akin to that of the mystic: the poet as priest. He announces theophany. And I do think he bears witness in a prophetic mode as would a disciple or evangelist. There was a kindred spirit between the two and, yes, I intuited that connection, as you said.

Kilcourse: How did you take the initiative in cultivating a fellow poet's exchange with Merton? Or was it his initiative? How much of a problem were the cloister and restrictions placed on Merton?

Seitz: Our initial meeting and conversation had indicated an appreciation of language. I've had that ever since I was a child. We both had written much before we met. My writing may have been of a very adolescent, romantic-like nature and needed to mature as his had. But I had been writing and, therefore, he could see the kinship and my appreciation of language. We'd speak back and forth, very cryptically and minimally sometimes; this happened very early. And also I think there was what you would call "a kinship of observation": noticing particulars in our response to our surroundings or, as they say, sharing "the poet's eye." We had a rapport of response. Often, when someone would say something, we would smile and look at each other; or we would encounter, as we took a walk, some image of nature and all at once I would experience this empathetic bond of response.

Tom was then curious to see some of my work. I had been writing quite a bit, and, of course, he would show me his work. But the meetings arranged by Dan later on, as I mentioned earlier, were short on time; so we transferred letters and phone calls. We would go to the guest house for a half hour to talk about this or that. But he was sometimes very impatient. He was on a strict schedule.

The restrictions of the monastery—well, they had these periods of time set aside for the monks' private readings, and that's when Dan and I would arrive and Tom would include me in this particular parcel of time. Sometimes it would only be fifteen to twenty minutes. Then when he would have to visit Louisville for a doctor's examination, he had the dispensation of the abbot to trust his judgment to do a few other things while he was in town. We did go to bookstores, libraries, and, of course, listen to jazz at a local club if he had to stay late that night and drive back. The cloistered restrictions, naturally, were a "problem," and he wasn't nearly as free then as when he moved to the hermitage, later.

Kilcourse: I complimented you in a review of *Song for Nobody,* saying that Merton responded to you because you knew how to be irreverent about the monk's persona; that you landed some hefty counterpunches in exchanging haiku, vaudeville, and wit with Merton. Can you tell us about his allergy to such a persona?

Seitz: It was only after I got to know him better, after a few years, with some of the other monks. You can imagine being a young student and encountering Merton's reputation and his work. I was somewhat intimidated for too long a time. I think we appreciated irony. I'm a great lover of Sophocles and Greek tragedy. We both loved Aristophanes—almost the absurd vaudevillian nature of people's eccentricities, oddities, idiosyncracies. And the culture as a whole: it was often disturbing and sometimes quite ugly and demoralizing. At the same time, there was that slapstick vaudeville element to all that and we sensed it.

The word "irreverent" is probably an accurate term because I wanted to be serious without being solemn and I think I found that in him. He was very earthy and could joke about very serious things, but I don't think he was ever scandalous or blasphemous. He could just see the underbelly of many things. He remarked in one of our long talks one time about how we had lost much of that vision in the Church. He loved Chaucer's *Canterbury Tales* and said it was a much healthier approach—to include the human foibles and the physicalities of our bodies. If you read *Canterbury Tales* you know what he's alluding to: the scatological humor. Still, that is not irreligious at all. Tom thought that was quite holy and sacred. Everything is blessed and we shouldn't be evasive about that.

As far as his allergy to this persona, the monk's persona is something I imposed upon him—something that many of us did. Initially, you might think you should do that too. I think he's got a poem or a letter to a severe nun where he advises us to watch ourselves and not try to be a Saint Jerome and throw ourselves in the thornbushes and flagellate with branches. Obviously, you don't have to do that. But Merton's guilty of some of that in *The Seven Storey Mountain* with the zeal of his conversion. He antagonized many people by espousing Catholicism so ardently. He was embarrassed later about being that myopic. But I think that goes with anyone's zeal of conversion. In spite of all that, the book redeems itself in so many other ways.

How Tom felt about that false persona was something I covered in *Song for Nobody*. He was uncomfortable with that pious, plastic, saintly image because he knew all the time what he truly was. He was earthly, human, and he was a sinner. Later, one of the greatest conflicts in his life was that he almost became incapable of realizing that God actually would accept Thomas Merton and love him in spite of his past, his secular life, when he saw himself totally "out of control," often excessively so. I hate to use the word "addictive" here because it's so current in the wrong sense of the term. But he did overindulge in many things. And his response to that allegation was that many people really knew all the "warts" and he didn't want to hide any of that. I think you'll find that in his private journals. Tom comes out and says he's quite ordinary, like the rest of us.

As far as our exchanging haiku, there is the economy of speech that you find in the poet, almost a cryptic, surrealistic exchange—minimalist bites of language that you find in *A Catch of Anti-letters*. He and Bob Lax did it much better. They had a real rapport—an empathy—one that was much closer than I ever established with Tom. Therefore, in that kind of bond you don't have to qualify your statements. You can just hint at this and that.

Kilcourse: You regularly infiltrated the monastery boundaries (and later the hermitage) by ferrying visitors to and from the monastery. Who were some of the memorable ones?

Seitz: "Infiltrate" is a strong term. It wasn't undercover like the Navy Seals at night with a black suit, over the wall with hooks, like prison. But I did volunteer for that. I thought it was a privilege and honor to meet someone at the airport. Some of the people I should have known (they were prominent theologians, philosophers, and poets). Others I did know and one of the most enjoyable ones that I spent a couple of days with prior to taking him out to the monastery was Brother Antoninus (William Everson)—the West Coast Dominican monk and one of the first San Francisco Renaissance poets with Kenneth Rexroth before the Beats came along. He set the ground for that whole Beat movement of Kerouac, Ginsberg, and the rest in literature. After fifteen years of corresponding, Antoninus and Merton finally met.

I also met John Howard Griffin and knew him longer than Merton. I knew John for fifteen years and Merton for ten. J. Laughlin

(Tom's publisher and friend) visited at least once or twice a year, as well as Naomi Burton (Tom's so-called "agent" and friend-advisor). There are others I can't recall offhand right now (possibly Lax, Parra, other poets, a Sufi or Hindu or some Zen Master). I met Dan Berrigan at the hermitage.

John Griffin came in '65 (or was it '63?) and he spoke at the Memorial Auditorium here in Louisville. At that time, John had not regained his sight totally and addressed an overflow crowd downtown. We had never met. He spoke for over three hours about his book *Black Like Me*. In fact, Dan said, "He's obsessed with this racism." Griffin told me he had exhausted the educational possibilities in the United States at the age of fourteen and went to Europe to work with the French Resistance to help the Jews escape from the Nazis during World War II. He was blinded at that time. He was also doing his doctoral studies in musicology, "Gregorian Chant." He wrote his beautiful autobiographical account of that period, entitled *The Devil Rides Outside* (now out of print).

After Griffin's speech that night, we had breakfast together with Sally. We talked long and long, and we got to know each other. Then I led him back to the hotel where he was staying. He said he wanted to see my work. We started corresponding. When John came back later to write the official biography, he stayed at the hermitage and I would visit him, take him food and his mail. I stayed with him back and forth for a month. Another time Tommie O'Callaghan's father had a place for John to work and we were together every day for about a month, but that's another story.

Kilcourse: I take it that you and Merton both critiqued one another's work.

Seitz: He mailed me copies of his work in progress and I did the very same thing. At that time I worked at a place where I secured teletype rolls. I'd rip off a section of the long roll and send him the carbon of poetry and personal letters and told him I was keeping the original, so "please just toss it in your fireplace or destroy it." I used some of that in *Song for Nobody*.

Later, Tom edited *Monks Pond* (a four-volume international literary magazine). That was during the last year of his life. It was quite interesting and only four issues were planned. It was eclectic and ecumenical. Some of my writing was put in there and now, looking back, it is quite embarrassing. I don't know if Tom was just being kind, a friend. I sent him so much material that he said, "I can't devote the entire issue to you." I'd write poems to him and about him, and he'd say, "They're very nice, but. . . ." Quite often, when I wasn't writing to Merton, he was still my audience of one. I wanted to bounce my work off him, not so much for approval, but for his response. He was honest enough to say that it was often excessive, full blown, or narcissistic.

I liked Tom's early work—the imagery of the monastery was concrete and arresting. There were fine similes there, and he would call them "pretty poems." But they were quite beautiful and effective. Obviously he was always ahead of me in his growth and evolution. When he shifted again into the apophatic period—those minimalist, concrete, sparse poems—I was also going that way. I was writing concrete poetry before I ever realized I was doing it. I had sent some to a magazine and the editor said, "We're not publishing concrete poems." I never knew what the hell that meant and only found out later it was what Lax was writing and what Tom was beginning as well.

Next Tom turned to the antipoem, his *Cables to the Ace*. This was Nicanor Parra's influence, but Tom had written antipoems earlier. We all had. You'll find some in *My Argument with the Gestapo* (his early novel). And when I protested, telling him that I preferred the "early poems," he said, "I'm not that man anymore. I'm not that guy who wrote those poems. I'm writing these poems and that's who I am." I had to become familiar with and accept that. In our exchange of poetry, sometimes I was put off. I'd say, "You've lost it" or "this is garbage." I'd be that frank about it. Of course, he was kinder in calling mine "gibberish."

Kilcourse: Merton obviously taught you much about writing, especially about writing poetry.

Seitz: He taught me much about writing, but as regards style, no. There are other poets who influenced me extensively: Dylan Thomas, some of the Beat poets (Kerouac, Ginsberg, and Corso), the French surrealistic poets, and even Pound, Eliot, those kind of people. To me, being a poet is a way of responding to life and a way of interacting. I think it is a way of appreciating life and bearing witness to it. I understood that Tom's vocation as a poet was just that. I began to see poetry as prayer, the sacredness of speech. That's the kind of influence he had in my development, as my mentor. But in many of my contemporary poems, the rhythms and the energy were from the city and the culture that I was enveloped in at that time (which was quite removed from Merton's home environment). But he taught me to "trust my vision and the subject matter."

Kilcourse: How would you say Merton influenced your own spirituality?

Seitz: I had options: to be a poet, to be a monk, or to get married. I realized the problem of being a poet and a monk simultaneously. I found out that I could not be self-indulgent in my writing at the expense of my spiritual life. Writing was my spiritual life, this was my calling. Possibly it's not the highest one. Even Merton (early) said the highest vocation was to be a contemplative monk and, down the line, maybe a writer. He tried to purge himself of that prejudicial spiritual hierarchy, and I had the same sort of conflict. After all, there is a spirituality of aesthetics.

Paul Tillich expressed beauty as theophany. And that's true, even in my vocation of marriage. I'm a "cradle Catholic" and was taught the old religious hierarchy: you could be a cloistered contemplative, then you drop to the mere priest, then the brother, then the lay single person, and finally, the lowest common denominator, those who marry. Those married people still had a spiritual life, but it was almost negligible. I reconciled these things, rid myself of such notions. Tom helped me through that. (Who better a teacher, with his exposure of such?)

Kilcourse: You are a native Kentuckian and, as you stated, a "cradle Catholic." How did that factor into your relationship with Merton?

Seitz: It was a factor in my relationship with Merton because I don't think he quite appreciated, at least for me, what an emotional trauma being a very sensitive young Catholic, quite impressionable, was like. I was maybe neurotically so. I was scrupulous. I took all this ritual and liturgy quite literally, and was quite moved by it emotionally (too much so, it appears). Much of it was due to my sense of sin and the guilt, the negative, joyless aspect of it. I suffered sort of a nervous collapse at the age of twelve because I couldn't come to grips with this idea of living up to my "perfect" expectations.

Tom, being a convert, approached the Catholic faith with much more sophistication and a different perspective, an adult one. Many of the major Catholic movers of the twentieth century were converts, and they were the most influential people. My experience of Christ and the sacraments and Mass . . . was somewhat polluted by all this emotional trauma and I couldn't come to a joyous openness to some of these things. I told him there was a difference in the way we approached that. I had to try to work it out.

Kilcourse: There is a splendid passage in *Song for Nobody* where you recollect your final conversation with Merton, the morning he left for Asia. It was obviously the climax of a long-standing conversation about faith and your own Catholic identity. Where do you now find yourself with this Merton legacy about faith?

Seitz: It didn't end there really, . . . it's ongoing. I'm still working out this East-West synthesis of spirituality that Merton was doing at the end of his life in Asia and Bangkok.

I recently spent three days with Frederick Franck, the Zen writer and painter, in a sort of "Eastern Spirituality Workshop." He worked with Albert Schweitzer, a Protestant, in Africa for six years. His other influence was D. T. Suzuki, a personal friend and mentor. And, of all things, Pope John XXIII was someone whom he loved dearly, spent time with, and of whom he did many portraits. Franck seems to be more where I am at the present. I always consider myself as embracing Tao. Taoism is very appealing to me and Zen Buddhism is not truly atheistic, as it appears to many Western thinkers.

I took books by R. H. Blythe to Merton while he was in the hospital. I like Blythe very much, especially his four-volume haiku collection, and his *Zen in Western Literature* and *Oriental Classics*. But Tom criticized Blythe's Zen as "too general." "Suzuki is the one to read," he told me. And I did that. At that time I used Alan Watts as an introduction to Zen to my students, but Tom said that Watts was "just a little too American" in his approach.

But, as I said, it's still going on with me. In the truest sense, I think the three basic premises of Vedanta are quite accurate. I often fill in the "religion" blank on official forms with: Native American Zen

Vedantist. Native-American religion is Christianity mixed in with their previous traditions, so I include them all as best I can.

Kilcourse: Merton once described your wife Sally as beautiful. Tell us more about her role in your friendship with Merton. Can you tell us more what Merton's friendship did for the family, how it has affected your sons?

Seitz: I was appreciative of his appreciation of her because, again, there was that kinship. We both did acknowledge and recognize and thank God eucharistically for the female. I realized that we both could love a woman. I don't know if Merton actually loved a woman prior to the monastery, but I know he sure had relationships and very much experience in that area. I considered him wise and earthy, healthy in that regard. Here was a monk to whom I could talk about my man-woman relationship with Sally (who, by the way, is quite beautiful in every sense of that word). I could talk about love. I could discuss sexual problems and I trusted that he knew what he was talking about. He wasn't abstract. To me, he was existential and concrete, having an immediate appreciation of a love relationship, and a knowledge and sense of wisdom about it all. He was a sensual man in all respects, as a true poet, a spiritual person must be.

Most women whom I've known who did meet Tom Merton were very fond and attracted to him; but more than a physical or romantic attraction, it was his openness and wide-eyed receptivity to them. And I have to say this—it's almost embarrassing—but women around Merton were sort of awestruck. I'm not referring to the guru who had his groupies, although that could easily have been the case if Tom had been so inclined. There was this "thing" that women (as well as men, I'm sure) saw—a full human being. I hate to use such words as poly-morphous sexuality attributed to Merton. What I mean by that, of course, is that he was sensually open and sensitive as a poet has to be, with all the pores open, all the antennae out, eyes wide open.

As far as my family is concerned, I think Merton affected my middle son, whom I named Sean Merton. Dan Walsh was his god-father. Merton visited our home right before he left that last time. Sean was only four years old then, and he kept asking after Tom had gone to Asia and died, "When is Tom Merton going to come back and see us?" And Sean still remembers and talks about Merton, and he reads Tom's Zen books. He loves him in that regard. Dylan, a year older, is interested as well in Eastern spirituality and Taoism. Casey was a little bit too young; he was only three. But he is very creative in his music and his art, just as Tom was.

Merton did something for the family. They still remember and appreciate the time he spent in our home with us.

Kilcourse: You spent a lot of time at the hermitage with Merton. And yet it was a place of solitude and contemplation—as well as extraordinary writing and work for Merton. How would you describe what the hermitage was for Thomas Merton in those years 1965–68?

Seitz: You say "a lot" of time. After reading *Song for Nobody* many people say, "My God, Merton's at the hermitage and you're always out there and you're having picnics all the time and doing all kinds of things when he's in town."

Well, no, that's not quite the case. Tom was living at the hermitage for three years, and a couple of years before that he had use of it. When you take all of those years and then compact the incidents I mention in the book, it sounds as if we spent more time together than it actually was.

But to get to more important points of your question. I sincerely think that Merton's anticipation of the hermitage, like mine of the monastery (and I hate to accuse him of that), was a little romantic and idealistic due to his appreciation of a few "saintly models." I remember once, after we first met, Tom reprimanding me for reading St. John of the Cross and Teresa of Avila. He said, "You're not ready for that. That stuff will screw you up. You're going to go off the deep end with that." And he was quite right. I was going off and much too fast; it takes time to get there. I also asked him questions about poetry. He said, "Why don't you read Rilke's *Letters to a Young Poet*"? He must've said that for three, four, or five years, and when I finally did read that book, I still asked him the same questions.

As you say, I think the hermitage was a place of solitude and contemplation for Merton. He did some extraordinary writing there. He was very prolific. He had discipline. At times I considered his life as having been out of control, and that he behaved compulsively. But at the hermitage he had a strict discipline. He had an idea of "I've got so much time to do this and that. And I've only got two hours a day to write and I've got to get things done." He had this schedule, and if I were even a little late for a meeting, he would be angry. He'd lose his patience and let me know about it. His schedule didn't allow that and he didn't want to be interrupted. It was time for him to have the opportunity to be silent, to be in solitude, and to do his true spiritual writing. As I mention in my book, it was a joyous time of creativity and spirituality for Tom. But after such a prolonged experience of this he became lonely, which, of course, is natural for any human being. I don't think Merton was a community person by nature, and I don't think that he was a true hermit in the same respect. He seemed to vacillate between the two. No doubt he wanted to be that, the solitary contemplative, but I think he was too sociable, too warm and expressive. He actually was a "people person."

Yes, Tom's life at the hermitage was an extraordinary time and a place of solitude and contemplation, but I don't know if he would have remained a hermit the rest of his life (at least not at a particular place, Gethsemani or otherwise). His hermitage would have been a moving "presence" wherever he went. The years 1965–68 at the hermitage were a very good time for Tom. For all of us.

Kilcourse: You intimate briefly in *Song for Nobody* that Merton confided in you about his relationship with the nurse in 1966. Last year in *The Merton Annual*, Jack Ford described it as an "infatuation." What more can you say about that?

Seitz: When this was going on I remember that it was extreme anguish for Dan Walsh. He was very upset because he was a very orthodox, traditional Catholic. Jack Ford is a much better man than I am, but I don't agree with him about this relationship just being an infatuation. I think that is what Jack would like to believe. I'm not accusing him of that, but so many others would prefer to judge it that way.

I think this was an experience of love for Tom (as well as the young woman). A true love. Quite analogous to a poem I wrote entitled "Girl." He liked that poem very much and he published it in his *Monks Pond*. There was a kind of love and attraction between the two of them that I could identify and sympathize with. It's not that I would necessarily condone all of this—after all, Tom was a cloistered monk, and this situation violated the "rules," but I can see it happening. I wasn't encouraging it, so to speak, but I certainly wasn't condemning it. I think Tom had to go through this experience because in his earlier life, before the monastery, he really did not have healthy relationships with women. They were, it appears, very "macho, patriarchal affairs." If you had listened to what he had to say about all of this, you'd agree. Tom had to confront that. He had, for too long, suppressed it. He did notice women. He looked at them and appreciated them. I'm not saying he lusted after them, but had a healthy attraction to their feminine beauty. I think he had begun to come to terms with this feeling. It's in his love poems. He wrote that he must correct the distorted way he had related to women. He had to cure that. He wasn't using this woman as an experiment. I don't think he was leading her on or exploiting their relationship at all. I think he was very sincere but, at the same time, admitted that he had not had a mature understanding of women. He did respect them. But there had been a deep sexual problem. I had it too. I still struggle with this because my relationships with women had been either romantic or physical. For many men, myself and (I think) Merton included, it's often difficult to relate to some women on intellectual, artistic, or other levels as well. It takes a breaking through a barrier for that.

Really, I don't know if Merton ever resolved this issue or not, because in *The Asian Journal* he still talks about how maybe monks do not have to be celibate: "After all, these Tibetans aren't; these Hindus or these Buddhists aren't." Much of that was stated sort of "off-hand." I don't think he felt any guilt about his recent "love experience" too much. He was torn between these things. It was an awful conflict in him—that you can't have both: be a monk and still love a woman. I think it was the summer before he left—he waited that long to burn her letters. Some people say it ended then, but I think that he might have carried that with him till his death. I'm not saying he would have married or anything, but he could not help but be more a whole person and more appreciative of the vocation of marriage. It gave him a much better perspective about human nature.

Kilcourse: You have described your perplexity with *Cables to the Ace* when typing pages of Merton's antipoems for him. Tell us something about how you saw him developing with this new genre of antipoetry in *Cables* and in *The Geography of Lograire.*

Seitz: My poems were hard, noisy, city-busy, and Merton was isolated from that urban climate. *Cables to the Ace* doesn't seem to work as well as J. Laughlin thinks. Merton was not living in the total home environment of the city. *Cables* has an "electric" rhythm to it. Its sound is static, the language is often harsh, fragmented, and splintered.

At the time, I was taking him books out there to the monastery, some City Lights paperbacks by contemporary poets. Not to say, "This is how you should write," but to expose him to the vision of our particular generation, which I considered him part of—the Beats, with Ginsberg, Kerouac and others. In fact, I was part of it, and we were all one in that. But there was perplexity early on about Tom's aesthetics, his poetic expression of the consciousness of the American experience. I thought that what he was trying to do, *Cables*, wasn't working. In rereading the book, I do find isolated sections that are quite beautiful, quite effective, and there is a jarring fragmentation there, but far more on the page than the sound of his voice. It lacks the rhythms that you find in jazz, in a John Coltrain saxophone solo. It lacks that musicality. There is almost a John Cage cacophony of sound needed in a book like that.

The Geography of Lograire was still "in progress" when published. It wasn't a finished product. I remember taking *Religions of the Oppressed*, a book by a fellow named Lanternari, out there to the hermitage. It's excellent. It's about all the messianic cults, cargo cults, the ghost dance and all that. And I took Rasmussan, the Norwegian anthropologist, who did work with the Eskimos. In fact, in my poem "When Writing Merton," I allude to that—how the Eskimos would sit there in the cold and the dark and wait for the poems to pass through them; they were open, empty vessels.

In *Lograire*, when Tom did the opening prayer-passage—it's very Joycean. But when read aloud, it does not work as well as Joyce. For me, *Lograire* comes full circle back to Tom's macaronic method that you find in his early *Gestapo* book. I allude very briefly to that in *Song for Nobody*. Tom had passed through his "choir" poems, his "desert" poems, the apophatic period. Then he was freed up! It was like going through a black hole. His vision becomes dense, then comes out the other side full blown, like Faulknerean prose. *Lograire* has some of that. But in many of the passages, the way he puts it together, it's somewhat like Williams' *Paterson*, but it doesn't work as well. Maybe the final version of the book would have worked if Tom had lived to rewrite it and add to it. But as it stands, that's the way it should be.

These last two poetry books, *Cables* and *Lograire*, are in sharp contrast to the early monastic poems. There the imagery of the liturgy and ritual of his religious life is monastic, beautifully expressed. I don't consider those works "inspirational" but Tom often did. He looked upon them derogatorily, as "those sickly sweet falsely pious poems." No, they're some of his best works. In the last books, Tom was experimenting with the American avant-garde (at the expense of his much better affinity with the French surrealistic and Latin poets). But he was at that time in the hermitage, again a climate not conducive to that consciousness. It's true that a few times we went into town to listen to jazz, and he had a few records to listen to, but that is not enough immersion in your culture to be able to echo it and bear witness to it.

Overall, I think Merton would like to have accomplished what the Peruvian poet César Vallejo did in his work—that is, maintain his natural vision of being a lyrical surrealist while expressing his social conscience. This was Tom's challenge (and what he often reminded me in the last years): to overcome the temptation to remain in the aesthetic ivory tower of a Rilke, and to meet the obligation of voicing the social-justice concern of a Camus.

Kilcourse: You were close to Merton during the antiwar protests and his work with Jim Forest and the I.F.O.R. (International Fellowship of Reconciliation). The Cistercian censors had silenced him, yet he circulated his *Cold War Letters*. How do you remember him dealing with this ordeal?

Seitz: There was, of course, some anger. And it was often more than righteous indignation. Tom sent some of his materials to Ping Ferry at the Center for Democratic Studies in Santa Barbara to circulate them. The paradoxical, contradictory thing is that the *Cold War Letters* are dealing with peace, which is supposed to be at the root of spirituality, Christianity, Catholicism. Merton considered the rigidity and conservatism of the hierarchy and the administrative bureaucracy of the Church stultifying and suffocating. The *Letters* express a frustration and disappointment in his own Church. And he wasn't being judgmental so much; he was just impatient. Prophets always are. They don't predict the future; they see things as they are now. And it always takes any institution a while to catch up to that—what mythmakers always have to contend with. And I don't think Tom was disobedient to protest for peace in the way he did. Somehow, his was "legal" as regards the Order. Like a lawyer, he'd found a loophole in the censorship rules, and distributed these writings in a mimeograph network. It was somewhat of an ordeal, but he did get through that.

When Jim Forest visited Louisville (infrequently) he would sometimes stay at our home. Jim was, I think, very much of a youthful, idealistic, rebel, a purist-pacifist. He was very much like myself; we were "true believers," as Eric Hoeffer would say. But he liked to laugh a lot, much of it self-deprecating humor. He was unlike Jim Douglas, another pacifist friend of Merton's, who visited Bellarmine one year and taught theology. Jim is somewhat more solemn about all of this (having written one of the seminal works on pacifism, *The Non-Violent Cross*). These two Jims are still deeply involved with the peace movement.

I haven't mentioned the civil-rights movement here. It's difficult to separate it from the peace movement. Tom discussed that relationship a lot too. He wrote passionately about civil rights, as well. In fact, John Griffin said Merton knew more about the problem of race than any American writing at the time. And, as I stated earlier, Griffin devoted his entire life to the race problem here in America after contributing to the Jewish liberation during World War II in France.

I went to Selma with Martin Luther King. I was privileged to do that. And I worked with Dick Gregory during the open-housing demonstrations here in Louisville. I also participated in the many peace marches at this time. Tom wanted reports of all that when we got together. About that time he had counseled a conscientious objector in Louisville and got in a little trouble for it. He told the young man to follow his conscience in this, and many people in Kentucky thought he was provoking draft-dodging (as reported in the local news) and advocating that sort of thing. There was much misrepresentation and misunderstanding of the entire issue. Tom tried to disengage himself from all this, but he was becoming quite confused about the entire peace movement's tactics. He felt an allegiance, and, at the same time, some of the extreme radical activists disturbed him. It appeared that Jim Forest and some of his fellow Catholic Workers were taking it all too far. And it's possible that Jim was then somewhat of a zealot. I don't think Jim is myopic and this is all he can think about, but that's exactly what Dan Walsh said Griffin had succumbed to regarding racism. The just cause could be grotesquely bent out of shape.

In large part, the Church did somewhat silence Merton on the peace issue, but I don't think it was an ordeal that did him in. After all, there were the *Cold War Letters*, eh?

Kilcourse: We've already talked about how Zen Buddhism has affected your own poetry. Can you comment on its influence on Merton's poetry?

Seitz: As I've said, Tom's early, apophatic period evolved into his Zen humor. He often spoke (and later wrote eloquently in *Zen and the Birds of Appetite* and *The Way of Chuang-Tzu*) of the sense of irony in life, and all the seemingly paradoxical and contradictory nature of most things. But rather than having a negative response to the apparent absurdity of much of our lives, Merton (as Aristophanes) could laugh at the slapstick incongruity of it all. Self-deprecating and self-effacing humor was his response to "God's koan of Creation" (as he put it). So I did see this Zen influence in his writing.

Yes, the Buddhism affected my poetry and it had an influence on Merton's poetry as well, even if indirectly. *Cables to the Ace* is not pure Zen. The work, as mentioned, was surrealist, sometimes minimalist, and might even be called expressionistic antipoetry. But there are these contradictions and incongruous images that are quite obscene. He used obscenity to mirror obscenity. He showed us that we are, our culture, obscene you know, in the sense of dehumanization. Tom, without censoring, presented (often in pain) much of secular society in all of its grotesqueness to remind us of our "collective sin." At the same time, there were interludes and small poems that were Zen counterpoints of beauty and compassion and joy. Yes, reading Zen did influence Tom's poetry. I think it made him less solemn, though still serious. It made him far more concrete, existential, and immediate—"in the flesh"—in his poetry.

Kilcourse: In what ways did you see the 1968 trip to California (in search of a more remote hermitage and anticipating the trip to Asia) affecting Merton?

Seitz: He was excited. The hermitage, as I said earlier, was not too solitary. It was still, in a sense, somewhat structured, though not quite "institutionalized." Tom had been wanting for many years to travel. He had only made that one trip to see Suzuki in New York, and that later trip out to California, and his trip over to New Mexico. He enjoyed those immensely. How it affected him? I think it was very liberating, healthy. He had been reading much, as we all do, and now he was anxious to get firsthand experience. That had been the case with his interest in the Native Americans. Sometimes our intentions are quite serious, but we tend to romanticize. I think by visiting Asia, Tom could see what was going on in the East directly. He found out (or reaffirmed) that there was a deep mystical contemplative tradition in his own Western life and vocation. Therefore, he wouldn't have to always see the other as possibly being better. I have that tendency to see the Eastern as better than the Western because I'm so disenchanted, mostly with myself, and I project it onto the culture. I think Tom had to find out that there was this synthesis of the two and he could bring that back home. Earlier, in his studies, he discovered that many Easterners were now appreciating some of the Western contemplatives. It was good for him to see that firsthand.

Kilcourse: Where do you see Merton twenty-five years after his death, in terms of a figure in American poetry and literature?

Seitz: J. Laughlin is very disappointed at Merton's place in American letters. As mentioned earlier, he expected *Cables to the Ace* and *Lograire* to win some sort of national book award or be critically acclaimed as major works. They almost went ignored. Merton's not anthologized that much if you look in any poetry collections. He's not considered a major figure in American poetry, and sometimes not even minor. You can find some collections that don't even include him. But he was probably aware of all this. I remember him saying, "I'm going to do nothing for ten years but read and write poetry because all of this other stuff is a distraction." It's obvious that his prolific outpouring of "writing-on-demand" was diluting and polluting his poetic vision. Tom wanted to be a pure poet as T. S. Eliot was. He recognized the superiority of such work and he loved reading *The Four Quartets* aloud. And Dylan Thomas.

Sometimes it's a crooked curse and blessing to be a poet. It is difficult to socialize, to relate to other people in "normal" situations. There is a little bit of psychic dishevelment going on (a condition that sometimes expressed itself in Tom at his rare public appearances)— but, again, that's another issue altogether.

Tom wanted that total commitment to his vision, to the language, to the craft of poetry. But he spread himself so thin with all his other writing. He had a genius for literature, no doubt about that. But if he had focused, had been exposed more to the culture and the creative climate of other poets, he could have reported on it much better.

So in American poetry and literature now, a quarter century after his death, Merton is not recognized as a major figure other than by those people who read all of his work (they read his poems as well). I don't know if you agree, but many have said that Tom's genre was as a diarist, writer of journals. There are prose poems throughout that writing and there are poems throughout *The Seven Storey Mountain* and the novel *Gestapo*. I consider all honest writing, including prose, as basically poetry anyway. But in terms of Tom's place in contemporary American poetry, he's almost a ghost.

Then again, Merton's output is so prolific—sixty or seventy volumes. Down the line—I don't know how it's going to be judged. Some of his writing is quite uneven. He rushed it out, much in first draft with little editing.

Kilcourse: Writers like David Cooper have ventured some penetrating new interpretations of Merton. Cooper, in particular, has made some critical judgments about Merton's work, refusing to canonize him and everything he wrote. What is your judgment?

Seitz: Thomas Merton's Art of Denial is an important book and David Cooper is very insightful and intelligent as far as I'm concerned. There are decent insights into Merton's personal and psychological makeup here. But some have said that the shortcoming in Cooper and others like him is that they are blind to the monastic-contemplative vocation, they just do not have an appreciation or empathetic understanding of this at all. I think primarily you've got to look at Merton as a Catholic priest. You start there. He's a Christian contemplative. He is a monk and belongs to the Cistercian order. That reality cannot be denied, it is pervasive, a "contagion" that infiltrates everything he does in all of his writing. If you ignore that dimension, which Cooper often seems to do, then you've got just a partial view of Merton's life and work. There are big holes and gaps.

Some of Cooper's insights in his *Art of Denial,* such as Merton's problems relating to his parents, appear plausible. Tom might have entered the monastery out of guilt. As admitted, he wasn't the best community person or the ideal hermit. He failed in this and that. Well, we all fail in our aspirations to be "saints," and that's what he wanted to be (as we all do, eh?). There are many things Tom had not worked out psychologically. He was starting to read some on this matter later, near the end of his life. But there's so much of this jargon, pop humanistic psychobabble out there, and he wanted to avoid much of that. We have quite a bit of that today in what we call holistic psychology, esoteric views of religion and anthropology—all that New Age millennium stuff.

Concerning Cooper's *Art of Denial*, I think it's time we have some of this kind of criticism. It's not negative. I think it's an honest appraisal. It may not be totally accurate. Cooper is merely questioning Merton's motives for much of what he has done and asking if Merton did deny these things. We are into this whole contemporary concern about addictive personalities and denial, alcoholism, obsessive-compulsion—all these "problems" come up in this book. I guess some of this "analysis" is relevant and the diagnostic terms might apply to Merton as well as anyone else, and we have to come to grips with that, if accurate. So, I appreciate what Cooper has attempted in his book.

Kilcourse: You had the privilege of being a friend of Thomas Merton. How would your friend, Thomas Merton, want to be remembered?

Seitz: I guess I'd have to quote people like Emerson who said, "It's not who wrote the poem, but that the poem exists." I've got one line in a Merton poem that reads: "There's not a cloud-wisp of tracery in our passing through." Merton preached this in most of his writing (possibly talking to himself as much as his audience). He believed that you don't leave behind evidence or testimonials or monuments to your achievements. Some of the greatest saints are those who are anonymous and didn't leave the trace. They exist in their work and influence, but not in their name, their identity, or fame as a personality. The author is the work. It came out of him. He was the creator, here's the creation.

As a personality, I'm sure Tom wouldn't want to be on holy cards (like baseball players are) because he was aiming to get rid of the ego. But about his "being remembered," he knew it was inevitable when he established the Merton Collection. He said, "It's going to happen. I may as well go along with it for these scholars. I will help them." I think he was very compassionate in doing that because it was hard work.

How he wanted to be remembered is a difficult question. In fact, the entire notion appears contradictory in light of his vocation. I don't think he was as self-conscious about himself at the very end. He was not too much enamored with the persona of the "famous monk." He said, "I have wasted so much time." He wanted to make the few years he had left "meaningful" (in the sense of his being "spiritually realized").

You know, Jung divides life into two major phases: the early heroic phase of youth, then the phase of the "sage" or wise person in our elder years. I think Merton had lived out that first heroic stage. But it's a paradox that in his spiritual direction as a youthful novice-master, and in his writings at that time, he was the sage. But in his everyday life and habits and inclinations, he was still the hero. Tom appeared to be aware of this contradiction, and that's why he made the late remark about so much of his life being a waste. I think he was anxious to get over that hurdle and enter into a life of true humility.

Many say that Merton had an "untimely death," but all deaths are untimely. And at the end he still considered himself as lacking "the freedom of love." I think he tried to evolve from *The Seven Storey Mountain* persona to that of a Chung Tzu. *The Way of Chung Tzu*, I'd say, is his true autobiography because of the self-effacement you find there. There is this holy indifference, this freedom from all of those "religious" hangups he had much of his life. I think he would have liked to be free enough to trust his vision and his liberty. The "real" Merton (just listen to his tapes) was extemporaneous. He was spontaneous. He was creative in the moment. He improvised all the time. That is the kind of life he wanted to be able to trust himself to live.

Much of Merton's life was "busywork"—his conferences, his publications, and his response to others' interest in him. I'm embarrassed that I added to that. I think much of the conference work being conducted in his name since his death is busy academic work, with very little relation to who he was. Most of the people attending these meetings are sincerely interested and moved, and the speaker-scholars are truly inspired and dedicated in their work. In spite of this, Merton would not be comfortable attending such conferences. They seem to be a bit too formal. Not at all the climate of humor and freedom that Merton enjoyed.

One last thing about my book, *A Song for Nobody*. Again, I am somewhat embarrassed by it. It is about a "relationship," a very close one (for me, anyway). Some people say it almost reads like a love letter to Merton. Well, I hope I'm capable of that. I do miss him. There is a deep loss, a nostalgia of longing—my memory of the few years I was blessed to be in his presence.

I have always been somewhat perplexed as to why Merton befriended me in the first place. Other than that he saw some of the same imperfections in me that he had in himself, and that there might have been a sort of bonding in that regard. We struggled with many of the same conflicts (although obviously on different levels). He was a perfectionist (as I am), demanding so much more of himself than others.

I truly believe that Tom's final breakthrough was his realization that God did love him, that he was forever forgiven, and that he was unconditionally accepted. I don't think that happened until the last few years, maybe the last few days, of his life. And that's an awful cross to carry for half a century, his continuing conviction that "I not only am not loved, but unable to love." And, through the unbounded mercy of God, the laying down of that self-imposed load of living hell is, to me, the final celebratory, triumphant act of victory in Merton's life.

"Easter Fugue" out of a "Great Spiritual Silence": 1993 in Merton Scholarship and Publication

George Kilcourse

Publications in this year leading up to the December 10, 1993, twenty-fifth anniversary of Thomas Merton's death are best described as revisionist. We enjoy the poet and literary figure of Merton in a fourth volume of his selected letters (this one to writers) and in a fellow poet's "memory vision" tracing a decade of both friendship and apprenticeship. This pair of books affords an antidote to the sometimes claustrophobic effect in presentations of the cloistered, univocal monk-Merton. We need a simultaneously binocular appreciation of both the poet and monk to perceive the true depth of his lived monastic charism expressed through his literary gifts.

The uneven selection of Merton books for this year will undoubtedly be mirrored and multiplied in the avalanche of 1994 publications that have been spilling from the twenty-fifth anniversary symposia, conferences, and remembrances. However, other authors launched 1993 journal articles challenging the lingua franca of the Merton scholarly establishment and its image makers. Such signs prompt that we are indeed maturing into a more scholarly appraisal of Merton's strengths and lacunae, as well as of the weaknesses in earlier scholars' uncritical enthusiasms and oversights.

With the publication of more Merton letters and the first-person reminiscence (alias "memory vision"), new questions occur. How are the letters to be weighed as autobiography? What real distinctions demarcate the genre of letters from journals? Or from some journal-like entries in the "working notebooks"? With the publication of seven volumes of Merton journals now projected, these and related questions deserve attention. Not only do we wrestle with these Merton sources, but the first-person-narrated reminiscences of friends of Merton will undoubtedly multiply. Where do we draw the line between a recollected matter of fact and an interpretation? What to do in the event of conflicting reports of facts, let alone the inevitable clash of interpretations? In the midst of such musings, I remind myself that Michael Mott's *The Seven Mountains of Thomas Merton* only grows more authoritative as a meticulously researched and reliable Baedeker to the essential Merton. Mott's biography deserves a wider reading public as both introduction and source of interpretation. Despite more recent quasi-biographical efforts, Mott's highly readable and probing effort remains without peer. The pairing of Anne Carr's concise preface with Lawrence S. Cunningham's well-organized introduction to *Thomas Merton: Spiritual Master* complements Mott's volume by refining the monastic identity and vocation. But those essays emanate from a very different project. More of this conversation later, but now for a survey of 1993 Mertoniana.

Books

Thomas Merton. *The Courage for Truth: Letters to Writers.* Selected and edited by Christine M. Bochen (New York: Farrar Straus Giroux, 1993). xiv + 314 pages. Hardcover $27.95.

Toward the end of *The Courage for Truth* we find a magnificently candid series of epistles addressed to an unlikely correspondent for a Cistercian monk: the controversial and provocative Henry Miller. Their mutual respect engendered some of the most unguarded Merton letters. His free voice and often irreverent tone characterize the bulk of this fourth and best collection yet in the projected five-volume series of Merton's selected correspondence.

Two passages, one to Henry Miller and a second to poet Louis Zukofsky, set the poles for this collection. When Merton judges the failures of today's religion as "the greatest orgy of idolatry the world has ever known," he frankly confesses in the August 1962 letter to Miller that even as a priest he ought "to be able to give Christ's answer. But unfortunately . . . it is no longer a matter of answers. It is a time perhaps of great spiritual silence." Merton writes to Zukofsky nearly five years later that his own poetry has recovered the paradise vision that he lauds in the musicologist's own poetry. And we move from the great spiritual silence to Merton's description of Zukofsky's work " 'A' 7" as "a most marvelous Easter fugue":

> . . . You are in fact sacred music but as it should be, not just Church music. With the kind of secularity that is in Bach. And the compassion. The great Lenten compassion and sense of rising from the dead that must happen, that happens, that art is all about. The victory over death. This is the real witness to the world and you are the one who is saying it most clearly. . . . I really get the breath knocked out of me completely by some of those "A's." The way in "A" 7 the perspectives fuse in and out of each other and the dead and the alive interchange and come into focus, and the echoes of the psalms in scorn of idols, the dead wood, the dead and living horses, oh my. Such praise.

The Courage for Truth records Merton's own fugue spoken out of the great silence. In these pages he celebrates the poet's freedom to scorn the orgy of religious "idolatry" by fusing death and life in poignant, even intimate letters to fellow writers, most of them poets and many of those poets from Latin America. Two years after the letter to Henry Miller he quips about the novelist's remarking a striking resemblance to himself in a photo Merton had sent; Miller also thought the monk's companion in the photo, poet Miguel Grinberg, resembled an ex-convict. Merton replied: "In a world of furnaces and DP's it would be hideously immoral for someone, especially a priest, to be well, totally sane, perfectly content with everything, knowing which end is up. . . . Yes, I have got some good hellburns all over me."

Since so many of these Merton correspondents were later contacts from Latin America, readers will savor the liberated monk of the 1960s in these relaxed paragraphs. To his former novice, Nicaraguan Ernesto Cardenal, he confesses that he feels more a part of the scene in Spanish American poetry than in North America "where I am a bramble among the flowers." This kinship with Latin America ripples in concentric circles throughout these letters. Perhaps the collection of letters addressed to Cardenal is the most valuable because in them Merton's identities as contemplative, poet, social critic, and Church-person all converge. At times he speaks as the spiritual director; or the fellow poet; or the social visionary forseeing the unity of the Americas, which he then lamented as "the rootless culture . . ., a sort of cancerous orchid transplanted from somewhere else." So he recommends to the Nicaraguan priest the task of "spiritual reconciliation . . .[,] a redemptive and healing work that begins with *hearing*. We already begin to heal those to whom we listen." He can speak candidly to Cardenal about his own aborted efforts to leave Gethsemani, and eventually he redefines his monastic identity in his letters to this liberation theologian because their friendship is multifaceted and anchored in poets' souls.

In a lengthy May 16, 1960, letter to the Polish poet, former diplomat, and writer Czeslaw Milosz, Merton remarks about a manuscript, "I do not say it represents much but it is my own authentic voice of the moment. . . ." Thus he unwittingly names his own metier. Less than a year later he writes again, resonating with Milosz's metaphor of the "spellbound dance of paralytics" to describe our obsession with a "fog" of concepts, knowledge, and techniques to address "illusory answers to illusory problems." He points to the "poison" of our evading the expression of what is most important to us.

But there is nothing evasive about Merton in this fourth volume of letters. He speaks throughout of the reality of the post-Christian world. In 1961 he writes to Brazilian scholar and teacher Alceu Amoroso Lima about Christianity "vanishing into an age of shadows and uncertainty." He chides his own monastery as a deceptive greenhouse: "And grains of error planted innocently in a well-kept greenhouse become giant poisonous trees." Death and life wrestle in Merton's fugue as he concludes to Lima with an unmistakably mature faith: "Our faith can no longer serve merely as a happiness pill. It has to be the Cross and Resurrection of Christ. And this it will be, for all of us who so desire."

Readers of this fine selection of letters edited by Christine M. Bochen of Nazareth College will find far more than might be expected in a volume quietly subtitled "Letters to Writers." Merton struggles openly with the "authentic voice of the moment" on issues ranging from monasticism to his ongoing struggle for his identity as a true self. The "hellburns" he admitted to Henry Miller are amply illustrated as he agonizes over having shadowboxed with a medley of false selves and personae. To Clayton Eshleman, University of Indiana translator of Pablo Neruda and César Vallejo's poetry, Merton writes in May 1966 that "there is no question that the great issue is freedom. From Urizen's goddam hammers." But Merton elaborates important definitions of religion, spirituality, and the Church itself in these porous letters. They are the treasure chest of his spiritual legacy. To Pablo Antonio Cuadra in 1963 he laments the obsession with technics and results that lead the human spirit to be "overwhelmed by the riot of its own richness, which in the end is the worst kind of poverty." He concludes by seeking truth, "constantly discerning it from the obsessive fictions of the establishment everywhere."

The range of correspondents in the letters is remarkably diverse, including Evelyn Waugh, Jacques Maritain, Walker Percy, James Baldwin, and Lawrence Ferlinghetti, among others. In a 1967 curriculum vitae addressed to Jonathan Williams, Merton proves self-deprecating as he writes, "Autobiography 1948 created a general hallucination followed by too many pious books. Back to poetry in the fifties and sixties. Gradual backing away from the monastic institution until now I live alone in the woods not claiming to be anything, except of course Catalan." Indeed, the woods surrounding Merton's hermitage figure prominently in his enthusiastic reports to correspondents. For from the environs of the hermitage, amid a great spiritual silence, Merton voiced his own authentic moments in an unmistakable Easter fugue.

Song for Nobody: A Memory Vision of Thomas Merton. Ron Seitz. Ligouri, Missouri: Triumph Books, 1993. 188 pages. Hardcover $19.95.

Midway in the opening part of this provocative portrait of Thomas Merton, Ron Seitz names the immediate emotion engaged upon remembering his friend: "a run-on endless heart movie I can hardly control." *Song for Nobody* begins with a flashback to twenty years earlier and the death of Merton of Gethsemani in 1968. Gloom. Doom. It is a dicey, brooding overture with its own disonnance and abrupt lurches ahead. We fast-forward and it is December 1988. Seitz teases his strength and foolishness to imagine again Merton. He quickly finds himself heading for the abbey "to wipe clean my vision, to begin again fresh with memory—the only instrument of inspiration and creativity to compose a portrait of the Thomas Merton I knew." On the twenty-fifth anniversary of the monk's death we receive a poet's rendering.

This is a book calibrated with the eyewitness fervor of other intimate friends' remembered visions—the likes of John Howard Griffin, Bob Lax, Ed Rice, and Jim Forest. But its author is more transparent than the others. This is a book as much about the author's ongoing conversion and search for a spiritual foothold as it is about his famous monk-friend. Seitz's voice sometimes whines rather than laments. There is an echo of Jack Kerouac's bravado that Seitz admits is often counterfeit. The most apt image I find to describe his venture is that of the tightrope walker dangling over a perilous chasm of the maudlin. Seitz even quotes Merton once sarcastically describing him as "gargling with language." But there is an uncanny quality about this book that refuses to let the reader look away. By the final pages, the author's confidence has steadied him across the tightrope. What has emerged is the story of a unique ten-year relationship between monk and professor-poet-beatnik-husband-father-spiritual questor.

If ever we needed an antidote to Merton's self-admitted concern that he would be turned into a myth for parochial school children, *Song for Nobody* writes the prescription. Beneath the problematic veneer of Seitz's hero worship and sense of loss is the sometimes temperamental, always human monk. The personae fade in this earthy, vibrant, and sometimes unpolished rendition of the sinewy poet-prophet. At times Seitz recollects an irreverent Merton who demolishes monastic observances when they distort a deeper spiritual identity. The much-discussed polarization of contemplation and art are reconciled in Merton's own telling, remembered by his poet-confidante. Perhaps Seitz puts it best early in his memory vision when he judges that from the beginning "Tom was a 'Body Poet.'"

> I think that the spirit of Eros had finally reclaimed him in his last years—that he was open to touch others in the concrete, the immediate, the (if you will) existential flesh. I think that, at long last, he had "let go" for the free fall that comes with the final acceptance, the trust, and love of one's own person. . . . He was "at home with/in creation."

Such insights gauge Seitz's affinity for the key themes of Merton's spirituality: the true self, contemplative awakening, the cosmic Christ, the "hidden wholeness," the desert experience, paradise consciousness. If he unabashedly promotes Merton's identity as poet he compels readers to be persuaded that this was Merton's natural, even primary, gift. The scholar-theologian-philosopher identity fares poorly in Seitz's recounting the monk-hermit's story. But Merton himself fueled this critique with the banter and self-deprecation he exchanged with the poet with whom he indulged an uncommon intimacy. It is obvious that Seitz's flirting with a monastic vocation in 1958, combined with his irreverence for what Merton called "simulated monasticism," made him an engaging poet-comrade. The exchanges of Zen archery, haiku, and sarcasm evidence Seitz's deft counterpunches in response to Merton's leading. The two men grew to love each other. There lingers throughout their relationship something of the surrogate father and son quality. The fact that Seitz's spiritual mentor was Dan Walsh forged an even stronger kinship.

Where biographers and commentators have overlooked Merton's prowess as a poet, Seitz explores and ends up quarrying rich spiritual ore. He appreciates the apophatic mysticism of silence where words run out. But out of such silence emerges the poet's word. He can name the "language tangle" of discursive thought when he and Merton come to an impasse. But the exchange of glances, like the images in a poem, communicates the contemplative's letting-go of self-consciousness for the no-mind that accepts and celebrates things just as they are. Merton had taught Seitz to use his camera as such a contemplative instrument, "to stop looking and to begin seeing."

While few have attempted to integrate Merton's late, lengthy antipoems, *Cables to the Ace* and *The Geography of Lograire,* into his spiritual vision, Seitz offers an interpretation of these poems in terms of the monk's lyric essay "Rain and the Rhinoceros." Both are directed against subtle modern totalitarianisms. One wishes that he had made stronger connections with Merton's protest against racism and urban violence, war, and secularization in his attention to Merton's meandering antipoetry.

The final days with Merton before the trip to Asia are narrated with intense feeling. There is melancholy as he describes the final minutes at the hermitage and the last meal with a circle of friends in Louisville, the scene of some apparently large egos clamoring for Merton's attention. More poignant is the playful lunch Seitz and Merton shared with Seitz's toddler sons and his wife. The final morning before driving him to the airport, Seitz pleaded with Merton for a dialogue on the absolute essentials of the Christian faith. The monk unfolded a last testament on the cosmic Christ and Christian hope that offered the author "some kind of peace to a proud, but troubled soul." This summons to trust in the ultimate goodness of creation resonates well with Merton's spirituality and indexes Seitz's insight into his friend's soul.

Like other books on Merton, Seitz's suffers from a certain one-dimensionality. He so focuses on the poet that he risks overlooking the total integration of monk-social critic-ecumenist-mystic-theologian. The very strength of his portrait is also his weakness. But Merton scholarship grows with the cumulative effect of such converging studies. Seitz gives us access to the affective and childlike side of Merton which often evaporates from the dense pages of his prose. His poetic profile of Merton has forced us to reconsider the relative balance in a multifaceted personality.

Laughter: The legacy that ultimately effervesces from the pages of *Song for Nobody* is the rib-shaking, face-creasing, belly laughter shared between Thomas Merton and Ron Seitz. There is something of the vaudeville exchanged between two clowning wits. A mocking, ironic humor volleys between these poets with whiplash speed. It is refreshing to hear Merton described by one of his intimates as vulnerable enough to laugh and to weep. Seitz accuses some of Merton's detractors as misinterpreting the vulnerability as naiveté. He interprets the monk's relationship with a student nurse in 1966 as just such a misinterpretation. The gamut of Merton's spirit enlarges with both the weeping and the laughing.

Song for Nobody is not an easy read for those expecting a linear biography. The syntax, cryptic haiku, "song space," sentence fragments, and other evidences of Seitz's poetic license challenge and occasionally escape even alert readers. The mixture of stream of consciousness, poetry, letters, sarcasm, mock humor, private meanings, and Zen all combine for a playful but rewarding effort. Over thirty black-and-white photographs of Merton and his abbey environs (most from Seitz's own camera) grace the book.

A final caveat: Not since Ed Rice's *The Man in the Sycamore Tree* have we encountered so much interpretation "remembered" by a Merton intimate. The sheer volume of material, including dialogue, which is recorded in this volume (and Rice's) raises questions for scholars about the first-person attributions these authors make. This is not to discredit in any way their contribution. But Merton research and scholarship needs to find a method to integrate, to assess, and to critique the relative significance and merits of this genre of the remembered Merton.

Meditations With Merton. Nicki Verploegen Vandergrift. Ligouri, Missouri: Ligouri Publications, 1993. 80 pages. Paperback $4.95.

This modest book uses excerpts from Merton's writings and launches into meditations on a series of spiritual themes. The author describes her effort as "an attempt to reflect on [Merton's] words in light of everyday living." A related Scripture passage and original prayer complete each entry.

The resulting collage reads more like a contemporary commentary on excerpts from *New Seeds of Contemplation,* the text most heavily quoted. In fact, one of the weaknesses of this volume is the disproportionate use of that single text, although several passages from *Conjectures of a Guilty Bystander* earn a place as catalysts for the meditations. The passages are well selected, concise, and represent some of Merton's best spiritual writing. While the text is arranged into ten sections— Personal Integrity, Sanctity in Life, Seeds of Identity, Integration, The God Within, Labor, Solidarity and Service, Words of God, God's Will, and Love Is a Foundation—the overall structure is not apparent and seems random.

No doubt these meditations are deeply felt and well-written spiritual reflections. However, the genre of such spiritual meditations might be represented in some more accurate manner than through the description "with Merton." There is a contemplative sensibility in the meditations coupled with a sense of Eastern as well as Western spirituality. What seems to be lacking is the deeper social consciousness and compassionate protest that characterize the mature Merton. Because he grew beyond the classical expressions of *New Seeds of Contemplation,* Merton's later works deserve more attention in these meditations. The thirty-two brief meditations do make for good spiritual reading in their own right. This is a book that might be used for Lenten spiritual exercises or as a retreat instrument.

A Seven Day Journey With Thomas Merton. Esther de Waal. Foreword by Henri Nouwen. Photographs by Thomas Merton. Ann Arbor, Michigan: Servant Publications, 1992. 114 pages. Paperback, $12.99.

Esther de Waal's reflective and handsome volume succeeds where Vandergrift falters. A Benedictine and Celtic spirituality scholar, she intentionally sketches the "retreat design" on her seven days' journey as an effort to gauge Merton's effect on her own spiritual life. But she insists that hers is "not a book about Thomas Merton" and for that reason her well-selected borrowings incorporate his insights without eclipsing the primacy of the reader's discovery of the contemplative awareness of God's presence in life. De Waal's second chapter, "Thomas Merton's Journey," however, does offer a cogent interpretation of his monastic identity and his holistic spiritual attitude that incorporated body, mind, imagination, spirit, and all the senses. Her interpretation of Merton's story as a paradigm for all of our stories is well wrought in terms of the parable of the Prodigal Son.

The seven days that structure the book mark progressive moments toward an integration that equips the retreatant to resist the ambush and imperatives that rob us of time for contemplative prayer. In the first chapter, "The Call," de Waal relies upon John Howard Griffin's experience of silence and solitude to appropriate Merton's eremitic life as an awareness of vulnerability. When the illusion of strength is broken, then we cannot escape the awareness of God's mercy. Chapter 2, "Response," follows this perception of weakness, failure, darkness, and sin with a poignant reflection by Merton on compunction. The familiar Merton theme of the "true self" is ably unfolded in chapter 3, "The Solitary Within," where she deftly retrieves from the prologue of *The Rule of St. Benedict* the monastic therapy for sloth. This avoids both the torpid, semiconscious, half-alive and half-awake existence and the false self's need to be fed by achievement and acclamation.

The final four chapters, "Encounter with Christ," "The Demands of Love," " 'Common and Natural and Ordinary,' " and "Integration," borrow from Merton an especially strong Christological focus. The affective dimension of the heart engages the mystery of the cross; Christ's love is portrayed as a forgiving love. This allows the retreatant to return to the world with an authentic love for others that relaxes its illusions and grasp, "since I no longer need their dependence." De Waal concludes by proposing the key to Merton's own journey from a *Seeds of Contemplation* text: "All our salvation begins on the level of common and natural and ordinary things." This plumbs the depths of Merton's sacramental consciousness and eventuates in his "wholeheartedness . . . which finds the same ground of love in everything." This sacramental principle allows us to rediscover the spontaneity to celebrate the sacredness of life.

One of de Waal's most effective tools in presenting excerpts from Merton is her arrangement of prose quotations in the form of lines of poetry. Such "found poems" evidence well his metaphoric gifts as a writer and halt us when we would ordinarily miss his meaning. Her first chapter, "How Do I Use This Time," offers unique practical notes and suggestions for the use of psalms and twenty-eight of Merton's photographs, which have been carefully chosen for their contemplative and artistic qualities and are masterfully interfaced with the text.

The only frustration in using this splendid volume concerns the "Notes and References," which are placed at the end of the book. It proves clumsy to identify quotations without footnotes and a few quotations are not identified. The unfortunate printing error that mispaginates the references in the last chapters needs to be corrected in future editions. The book is well researched and exhibits a careful and reflective familiarity with Merton's classic writings and more recent publications, such as his letters to religious in *The School of Charity*.

Swimming in the Sun: Discovering the Lord's Prayer with Francis of Assisi and Thomas Merton. Albert Haase. Cincinnati: St. Anthony Messenger Press, 1993. 216 pages. Paperback $9.95.

Franciscan Albert Haase's *Swimming in the Sun* is a book of contemporary spirituality, drinking from the wells of Francis of Assisi and Thomas Merton. It integrates three elements: (1) the importance of practical experience; (2) psychology; and (3) the wisdom of the world's relations, with an emphasis upon Christianity. Haase identifies the five important elements of personal spirituality as (1) one's image of God; (2) the present moment as the place of encounter with God; (3) community; (4) personal commitment to God's dream of peace, love, and justice; and (5) the practical importance of asceticism. The title of the book comes from Merton's description of the Lord's Prayer in *The Sign of Jonas*.

The design of this book will prove attractive to those who are seeking a more applied spirituality. The author has designed chapters to appropriate phrases from the Lord's Prayer in terms of Francis's and Merton's "spiritual wisdom." To this end he excerpts fine quotations from the writings of both (including Merton's poetry), plus some pearls from Merton's very effective Credence Cassettes tape recordings on spiritual titles. The author's illustrations and anecdotes abound, making this book more homiletic than scholarly in character. Although the breadth of sources Haase employs from the Merton canon evidence his scholarly abilities, each chapter concludes with a very practical list of questions labeled "Points for Reflection."

Swimming in the Sun offers a popularization of Merton's spirituality. The colloquial style and contemporary vernacular provide a user-friendly context and threshold for some of Merton's more polished and sometimes dense prose as well as for the biblical scholarship that Haase incorporates into the book.

Follow the Ecstasy: The Hermitage Years of Thomas Merton. John Howard Griffin. Edited with foreword by Robert Bonazzi. Maryknoll, N.Y.: Orbis, 1993. xv + 158 pages. Paperback, $12.95.

Although this biography of Merton's final three years in the hermitage was originally published in 1983, this new Orbis edition deserves a note. Merton's friend John Howard Griffin was originally charged in 1969 with the project of the official biography. However, even after ten years his task remained incomplete and the debilitating effect of diabetes forced him to resign his commission. From his drafts of material his family and Latitudes Press have extracted the chapters on Merton's final years because, explains editor Robert Bonazzi, this period had most fascinated Griffin and it had been freshest in the memories of those he interviewed.

Bonazzi's extraordinary foreword captures the spiritual affinity between Merton and Griffin in poignant descriptions and insightful intuitions that warrant Merton readers' attention. He sketches three characteristics of Griffin's work that permeate his immersion in Merton's hermitage and the interpretive biography that resulted: (1) the reality of Griffin's experience of solitude; (2) the objective portrayal of Merton's 1966 romantic relationship with a young nurse; and (3) the illuminative, personal quality of Griffin's prologue ("Les Grandes Amitiés") and epilogue ("The Controversial Merton").

Griffin's gifts as a writer uniquely equipped him to render his monk-artist friend's experiences. The selection of materials from letters, journals, and notebooks is deftly woven into his narrative. Above all, a contemplative kinship between the biographer and his subject engages the reader. Ten years after first reading these pages I was again moved and mesmerized by Griffin's graceful interpretations. But two questions deserve to be raised about this volume. First, why does Bonazzi go to such lengths to reach for overstatement in diminishing Michael Mott's biography as "mainly a book of facts and scholarly interpretations from which the essential Merton does not emerge" in comparison to *Follow the Ecstasy?* This unnecessary and misleading exaggeration blemishes an otherwise excellent foreword. Second, for all the value and insight of Griffin's narrative of the hermitage years, the publication of this segment with its focus upon Merton's late romantic relationship risks a sensationalism that is disproportionate to Griffin's whole effort. One hungers for the remainder of his manuscript, even in rough form, for John Howard Griffin's presentation of the hidden wholeness of Thomas Merton. Perhaps this hope can one day come to fruition with Robert Bonazzi's able enterprise.

Articles

Robert E. Daggy, "Choirs of Millions: A Reflection on Thomas Merton and God's Creatures," *Cistercian Studies Quarterly* 28:1 (1993) 93-107.

This article presents an eclectic collage of Merton's various celebrations of creatures now endangered or mistreated. The curator of the Thomas Merton archives at Bellarmine College offers the context of the monk's apocalyptic mentality concerned with human survival vis-à-vis the modern world and projects him as a guide and mentor for our ecological era.

Daggy points out that Merton's Thoreau-like reverence for nature and the creatures of rural Kentucky extended throughout his monastic life, although it intensified with the solitude and seclusion of his final three years in the hermitage. As forester at the abbey, Merton's long-standing attention to the woods is duly chronicled. Asian religious respect for nature and Merton's study of these traditions is acknowledged by a Taoist-inspired poem.

The suggestion in this article that Merton's theology of creation is synonymous with contemporary "creation spirituality" warrants critical scrutiny. The identification of this term with the work of Matthew Fox gives theologians pause about such an easy identification of Merton with this unorthodox trajectory. Future attention to Merton's ecological interests would do well to examine the effect of the imagery of the psalms, the backbone of the monastic Liturgy of the Hours, on his appreciation of creation. Merton's poignant prose-poem on *le point vierge* in *Conjectures of a Guilty Bystander* also deserves a prominent place in his understanding of creation.

Karl A. Plank, "The Eclipse of Difference: Merton's Encounter with Judaism," *Cistercian Studies Quarterly* 28:2 (1993) 179-91.

This Davidson College professor's article will prove important not only for the immediate assessment of Merton's encounter with Judaism, but as a critical analysis of the monk's efforts to deal with the particularities of "the other" as other in dialogue. Plank speaks of "a certain flaw" in William H. Shannon's 1990 *America* essay, "Thomas Merton and Judaism," and proceeds to probe the effects of Merton's language addressed to Jews or about Judaism, which Shannon has neglected. The results are illuminating and radically revise our understanding of Merton's correspondence and dialogue with Abraham Heschel without diminishing the merit of his desire to appreciate Judaism.

Plank evidences careful scholarship on the Second Vatican Council's declaration on non-Christian religions, *Nostra Aetate*, and its unsatisfactory solution to the question of conversionism. The question is not only the matter of the Church's proselytizing, "but the value of the Jew *as Jew*." In this regard he borrows from feminist liberation theologian Sharon D. Welch, who recommends a "communicative ethic" of risk, allowing distinctiveness and difference and refusing the universalisms of the lowest common denominator, that is, the "Judaeo-Christian tradition." Plank connects this emphasis upon difference to postmodernist critiques. He interprets Heschel as challenging Merton about the Church's arbitrary and manipulative "attempts to define Judaism relative to the theological claims of Christianity."

Although Plank credits Merton with reminding us that anti-Semitism is an attack on Christ, he claims that such a statement diverts us from the immediately concrete vulnerability of historical Jews. Merton, he finds, relies upon the Christian lens as a single frame of reference. Plank carefully concludes that Merton's emphasis on kinship is partial rather than wrong and certainly is not an intentional wound but "a conspicuous omission." In fact, he finds foundations for better Jewish-Christian dialogue in Merton's *The New Man* (1961) with its critique of Prometheanism. But he finds even more fruitful that book's reflections on human persons' ability to share in God's capacity for speaking freely *(parrhesia)*, because if dialogue is grounded in the perception that the Jew has challenging words to speak, then such freely spoken words might be seen as the Jew's attempt to love the Christian—and the Christian's vulnerability to being loved.

Victor A. Kramer, "Forgetting in Order to Find: The Self in Thomas Merton's Poetry," *Cross Currents* 43:3 (1993) 375–88.

The author of *Thomas Merton, Monk and Artist* returns to Merton's poetry to examine how it best reveals his changing self-perceptions. In this regard Victor Kramer follows the lead of Anthony Padavano, who has argued persuasively that Merton's poetry was the true barometer of his soul. Kramer's study proves especially valuable because he traces patterns in the basic stages of the monk's poetic self that simultaneously reflect his changing concept of self. We discover through this study the voice of an unselfish and less self-conscious poet who interacts and grows into compassionate awareness of others.

When he identifies Merton's "elusive *core*" as silence, awe, and forgetfulness of self, Kramer offers a compelling revision that contrasts with other attempts to isolate what he calls the pious monastic Merton of the 1940s, the angry Merton of the 1950s, or the earnest and ironic Merton of the 1960s. The strength of this essay is the appreciation of contemplative prayer and the transformation it effected in Merton's life and poetics. The analyses of particular poems from the early and middle Merton canon afford a clear and cogent interpretation from this perspective.

Not only does Victor Kramer offer his hermeneutic for Merton's poetry but also for the much-neglected "antipoetry" of the final years of the hermit's life. *Cables to the Ace* and *The Geography of Lograire* yield new dimensions with this appreciation of how Merton comes to "make room for all," especially the marginalized, the excluded, and the exploited, whose lives and stories echo in his global canvas of Western culture's sins. It provides an index of the radical changes Merton witnessed and the challenges he prophesied for his audience.

When Kramer judges Merton's success with the theme of self-forgetfulness, he appraises it as the work of a minor poet having "major spiritual importance." Readers will look for continuing attention to

Merton's poetry and various interpreters' analyses of that spiritual importance. Its exact nature will undoubtedly be the central concern of a wide circle of discourse.

Richard E. Getty, "The Polychrome Face of Contradiction: Assessing Inconsistencies in Thomas Merton," *Cistercian Studies Quarterly* 28:3/4 (1993) 281–96.

Getty, a licensed clinical psychologist in private practice, opens a series of questions by analyzing what he terms "contradictions" in Merton's work and life. He begins by asserting that contradictions are not to be explained away. He finds that the challenge "is rather to come to terms more honestly with the human condition that contradictions illustrate and the ramifications of this condition for grace and salvation." Borrowing from an impressive number of sources and Merton commentators, Getty finds Merton's autobiographical search for identity and his discoveries of the true self critical to our attraction to and understanding of the monk.

Silence, poverty, and conversion of life are topics selected to illustrate inconsistencies in Merton's writings. Getty identifies evolutionary growth, a dialectical temper, dissatisfaction with formulations, multiple persons influencing his thought, and Zen Buddhism as reasons explaining the contradictions in Merton's life and personality. Plausible as these may be, Getty's work challenges the interpretations of many who find more continuity in the Merton canon. Others have interpreted his writings in terms of "paradox," or seeming contradictions, rather than explicit incongruity. Getty's judgment that Merton's "indulgent living" (for example, his books and camera) and "acquisitiveness" marked failures (and not just contradictions) in his vow of poverty is certainly a revisionist and harsh appraisal. Likewise, while he quotes Merton's abbot, Dom James Fox, to attribute a "lingering propensity to think in terms of exclusion," there is another stream in Merton that insists on inclusiveness and a "hidden wholeness." What Getty provides is an insistence that our specific biographies narrate how "we are saved *through* our humanity and not *from* it." One hopes that he will expand and develop more precisely his larval and global reflections on Merton's story as one of "graced individuality" or "personality."

Breaking New Ground in Merton Studies

What has begun to happen in Merton studies evidences a subtle, almost imperceptible shifting away both from attempts to romanticize his monastic life and vocation and from efforts to domesticate his role in the Church and culture-at-large. The revisionist direction of some of the 1993 Merton material represents a turn to a more critically analyzed, integrated Merton. And the ongoing publication of primary Merton sources itself contributes to this breaking of new ground.

At the beginning of this review-essay I raised the question of the distinctive genres of Merton's own work. It is intriguing to find buried in the early pages of *The Courage for Truth* a 1962 letter to Jacques Maritain where Merton himself ruminates on such a query. He is cautioning his philosopher-friend against publishing for the general public his recently deceased wife, Raissa's, journals in their entirety. His fear is that such an intimate genre would be received with only "flippant respect" because of people's fear, a fear he says "mocks their own inner light and beauty." Three years later he writes to Maritain after having read his fellow Frenchborn friend's published "notebooks" (Merton uses the French word, *carnets*). Merton confesses that his own just-finished work, *Conjectures of a Guilty Bystander*, "is itself a kind of carnet (rather than a Journal) but with quite a lot of poetic and descriptive stuff too." This poses the hermeneutical question: What kind of autobiographical gravity do Merton scholars and aficionados give to these varied genres: journal, correspondence, diary, working notebook, prose-poem, lyric essay, poetry? We expect the six editors of Merton's forthcoming journals to clarify the equivocation of scholars—and Merton himself—in using these designations.

A second new vein of research, signaled by its prominence in *The Courage for Truth*, centers upon the theme of marginality for interpreting Merton's monastic identity. This theme also intersects with his identities as poet, social critic, and explorer of interreligious dialogue. It would profit us to examine the ecclesiology expressed in monasticism itself. How is contemporary monastic life, with dwindling numbers, reinterpreting this charism? Merton's insistence that monasticism is a lay countercultural movement has retrieved for us some compelling arguments to contribute to the often agonizing discussions about future directions for the life of the Church. It is frighteningly easy to mistake his vectors and retreat to monasteries for a spiritual recharge when Merton was arguing against such a distorted, trivial imitation of simulated and juridical monasticism.

Along these very lines runs another artery in Merton that connects with the monastic ideal: the contemplative identity. Parker Palmer has written that Merton's personality was not intrinsically monastic (with its observances of silence and cloister) but contemplative in a broader sense: it embraced his abilities as poet and accepted the created world in all its complexity and diversity. Scholars and commentators will give more attention to Merton's mature self-understanding as a contemplative without disguising his monastic status or his expressions of religious faith. We need to see in higher relief this distinction in order to fathom how contemplation centered his art and his social consciousness.

Finally, attention to the question of language and its relationship to the possibilities for human community in Merton's writing augurs well for our understanding of his legacy. The seminal papers presented at the October 1992 Abbey Center for the Study of Ethics and Culture at the Abbey of Gethsemani opened this question in an experiential process that resonates with Merton's intuitions. Rosemary Haughton has aptly reflected upon the elusive and necessary common language and our frustration over "The Fall of Babel" in her commentary included in volume six of this *Annual*. The International Thomas Merton Society's Fourth General Meeting also focuses on this issue and promises insights with Lawrence S. Cunningham's reconsideration of Merton's "A Message to Poets" and a medley of responses. One awaits for the lively conversation and rigorous reflections to unfold.

Reviews

Thomas Merton. *The Courage for Truth: The Letters of Thomas Merton to Writers*. Selected and edited with an introduction by Christine M. Bochen. New York: Farrar, Straus, Giroux, 1993. xiv + 314 pages. $27.95 hardcover.

Reviewed by Elena Malits, C.S.C.

The Courage for Truth presents a selection of letters to writers the editor of this volume describes as "in a special way Merton's literary friends, persons who shared with Merton a passion for writing as a life work." The writers addressed constitute an amazingly diverse group—internationally, intellectually, and religiously. Thomas Merton's "literary friends" include Evelyn Waugh and Henry Miller, Jacques Maritain and Ernesto Cardenal, Boris Pasternak, James Baldwin, and Czeslaw Miloz, as well as an assortment of younger poets from Argentina, Brazil, Chile, Cuba, Nicaragua, Peru, Uruguay, and Venezuela.

Merton always addresses the individual with whom he is corresponding in specific and concrete ways. He comments on materials they are sharing with one another, inquires about particular circumstances in the person's life, and points out what he most values in that writer's work. But there are common themes that run through these letters from the last twenty years of Merton's life.

One is struck by Merton's sense of identification and union with persons very different from himself. To Czeslaw Milosz he insists that "it is true what you say affects me deeply, seeing that we are in many respects very much alike. Consequently any answer must involve the deepest in me, and that is not easy." Merton expresses a profound affinity with Boris Pasternak. He writes to the Russian novelist "as to one whom I feel to be a kindred mind." Merton's response to Pasternak's account of his youth goes even further: "I feel as if it were my own experience, as if I were you. With other writers I can share ideas, but you seem to communicate something deeper. It is as if we met on a deeper level of life in which individuals are not separate beings." Thomas Merton gives Pasternak the ultimate compliment: "In the language familiar to me as a Catholic monk, it is as if we were known to one another in God." To Hernan Lavin Cerda Merton acknowledges his deep identification with Latin American poets: "I am not a North American poet, but rather a South American. I feel closer to them because of their sensitivity, irony, political point of view, etc."

Reaching out to his literary friends as people who understand what it means to be under attack, Merton is explicit about his own suffering, especially from fellow Catholics. He tells Ernesto Cardenal that he knows from experience "that one cannot write anything alive without being attacked, and sometimes quite fiercely, by members of the Church. Certainly the most virulent attacks on any work of mine have come from priests and religious." To Henry Miller Merton complains that "the religion of religious people tends at times to poke out a monster head just when you are beginning to calm down and get reassured. The religion of half-religious people doesn't bend: it bristles with heads."

In contrast to all the conflicts, he tells José Coronel Urtecho, a young Nicaraguan poet, of "the joy of being able to communicate with friends, in a world where there is so much noise and very little contact." Writing to Cintio Vitier, a Cuban poet, Merton speaks of their living in a time "where the printed word is not read, but the paper passed from hand to hand is read eagerly. A time of small letters, hesitant, but serious and personal, and out of the meaningless dimension of the huge, monstrous and the cruel." Friendship is, for Merton, at the heart of God's desires. To his good friends Jacques and Raissa Maritain, Merton exclaims: "How beautiful and simple God's plan for humankind is! That's it. Friends, who love, who suffer, who search, who see God's joy, who live in the glory of God."

Friendship and authentic community are the only defenses against mass society. "We must form a union of creators, of thinkers, of men of prayer, a union with no other 'organization' than charity and unanimity of thought," Merton writes to Pablo Antonio Cuadra. It is imperative, Merton tells this Nicaraguan poet, that "man, image of God, should be a creator, but not only as an individual person, but as a brother of other creators. Let us continue creating and struggling for the truth and the kingdom of God.''

And to another Nicaraguan writer, Alfonso Cortes, Merton sums up his sense of the mission of the poet: "It is truly the task of the poet to teach the ways of truth in the language of beauty.'' Such a task requires courage, Merton proclaims to José Coronel Urtecho, because poets "remain almost the only ones who have anything to say. . . . They have the courage to disbelieve what is shouted with the greatest amount of noise from every loudspeaker; and it is this courage that is most of all necessary today.''

This volume of Merton's letters, like the other volumes in the series, is filled with flashes of Merton's humor, irony, outrageous wit. It also reveals his preoccupation with never having enough time to get things done and his frustration with policies and practices within the monastery. But for the most part, *The Courage for Truth* gives us Thomas Merton at home with his own kind of creator: the writer. There is quite a lot of repetition—but how could there not be in anyone who wrote so many letters?

Thomas Merton. *The Merton Tapes: Fifth Release of Lectures.* Kansas City: Credence Cassettes. 1993. 6 Cassettes (60 min. each).

Reviewed by Steven L. Baumann.

Credence Cassettes' recently released (1993) tapes of Thomas Merton, originally recorded at the Abbey of Our Lady of Gethsemani during the 1960s, provide a unique access to key aspects of the history of monasticism and Catholic spirituality. A narrator states that the tapes were made for the benefit of the community of monks at Gethsemani. But the content and presentation transcends time and audience surprisingly well, except for Merton's use of noninclusive language, for example, the use of the term "man" to refer to human beings.

Like earlier tapes released by Credence Cassettes, these lectures reveal Thomas Merton to be a master educator and spiritual director. Merton's use of terms is superbly clear and well defined, so that an audience with limited familiarity with philosophy or Church history can follow and gain keen insights. Merton's humor and spontaneity come through far more in audiotape than in his edited and censored books. What the tapes lack in detail and comprehensiveness they make up in honesty and straightforwardness, the ability to get to the heart of the matter.

Technically the tapes have a few minor problems. For example, while the recorded quality of Thomas Merton's voice is exceptional the responses of his audience, a group of novices, are hard or impossible to hear. The tapes lack an outline or clear order, which might have helped the listener overcome minor problems created by editing and abrupt conclusions to some of the lectures.

The titles and topics of the tapes in the order in which they are coded are: "Obedience: A Means of Letting Go" (AA2616); "The Way of St. Basil" (AA2617); "St. Anselm: Reasonable Faith" (AA2618); "Created for Love" (AA2619); "In the Arms of God" (AA2620); and "Abelard's Loving Criticism" (AA2621). Thomas Merton's discussion of St. Anselm's "reasonable faith" (AA2618) exemplifies the value of these tapes and the gifts of the lecturer. By carefully situating the teaching of St. Anselm in its historical context, both secular and religious, and providing some useful reflections on the inner journey of St. Anselm, Merton provides the listener with considerable understanding of Anselm's struggles in a way that can give direction for spiritual growth and renewal today.

Merton's comments on the importance of integrating faith and reason and his discussion of Abelard's insistence on critical thinking (AA2621) are instructive. When Merton talks about St. Anselm's ability to combine philosophy and mysticism, writing and prayer, it is hard not to draw parallels to Merton himself as a "monk who thinks originally." He challenges the receptive listener to try to do the same. Merton's discussion of Anselm's ontological argument is a bit rushed and unfinished. St. Bernard's mystical theology and his understanding of the will of God underpin the tapes entitled "Created for Love" and "In the Arms of God." Merton's discussions of the writings of St. Bernard provide a vital retelling of the power of faith in the goodness and dignity of human being, the availability and effectiveness of grace, and the importance of "setting order in love."

The consequences of disordered love seem far more pressing today than at the time these conferences were given by Merton. He makes some intriguing and insightful comments, although somewhat

dated, on history, science, psychology, advertising, and world politics. His comments on Buddhist, Hindu, and Muslim religious traditions reveal his considerable knowledge and respect for these religions
and hint at the value of interfaith dialogues and exchanges.

In summary, these lectures make a valuable contribution to the
work by or about Thomas Merton, which continues to speak to the
challenges of being a Christian today.

Ron Seitz. *Song for Nobody: A Memory Vision of Thomas Merton.* Liguori, Missouri: Triumph Books, 1993. 188 pages.
$19.95 hardcover.

Reviewed by Thomas F. McKenna, C.M.

In a work of prose and poetry, Ron Seitz sketches the wavy yet
firm lines of his ten-year friendship with Thomas Merton. His book
is as much autobiography as biography as it probes the rich, transforming, and even numinous experience of two gifted people mixing
souls. It is a story of apprenticeship—lessons in the poet's craft, directions for following the gospel, wisdoms for living life deeply. Seitz is
the journeyman and Merton the master as the disciple recounts the
deepening of their bond over the monk's final years.

Seitz frames his account around two days. The first is a week
after Merton's death. The author sits alone through a dark and bitter
cold night and struggles to come to terms with his mentor's passing.
The second is another winter's day twenty years later, during which
he wanders across Gethsemani's grounds kicking over memory stones
to discover what of Merton lies underneath. Seitz writes, of course,
from memory. But it is one that he has fed and cultivated. There are
letters and cards Merton wrote him, notes and journals he kept before
and after the death, conversations with mutual friends, two decades
of reminiscing and mulling—all passed through the many-hued pal-
ette of Seitz's imagination. It is this last that Seitz claims gives his
recollection special power and truth. In his own words, this is a "memory vision" of Merton, a remembrance "of what it was to have touched
Tom in our passing-thru" (28).

The first day chronicles the rawness of loss and, to a lesser degree, the balm of remembrance. With Merton's other close friends,

Seitz is numbed by the suddenness. But other feelings seep in alongside the unbelief. Flashes of early hero worship come back. Vignettes of first meetings with Merton's close friends play out. Most vivid of all is the felt memory of Merton's innocence, his "awe and wonder at the 'first-time Gift of everything in Creation' " (25). For Seitz, Merton is quintessentially young, a marvelous open-faced laugh-er who was present to everything. It is Merton's entire motion that captivates Seitz, the "fluid, free movement" (31) of the monk's whole bearing. This is the *persona* the poet-friend would portray, though he knows from the start it is impossible to do. But so much of Merton's legacy is precisely the go-ahead to try such a thing. Memories of his encouragement to "reveal the inexpressible . . . in the concrete," "give Body images . . . as 'evidence' of Spirit," "leave residue-evidence of that journey to another country" (34) crowd Seitz's imagination.

The second day, calmer and more elaborated, is a memory tour of Merton's Kentucky homeland. As he moves across the monastery hills, the author hears his departed mentor tell him to become empty and open, a "voicebox of truth" (49), one of God's recording angels (64). Through memory, Merton continues to instruct in the mystery and arts of language. A pond trips off scenes of a picnic shared there in the spring of '68 when the older man spoke of writing and the struggle for the true self. Climbing a rise brings back the invigoration of Merton's simple presence.

Seitz spends the bulk of the day at the monk's hermitage. He stokes up the old fireplace, sits down in Merton's chair, even snoozes in the master's bed. Throughout, old declamations, one-liners, confrontations, sweet agreements, shared music, and mutual critique flood the visitor's awareness. He steps outside to sit on a stone wall made sacred by mutual revelations made on it twenty years before. For Seitz, it was wrestling with the monastic call. For Merton, it was a parallel grappling with "the nurse issue" (123).

The visitor continues into the woods, musing with his friend all along. He stops at a log the two of them used as a bench and hears echoes of instructions on the poet's art. The day wanes and Seitz returns to the porch to relive his last hours with Merton. The leaving for Bangkok—a stop at the author's home for a family meal and farewells, a quick trip to the newly founded Merton Center at Bellarmine, the dawn ride to Louisville and the plane waiting to take its rider Pacificward. Again, memories of place tease out memories of words and

silences. Leaving Gethsemani, Seitz pauses at Merton's grave to remind himself why he came here this day—"to remember, to remind
others who might have forgotten . . ." (179).

On the score of personal tribute to Merton, Seitz's book succeeds.
It is personal because the younger man speaks from the privileged spot
of intimacy. He conjures up Merton's magnetism, zest for living, ready
humor, and disarming transparency. He catches—and mimics—
cadences of his teacher's speech. He translates favorite Mertonian wisdoms and themes into the warm and occasionally private coin of
friend's talk. Even when it is Seitz who speaks, Merton is present in
the words as backlighting and undertone. It is tribute because Thomas
Merton is woven so tightly into Seitz's soul. He is one with Seitz's
inner voice, prompting him to write, helping him to pray, encouraging him to be vulnerable. The book is believable testimony to the power
and subtle pervasiveness of communion.

On other scores, *Song for Nobody* achieves mixed results. To be
fair to Seitz, the genre, biography through autobiography, is a tricky
one. Seitz acknowledges this dual intent when at the beginning of the
book he proposes to paint a memory portrait of Merton and at the end
avers he has been "looking for the spiritual seed that Tom Merton
planted in my person" (183). There is no question that authors must
use their own experience as the prism through which to present their
subjects. The challenge is to remain on the proper side of that porous
line between revealing the other through the self and obscuring the
subject because too many of the writer's issues enter in.

In many parts of his narrative, Seitz stands where he should and
allows his man to come forward. This is clearly so, for instance, in the
recounting of their nights out (115ff.) and their rides to town (76ff.).
But there are sections where it is not easy to determine who the central actor is. At times in their extended conversations, I wondered if
the book were not more a vehicle for Seitz's wisdom and writing than
it was for Merton's. There are occasions, in other words, when the
author gets in the way and crowds out his master. The fine line here
is the one preachers hopefully try to keep before their eyes—how to
reveal the Word through one's person, but not cover it over by being
too densely personal. This is no easy divide to negotiate. At times
Seitz wanders across it.

Another reservation concerns literary quality. For one thing, the
narrative often moves quite rapidly between Seitz's use of prose and

poetry, the latter sometimes hiaku, sometimes other structured verse, and sometimes free association ("improvisational image rhythms of my head and heart at this moment produce a kind of spontaneous verbal play at poetry" [50]). While the transitions add vitality to the book, their suddenness at times jars and distracts. Second is the verse itself. Some of it sparkles, particularly many of the haiku and passages, such as Seitz's poem on seeing his wife for the first time (163). But other efforts do not work as well. Some of the verse is too private and compressed. It jangles the ear, disrupts the flow ("the 'see-through' light a breath of aura-breath to me. The birds . . . shifting shape in a sway-lift . . ." [31]), and again borders on drawing too much attention to itself.

The reader might find interest in a parallel reading of George Kilcourse's recent work, *Ace of Freedoms*. Both books take explicit aim at Merton the poet, yet each sights him through a different scope. Kilcourse's is a more systematic and developed treatment of Merton's poetic theory and fills in places that Seitz's more memoir-like treatment (necessarily) passes over. But Seitz puts the more fleshy texture of face-to-face initiation by the master onto Kilcourse's analysis. The authors comment on many of the same themes (e.g., looking versus seeing, developing "the paradise ear," primal movement, art as residue of the journey, etc.) in complementary ways.

These cautions made, Seitz is worth reading. His insider knowledge of his mentor is arresting stuff. His simple love for the man and wonder at his life-giving profundity shine through the occasional flaws in Seitz's literary lens. The book title is lifted from one of Merton's poems about the pure livingness of things. Flowers and all creatures sing golden songs "for nobody": they sing simply because they joyously are. Seitz's memory portrait catches much of the exhuberant music that was sung by his beloved Tom.

Esther de Waal. *A Seven Day Journey with Thomas Merton.* Ann Arbor: Servant Publications, 1993. 114 pages. $13.00.

Reviewed by Dianne Aprile.

A spiritual retreat, carried out alone in silence, is by definition a private and personal journey. Anyone anywhere who has tried to meditate daily—be it in the quiet of a predawn kitchen or within the four walls of a monastery room—knows that the path to prayer and spiritual growth is by necessity a tailor-made trial. While you and I both may find Merton's writing a good companion for the trip, it is a fact that we will be stopped in our tracks by different passages along the way, just as we sometimes will be led to very different places by the same passage.

That is the beauty of it, of course. You cannot predict prayer or organize it or even honestly plan it. You can only await it with an open heart. I'm reminded of the lines in a poem called "Traveling at Home," by Kentucky writer Wendell Berry, that address the challenge and rewards—and, yes, surprises—of walking a familiar path: "Even in a country you know by heart / it's hard to go the same way twice. / The life of the going changes. / The chances change and make a new way." A personal retreat is not so different. Surrender, acceptance, and spontaneity are what is needed, not a road map.

With this in mind, the challenge taken up by Esther de Waal in her new book, *A Seven Day Journey with Thomas Merton,* is clearly an ambitious one. Her mission is to offer readers a stimulating mix of Merton writing and photography, day by day, for one week. A different theme is addressed daily in chapters with titles such as "The Call," "Response," and "The Demands of Love."

"This book is meant to become a prayer," de Waal writes in her opening chapter, subtitled "Some Practical Notes." "It is not a book about Thomas Merton," she continues. "It simply shows the succession of steps taken by one woman in trying to draw closer to God with Merton's help. I do not follow any accepted scheme or pattern, but have devised something which seemed to make sense for my own needs at the time."

This Merton-infused field guide to prayer is intended to inspire meditation and not prescribe it, she states. Passages from his essays, poems, and journals are offered as nudges in the right direction, as are the black-and-white photographs scattered through the text. When the author sticks to this stated mission, the book resonates with Merton's spirit, buoyant and generous. Yet there is often a less comfortable feeling of being led by the hand as you read the book. It is true, as she notes, that it is hard for many people today to carve out a slot in their busy lives for prayer and solitude. But is the answer to save them the time and trouble of figuring out how to do it—and to supply them, instead, with step-by-step directions?

In her opening salvo, de Waal demonstrates a sense of adventure and willingness to break out of routine that her spiritual mentor would surely approve. She suggests keeping a journal or sketch book, lighting candles, taking slow meditation-walks outdoors, and collecting stones or shards of bark to bring back to one's usual place of prayer for comfort and encouragement. This openness to improvisation and to sharing a bit of herself with the reader gives an air of intimacy to the book that is inviting from the start. De Waal candidly describes the structure of the book as "entirely of my own devising. It has not been dictated by anything other than what I perceived as my own need to be refreshed and to gain some new perspective in my life."

Private inspiration is a good place to start writing such a book, but de Waal's highly individualized response to Merton's work and her random way of presenting it to the reader is part of what makes the reader, in the end, feel curiously left out of the experience. It is not that de Waal's personal feelings get in the way or that her conclusions about Merton's work are eccentric. It is the format, the catch-as-catch-can framework she personally found so helpful, that diverts attention from her stated mission.

It is as if de Waal could not decide which book to write: a memoir of her own experiences with Merton and prayer; a how-to book on self-styled retreats; a beginner's guide for Merton readers; or a meditation manual. Any one would work. Trying to combine them all is a far trickier business. One can almost hear Father Louis, red pen busy on the page, whispering: "Simplify. Simplify. Simplify."

The 114-page book, cram-packed with Merton material as well as her own, often tries too hard to flesh out the spirit of Merton's words and images. A little more faith in the power they wield on their own might have allowed her to relax and let Merton speak for himself.

The photographic portion of the book, for example, consists of a series of twenty-eight pictures—twenty-one shot by Merton, five by de Waal, and two (the front cover and frontespiece portraits) by his good friend and master photographer John Howard Griffin. After reading the introduction, which only noted the Merton photos, I wrongly assumed all the pictures were by him and found myself stumbling over the views of the French city of St. Antonin, where Merton lived for a time, and another of a cloister in the Pyrenees, near where he was born. These more conventional Old World landscapes somehow seemed out of place beside Merton's characteristic Zen-like images of stark wooden chairs shot in high contrast against a porch wall or a mandala posing as a common wicker basket or a primitive cross against an empty background—a brand burned into a cloudless sky. Were the unfamiliar, untitled, uncredited European photos among the "hitherto unreproduced photos" mentioned in the introduction? Even if they were, I wondered, why would the author include them in a contemplative book that emphasizes letting go of the busy, the overstated, the obvious, the complicated?

By the end of the book, after I'd read the photo credits that appear on the last page, I realized these were not Merton's photos, but de Waal's work. It was there I also discovered one of the book's many typographical discrepancies that confuse the reader—mistakes an editor should have caught. This one was a misidentification of a picture of what looks like a Zen garden. Intrigued by the shot, I had repeatedly flipped back and forth, twenty-eight pages, between the photo and its bewildering mistitle, "Stone wall in close up."

There are other such confusing lapses in editing, something that is an annoyance in any book but is a contradiction in a volume intended to quiet down the reader. Redundancies and cumbersome sentences show up throughout the book to frustrate even the most careful reader. For example: "And now his father was also now dying. . . ." Or de Waal's definition of holistic: "using my sight and imagination and senses." Or this head-spinning sentence: "There is a helpful image about how in solitude I am able to draw closer to those I love which comes in something written about Merton by one of his former novices." A good editor might have salvaged that line, made its meaning come alive.

The trouble with this book is not the mix of Merton's words and pictures but the hodge-podge of other material, a general lack of focus, the worrisome lapses in editing, and a footnote system that is far from reader-friendly. Because there are no numbers or letters attached to quoted passages and only some loosely organized notes for each chapter at the back of the book, it is impossible at times to know whose words you are reading without rustling pages back and forth. De Waal often breaks out passages by Merton and presents them as separate blocks within the text—but not always. Sometimes authors' words *about* Merton are also presented that way—but not always.

Nonetheless, de Waal's choices are excellent and worth recalling: pages from Merton's journals on the spiritual power of daily rituals; his reminder that we must always, each day, start fresh from where we are; passages from the Psalms that penetrate our everyday routines. Framed by Merton's photos of the basic tools of domestic life—ladles and ladders, a woodcutter's trestle, a wagon wheel—the Psalms of the Hebrew Scriptures take on an irresistible lyrical resilience.

As a personal narrator, Esther de Waal is enthusiastic, knowledgeable, invigorating and confident in her reading of Merton. But she is also intrusive. In the end, I wish in her writing she had heeded an insight she offers readers early in the book: "There is such a danger that I talk about God, and enjoy talking about God, and do not stop and in the silence of my heart listen to Him speaking."

Perhaps if she had allowed Merton's words to speak more directly to her audience and had surrendered her own desire to talk *about* him, *A Seven Day Journey with Thomas Merton* might have proved a more rewarding prayer companion. As Henri Nouwen says of Merton in the foreword, ". . . this ordinary man was a true guide to the heart of God and the heart of this world."

E. Glenn Hinson, editor. *Spirituality in Ecumenical Perspective.* Louisville, Kentucky: John Knox, 1993. 200 pages. $14.99 paperback.

Reviewed by Elaine Prevallet, S.L.

E. Glenn Hinson's *Spirituality in Ecumenical Perspective* is a collection of essays presented "In honor of Douglas and Dorothy Steere, beloved friends." The contributors are members of the Ecumenical Institute of Spirituality, a group begun shortly after the Second Vatican Council by two men, Benedictine liturgist Godfrey Diekmann and Douglas Steere, Quaker observer at the council. Steere believed in the value of a "functional ecumenism that begins with all of us encouraging each other to practice our own religious tradition to the hilt and to share our experiences with each other in every creative way we can devise" (9). To this end, he initiated annual gatherings such as this group in the United States and a Zen-Christian group in Japan, so that persons from various traditions could reflect together on issues of spirituality. A more important goal, however, was to provide the opportunity for committed persons of various traditions to share their experience, to know one another as friends. Many of the authors in this collection express their appreciation for Steere's ecumenical sensitivity, his deep and insightful work in the area of religious thought, and the extent and quality of his friendship. The book is a touching testimony to a great and greatly loved man.

Glenn Hinson begins the collection with a fine essay setting side by side the ecumenical spirituality of Thomas Merton and Douglas Steere, seeing them both in the light of the contemplative tradition. Merton wrote,

> At least this much can and must be said: the "universality" and "catholicity" which are essential to the Church necessarily imply an ability and a readiness to enter into dialogue with all that is pure, wise, profound and humane in every kind of culture. . . . A Christian culture that is not capable of such a dialogue would show, by that very fact, that it lacked catholicity (4).

"We must contain all divided worlds in ourselves and transcend them in Christ," he said (8). Steere perceived the Society of Friends to be a kind of "third stream," that is, neither Catholic nor Protestant "but part of the Christian mystical stream that has nurtured them all" (9). Friends are thus "naturally oriented to start at the right end of this ecumenical endeavor—namely, to begin from within and to draw the whole ecumenical process in this direction" (10). The freedom and openness of these two pioneers and their willingness to engage in "functional ecumenism," Hinson explains, results from their connection with the contemplative element at the very center of their traditions, or, more accurately, from "the love that those who take this route may experience at the center" (12).

In another essay later in the book, "Letters for Spiritual Guidance," Hinson reflects on Baron von Hugel and Douglas Steere as two masterful spiritual guides who often exercised their gift through correspondence. Quoting from the letters and writings of each, Hinson finds several commonalities: awareness that the work belongs to God, the capacity to be vulnerable, acceptance of individuals where and as they are, an ability to affirm the positive, and finally, patience, the willingness to "be there" for another. In both of these essays Hinson has selected quotations that both document and inspire, giving helpful insight into the work of these great-souled men, each of whom has provided light for spiritual seekers.

Tilden Edwards has written an instructive and stimulating piece entitled "Spiritual Perspectives on Peacemaking," in which he describes becoming a peacemaker as a process in which we are drawn to "gradually loosen our grip on narrowing identities" held apart from a more expansive and deeper awareness of self-in-God (143). His essay includes reflections on the inner process, along with a critique of the historical responses of the Church, and then moves to some requirements and practical suggestions for peacemaking. Edwards' approach, combining as it does both inner and outer dimensions of peacemaking, is exceptionally timely and helpful.

Only two of the twelve essays are written by women, but Mary Lou Van Buren's contribution, "Spirituality in the Dialogue of Religions," though short, seemed to me one of the freshest and liveliest. Reflecting on the advent of planetary consciousness in our time, Van Buren outlines *points of meeting:* spirit, common humanity, connection with nature, and conscience. *Points of struggle* must also be recognized, positive and negative; among them, exclusiveness, will to power and idolatry, as well as integrity, courage to listen, hospitality of mind and heart, and humility. Learning to greet one another with affection and appreciation, learning exchange and acceptance of another's gifts ("sharing as offering"), are fundamental for genuine meeting. The global community that is in-the-making requires gratitude for the truth at the core of each tradition. Van Buren concludes with a metaphor for ecumenism of the future:

> The way jazz musicians play together is instructive. They play with and to each other, bringing their artistry to the improvising moment. Each takes a turn while the others watch and listen, and then at the right moment they slip into playing together. The delight of the creative moment, the laughter and the applauding of one another spills over into the audience. I have been in an audience that itself rose to its feet while increasing its appreciative applause and then sat while its applause subsided, over and over again, as part of the musical dialogue. Each builds on the other. Each is unique. In solo and in company they make music (61–62).

Perhaps because this essay moves beyond the Christian and U.S. cultural ecumenical setting and opens onto the larger sense of need for planetary unity, which will have to characterize all ecumenicity of the future, it seemed to me an especially valuable contribution to this collection.

Other essays deal with the themes of work, action and contemplation, theological framework, listening, discernment, eucharist, centering prayer, spiritual reading. The collection is ecumenical in the sense that most authors draw in some manner on Douglas Steere's writing and/or on Quaker practice and use them as points of comparison with their own tradition. It is ecumenical also because the writers represent Episcopal and Roman Catholic, Lutheran, Methodist, and Baptist traditions. Overarching is the theme of tribute to Douglas Steere, a man whose great spirit and hospitable heart have touched each one of the contributors. My only regret is that there is not some way to pay equal tribute, in this collection, to Dorothy Steere, without whom, by Douglas' own admission, he could not have done what he has done. Glenn Hinson's dedication is completely accurate: Dorothy and Douglas are "beloved friends" to innumerable people throughout the world. This collection may help us carry their legacy into the future.

Mark R. Schwehn. *Exiles from Eden: Religion and the Academic Vocation in America.* New York: Oxford University Press, 1993. xi + 143 pages. $19.95 cloth.

Reviewed by Roy D. Fuller.

The title of this work emanates from a metaphor used by Clifford Geertz to describe the career of academics. Geertz observed that, for the most part, academics start their careers in research universities and then move to schools that are "lower down or further out." Geertz calls this phenomenon the "exile from Eden syndrome." Mark Schwehn has adopted this metaphor in this volume, which concerns itself with the relationship between religion and the academic vocation. Schwehn, on self-imposed exile from the University of Chicago to Valparaiso, has offered a work that must be taken seriously, as it exposes the hollow core that is at the heart of much higher education in America.

The principle reason for Schwehn's move and his primary motive for writing this book are connected. Schwehn left the University of Chicago because of the disparity between religion and the academic vocation; he wrote *Exiles from Eden* to explain how such a schism could have ever occurred. Unlike other recent works that have castigated American higher education (in particular see Allan Bloom, *The Closing of the American Mind*, and Page Smith, *Killing the Spirit*), Schwehn's subtle analysis focuses on the need for both vision and virtue as a cure for what ails higher education. Schwehn contends that only within religious community can both the vision and the virtues needed to maintain and perpetuate the connection between religion and academic vocation be found. This is not to suggest that higher education can only occur within religious community, but rather that the virtues which arise from such communities (humility, faith, self-denial, charity, etc.) are crucial if higher education is to recapture a more balanced sense of academic calling.

In spite of the fact that four of the six chapters of *Exile from Eden* first appeared as articles, there is continuity of argument and subject matter. Thus, chapter 1, "The Academic Vocation," describes the current status of higher education by examining contemporary conceptions of the academic vocation. Max Weber's essay "*Wissenschaft als Beruf*" comes under close scrutiny, with Schwehn concluding that Weber "urged us to retain the Protestant ethic while abandoning the system of religious beliefs that made such an ethic bearable" (13). Chapter 2, "Communities of Learning," primarily deals with the work of Parker Palmer and Richard Rorty, who, in spite of their often vast differences, demonstrate that the question of community has moved to the center of the debate on the relationship between religion and academic vocation. In chapter 3, "Spirited Inquiry," Schwehn makes his case for the virtues he feels are essential to higher education. Chapter 4, "Questions and Considerations," offers a change with its dialogical format. Here Schwehn attempts to address the sorts of practical considerations that have arisen in response to his work, most of which concern the questions of teacher evaluation and the difficulty of retaining virtues born in religious settings within a secular context.

If there is a weakness in the flow of Schwehn's work, it would be the inclusion of chapter 5, "Adams' Education." The Adams to which Schwehn is referring is Henry Adams and his work, *The Education of Henry Adams*. While this chapter does serve to illustrate

Schwehn's point concerning the connection between education and the quest for meaning, its presence disrupts the leanness of the overall argument. Schwehn recovers quickly and in the final chapter, "Conclusion: Adam's Exile," offers an inspired exegesis of Genesis 2–3, the biblical account of the exile of humans from the Garden of Eden. For Schwehn's purposes, "the most important point of the story is this: the pursuit of knowledge as power disrupts community and disorders the cosmos" (132).

Exiles from Eden offers both a description of the current state of higher education and how it arrived there, and a prescription for how academics (and their institutions) might pursue a small corner of paradise even while in exile. Merton devotees will find much of value in this work, especially those whose work involves teaching (at any level). Merton would seem to have embodied the academic virtues advocated by Schwehn. This essay should serve as clarion call both for institutions whose religious moorings have broken loose and faculties who have wondered why they find so little satisfaction in their work.

Kathleen Norris. *Dakota: A Spiritual Geography.* New York: Ticknor & Fields, 1993. 224 pages. $19.95.

Reviewed by Bruce H. Lescher, C.S.C.

Kathleen Norris' beautiful book *Dakota: A Spiritual Geography* defies classification. It is a tapestry woven of many strands: autobiography, nature writing, social analysis, cultural criticism, reflections upon monasticism, and above all, upon the slow, painful, and joyous process of conversion.

In her claim to write a "spiritual geography" Norris resembles Annie Dillard in *Pilgrim at Tinker Creek* (New York: Harper's Magazine Press, 1974), Gretel Ehrlich in *The Solace of Open Spaces* (New York: Viking Penguin, 1986), or even Belden C. Lane in *Landscapes of the Sacred* (New York/Mahwah: Paulist, 1988). Yet in the final analysis *Dakota* stands apart from all of these, and Norris speaks with her own unique voice. A summary of some of the strands woven into her book may give the reader a sense of its richness.

As autobiography, *Dakota* tells the story of Norris' move from New York City, where she was pursuing a career as a poet, to Lemmon, South Dakota, a town of 1,600 people located near the border of North and South Dakota. In 1974 she and her husband, David Dwyer, also a poet, moved into the house that was built for her grandmother in 1923. Since then she and her husband have survived by ''a crazy quilt of jobs,'' including (for her): librarian, free-lance writer, artist-in-residence giving writing workshops to school children, and cable television entrepreneur (4). The cultural transition from big city to small town, from the center of it all to the middle of nowhere, provides the narrative framework for Norris' insightful observations on nature and people.

As a nature writer, Norris shows her gift for close observation. Like Merton, she takes in the shapes and contours of the natural world and tastes them deeply. ''The beauty of the Plains,'' she says, ''is like that of an icon; it does not give an inch to sentiment or romance'' (157). The book contains beautifully rendered descriptions of landscapes, storms, rain, snow, and grasses. Many of these are contained in short ''weather reports,'' which are interspersed among the longer chapters. These descriptions are not so much objective reports as meditations on the interconnectedness of humans and the natural world. Her move to the Plains opened her to the many ways in which people are shaped by the environment in which they live. The vast emptiness of Dakota land and sky became, for her, an invitation to confront her inner emptiness and to pursue her spiritual journey.

Dakota also functions as social analysis. Here Norris reflects her work as a librarian. She delights in researching the history, demographics, and economics of her new home. Those who live on the Plains, she says, are ''forgotten people in a mass market society'' (26). She traces the growth of the Dakotas into the early twentieth century and then unflinchingly depicts the decline afflicting rural America in more recent decades: the economic inertia of the 1970s and 1980s, the subsequent loss of family farms, the migration to other areas, the devastation wrought upon the quality of life in small towns. The Dakotas, she suggests, have become ''a colony in America'' (33). The disregard for ''empty'' spaces and for the people who dwell there reveals a spiritual hollowness at the core of a society that ignores anything that doesn't turn a profit. Lemmon is ''a marginal place at the very center of North America'' (107).

Norris' book also functions as a critique of small town culture. She shows herself as keen an observer of people as she is of the natural world. Her move to Lemmon leads her to one of the central metaphors of her book: insider/outsider. Her family roots in Lemmon make her an insider, yet her education and New York experience render her an outsider. She notes that "outsiders are treated with an uneasy mix of hospitality and rejection" (7). She reflects upon the temptation to turn closeness into closedness. People become set in their ways: "Combatting inertia in a town such as Lemmon can seem like raising the dead" (49). Residents grow suspicious of professionals such as church ministers, who live among them for a while and then move on. Folks develop a tendency to hide the truth about their families and not tell the stories that really need to be told. The problems become compounded by the loss of population. Fewer people are left behind to carry out the same number of tasks necessary to keep the town running, and turf fights easily develop. At the same time, small towns hold the possibility of developing genuine bonds. Norris praises the community she finds at Hope Presbyterian Church, where she worships. And she has a wonderful chapter entitled "The Holy Use of Gossip." "I would argue," she says, "that gossip done well can be a holy thing. It can strengthen communal bonds" (72). In a small town, as in a monastery, telling stories can be a "safety valve" for people who know one another more intimately than they might choose.

Readers of *The Merton Annual* will perhaps be most interested in *Dakota* for its reflections upon monasticism. Here Norris demonstrates a close affiliation with Merton, who knew that monasticism held the potential to be an island of sanity in the midst of a culture gone crazy. The connection between the Plains and the monastery forms the central metaphor of *Dakota*. "When a friend referred to the western Dakotas as the Cappadocia of North America, I was handed an essential connection between the spirituality of the landscape I inhabit and that of the fourth-century monastics who set up shop in Cappadocia and the deserts of Egypt" (3). "The silence of the Plains, this great unpeopled landscape of earth and sky, is much like the silence one finds in a monastery, an unfathomable silence that has the power to re-form you" (15). Though she worships at a Presbyterian church, Norris becomes an oblate at a local Benedictine monastery.

Dakota is filled with references to the desert monks and monastic life. Monks, like Dakotans, live at the margins of society. Monks, like farmers, know how to wait upon the weather. Monks, like the people of the Plains, remain connected to the land and the rhythms of the seasons. Monks, like residents of small towns, live in all too close proximity to one another. The silence of the monastery, like the silence of the Plains, invites its inhabitants to confront their inner desert. Norris, like Merton, realizes one can carry monastic silence with himself or herself into action. The monastery can be an inner reality for people living in "the world." Readers of *The Merton Annual* are not likely to find anything new in Norris' reflections on monasticism, but her explorations of archetypal monastic energy are refreshing.

In the final analysis, *Dakota* is perhaps most of all a story of spiritual conversion. "I have learned," Norris writes, "to trust the processes that take time, to value change that is not sudden or ill considered but grows out of the ground of experience. Such change is properly defined as conversion. . . ." (145). Her book is a testimony to the changes wrought in her by the geography of the Plains. Her move to Lemmon, was, among other things, an attempt to put herself in touch with the faith of her grandmother: "[O]n the ground of my grandmother's faith I would find both the means and the end of my [religious] search" (93). The starkness of the landscape forced her to pay attention to experience, to where she was and what she was feeling. She found the same attention to the present in the monastic tradition. Living on the Plains taught her to slow down and appreciate the subtle beauty of land and sky, to reappropriate a faith to which she had become estranged, and to explore a monastic tradition that had not been a part of her spiritual heritage. Experience led her, in other words, to an appreciation of contemplation in the midst of a loud and brash culture.

Like all books, of course, *Dakota* is not perfect. Norris has a tendency, for example, to overdraw the distinction between "experience" and "theology," by which she seems to mean abstract, rational theological reasoning. Speaking of communal worship, for example, she says that "it is an experience, not a philosophy or even theology" (133). Such distinctions mark Norris as the product of twentieth-century Western liberalism rather than the world of her beloved Cappadocians, to whom such a distinction would have been incomprehensible. She does note that the "greatest gift" of monasticism "is how easily and even beautifully theology converts into experience, and vice versa" (117). Catholics, whose experience of theology includes symbol, sacrament, and liturgy, may find Norris' understanding of theology too intellectualized.

Norris also tends to work the outsider-insider distinction a bit too much. Here she resembles Merton, the loyal monk who consistently critiques and challenges the monastery. She dances along several borderlines: the New York poet living in her grandmother's small town, the ecumenical Christian worshiping in a Presbyterian church, the Protestant oblate of a Catholic monastic community. For all his struggle, Merton died a monk of Gethsemani, but where does Norris ultimately come down? Is she always an observer testing the possibilities of being a member? Does the monastic wisdom of vowing stability to one particular community challenge her desire to explore the outsider-insider border? If she ultimately remains an outsider, then her spirituality could fall victim to the same individualism she so trenchantly attacks for fueling American consumerism.

But these caveats must be put in perspective. *Dakota* is an engaging, warm, deeply spiritual book. Readers will be treated to a subtly designed and beautifully woven tapestry, one whose intricate designs and subtle colors will continue to delight.

The New Dictionary of Catholic Spirituality. Edited by Michael Downey. Collegeville, Minnesota: The Liturgical Press, 1993. 1,083 pages. $79.50 cloth.

Reviewed by Timothy J. Johnson, O.F.M. Conv.

The New Dictionary of Catholic Spirituality (NDCS) is a tremendous resource for those engaged in the contemporary quest to discover and appropriate the riches of the Christian spiritual tradition. This dictionary, edited by Michael Downey, treats the many-faceted aspects of spirituality with acumen and insight. In particular, the diverse selection of scholarly articles found in the NDCS provides the interested reader with an in-depth introduction to the concerns that comprise the emerging American approach to questions of spirituality. With this perspective, the NDCS offers a unique window on the American spiritual journey at the threshold of the third millennium. While the NDCS contains many of the same entries found in comparable European dictionaries of spirituality, the American background of the NDCS nuances and distinguishes it from them.

Contemporary writers, reflecting on the spiritual climate of the United States, note the pluralistic and experiential character of American spirituality. This is the natural outcome of the ongoing attempt to articulate and live out a spirituality reflecting some of the best, albeit somewhat misunderstood, qualities of American culture. As a result, the concern for exclusive confessional and dogmatic categories often takes second place, both on the academic and pastoral level, to the growing emphasis on the inclusive, pluralistic articulation and expression of the faith experience. This does not mean, however, that American spirituality neglects or ignores the need for rigorous theological reflection. In fact, the NDCS demonstrates that the present American interest in spirituality has fostered renewed research into traditional doctrines dealing with the Trinity, Christology, Mariology, and a host of others. These theological questions are approached with an openness characteristic of the American inclusive, pluralistic point of view. Consequently, many of the articles found in the NDCS emphasize the experiential participation in the mysteries of faith as well as an understanding of their intellectual content.

Given the ethnic diversity of American culture, it is not surprising that American spirituality is decidedly pluralistic. As Americans endeavor to discover and appropriate their particular spiritual traditions, there is a willingness among many to learn from traditions other than their own. While some could challenge the established view of America as a melting pot of different cultures and races, few would doubt that an incredible variety of spiritual traditions is represented within the borders of the United States. A Native American sweat lodge in Montana, a Buddhist temple in California, a Baptist church in South Carolina, a Moslem mosque in Ohio, a Jewish synagogue in Minnesota, and a Roman Catholic cathedral in New York all witness to the extraordinary spiritual landscape of contemporary America. The NDCS treats this mosaic of traditions in a number of articles dealing with Islamic, Protestant, Catholic, Jewish, Asian, Native American, African, and New Age spirituality.

It is perhaps in the area of experience and human relations that the American perspective on spirituality comes most clearly into focus. Not unlike many medieval women and men before them, Americans often consider human relationships as a mirror and model of the relationship between the human and divine. Consequently, the NDCS contains a significant number of articles that deal with the relational aspects of the spiritual journey such as friendship, family, children, community, marriage, single parenthood, divorce, the single life, intimacy, homosexuality, celibacy, and human sexuality. All these areas of human concern remind Americans that relationships are a privileged matrix where women and men are invited to encounter and learn the demanding dynamic of prayer. Experience indicates that traditional prayers and techniques are best appropriated when they are enfleshed within the circle of family and friends. Certainly the core characteristics of authentic prayer such as the acceptance of weakness and poverty, the ability to trust in another, the willingness to wrestle with desire, the openness to challenge and change, and the commitment to forgiveness and reconciliation are all discovered in the promise and challenge of human relationships.

The relational emphasis in American spirituality is also frequently illustrated, as several articles in the NDCS indicate, in an interest for the earth, social justice, gender sensitivity, and a desire to develop a life of contemplative prayer rooted in the mystery of God. The growing awareness in the United States of the increasingly fragile condition of the earth is giving rise to an appreciation of the ecological and social dimensions of spirituality. The universal call to holiness, so clearly enunciated at the Second Vatican Council and developed throughout the NDCS, requires a continuous attempt to integrate the struggle for personal sanctity with an evangelical concern for the health and welfare of all creatures. The locus of this struggle is contemplative prayer; it is in contemplation that women and men together discover that there is no dichotomy between a passionate love of the Creator and love of creation. Immersed in the mystery of God, contemplatives recognize that acceptance of the incarnation is impossible without an embrace of the earth, for all of creation groans for the redemption promised to the daughters and sons of God.

The effort to intertwine contemplation with life is evident throughout the NDCS. More than an outstanding collection of articles on spirituality, this dictionary emerges, in a sense, as a contemporary American expression of the ancient *lectio divina*. Article after article evidences a learned yet prayerful attempt to listen and respond to the Spirit of God at work in the world both yesterday and today. Students and scholars will certainly profit from a close reading of the NDCS; however, its value goes far beyond the academy. Many women and men who are involved in the ongoing process of spiritual formation in renewal programs, retreats, support groups, and adult religious education courses will find the NDCS to be a crucial tool for their spiritual journey.

A Review Symposium

Ace of Freedoms: Thomas Merton's Christ
by George Kilcourse
University of Notre Dame Press, 1993
xii + 260 pages, $34.95 cloth; $14.95 paperback

Participants:

Patrick Eastman
Diana Culbertson, O.P.
Donald J. Goergen, O.P.
Jean-Marc Laporte, S.J.

I

Patrick Eastman

The task of a book reviewer usually begins by identifying the aim of the author, asking what points are being made. This is then followed by an assessment of the validity of what the author has set out to do and an evaluation of the conclusions made. Fortunately for me, in this particular case, my task is only to lay out the aims of the author and the content of this book. I say this because I am neither a professional theologian in the academic sense nor well versed in literary criticism.

Before I begin a systematic look at the book let me make a few preliminary remarks. Sometime ago I published a paper in *Cistercian Studies Quarterly* on the Christology of St. Bernard of Clairvaux's treatise "De diligendo Deo." It was written under the tutelage of Dom Jean Leclercq. In that essay I pointed out the centrality of Christ in the monastic life. In the early Church a favorite expression for the baptized was that they were "in Christ." To be in Christ was the moderating factor in all their life. Monasticism as a specific way of living the baptismal life was similarly to be a life immersed in Christ. If, then, Christ is to be the essence of the monastic life, and St. Benedict makes it clear that it is, an examination of a monastic author's Christology should lead us to the essence of that particular monk. We can take this one stage further, for if Christ is to be the governing factor of one's life then the Christology will not only be there in explicitly theological writing but it can be recognized implicitly in all other writings.

George Kilcourse has recognized this, so in his exposition of Merton's Christ he examines not only the explicit references to Christology in Merton's religious writings but also the influence of that Christology implicitly in the poems, journals, and literary essays. Indeed, perhaps that which speaks most authentically is not the consciously theological, but the hidden Christ of poems, parables, and ponderings. Kilcourse has in some ways used a Merton method upon Merton himself. In his conclusion to the book Kilcourse writes of Merton's "untiring struggle to recognize the hidden Christ of *kenosis*, as manifested in the myriad parables and ambushes of autobiography, self identity, and a post-Christian history's discontinuities." Kilcourse goes on to say that he has taken the whole mixed bag of the Merton corpus and examined it "through the master lens of his sustained Christocentric spirituality," saying that it all radiates from "his distinctively kenotic Christology" which gives his life and work "a hidden wholeness." The whole of this book is based on the assertion that "an author's metaphysic underlies all his writings."

In general terms it also needs to be pointed out that Merton was thoroughly monastic in his theological method. The Second Vatican Council saw a fundamental shift in the predominant method of theological investigation. It was a return to the way of the early Church, a way that had never been entirely lost in monasticism. The early Church began with the experience, and the theological principles emerged from prayerful reflection on that experience. It was an inductive theological method that enabled the fourth-century Evagrius to say that "the one who prays is a theologian and a theologian is one who prays." In the mainstream of Catholic theology this method was to be overtaken in the Middle Ages by the deductive theology of Scholasticism. Merton's method of rooting his theology in his own experience is no doubt the reason why he describes Julian of Norwich as being one of the greatest English theologians. As Merton writes, "First she experiences then she reflects on that experience." Kilcourse refers to the method in his opening chapter, describing it as "[t]he shift to the autobiographical voice." He goes on to identify the philosophy of Duns Scotus, the poetry of Gerard Manley Hopkins, and the theology of Bernard of Clairvaux as early sources "nurturing Merton's turn to experience."

In the second chapter of his book Kilcourse begins by pointing out Merton's discovery that the very nature of God is simply to exist, which led him to hunger for sharing the life of this God. In this same chapter Kilcourse goes on to point out that Merton's notion of the true self is "the inner self in Christ." It is the "paradise consciousness" of this inner self identified with Christ wrestling to be free of the illusory false self that Kilcourse suggests transcends all Merton's poems. The main thrust of this chapter is to demonstrate that the symbolism of the poetic images ultimately reflects Merton's struggle. "It is this 'true self' (or 'inner self') and the assaults upon it by contemporary society which Merton develops throughout his spirituality. He prescribes no technique, but speaks in terms of 'awakening' and 'discovery' of the inner person beneath our superficial pursuits. The poems of paradise consciousness already have manifested this dynamic." Kilcourse suggests this awakening and discovery is symbolized by the frequent references to the "shy wild deer" in Merton's poetry. The awakening to the true self comes from stillness and silence. Kilcourse points out it is a spirituality that Paul Tillich categorizes as a mystical or a symbolic type of faith. Tillich's schema outlines four types of faith: the moral, which is divided into law and prophecy, and the ontological, likewise divided into mystical and symbolic. Kilcourse states that "Tillich's schema suggests that the mature believer integrates dimensions of all four possibilities rather than isolating in only one of the four." Although it does not explicitly use these categories as a yardstick to assess Merton's development, evidence of each category emerges in Kilcourse's detailed examination of all Merton's writings.

Kilcourse, when dealing more explicitly with Merton's personal spiritual development, begins by pointing out Karl Rahner's distinction between two types of Christology: The "incarnational," where "emphasis is placed on the descent of God's Word into the World," and "the salvation-historical Christology [where] the story of Jesus' life is central." Kilcourse traces Merton's development through an examination of some of Merton's significant works. He begins with the 1949 classic *Seeds of Contemplation,* progressing through *The Ascent of Truth* and *No Man Is an Island,* all of which he uses to illustrate Merton's emphasis on the divinity of Christ giving rise to a general rejection of the world. Beginning with *Thoughts in Solitude,* published in 1958, a year Kilcourse sees as "a watershed for Merton," he traces Merton's development to a more balanced Christology where the two natures of divinity and humanity are united in the one person, Christ. The result, says Kilcourse, is that "[c]ontemplation is demythologized, no longer a special state that removes or separates a person from ordinary things because God penetrates all . . . the contemplative participates 'in a concrete action of God in time.' " This conversion Kilcourse follows through *The New Man* and *New Seeds of Contemplation,* culminating in the 1964 essay "The Humanity of Christ in Monastic Prayer." This integration of the incarnation, cross, and resurrection is centered in the historical Jesus. Merton grew in his sapiential understanding of this Jesus through his own experience and the influence of the Scriptures, the Desert Fathers, and patristic literature. Kilcourse asserts that Merton's study of patristic writers like Henri de Lubac and Hans Urs von Balthasar exposed him to writings of Gregory of Nyssa and Maximus the Confessor. The patristic tradition opened new vistas on soteriology and the *kenosis* of Christ, that early monastic Christology that was strongly influenced by Paul's writings (especially that in Philippians 2:1-11), giving great emphasis to Christ's *kenosis.*

In Kilcourse's book we are given a detailed account of Merton's movement to a salvation-history Christology by an examination of the influences that Karl Barth, Dietrich Bonhoeffer, Eastern Orthodoxy, and Teilhard de Chardin had upon him. This movement, we are told by Kilcourse, leads Merton to explain in *Seeds of Destruction,* that "the contemplative life cannot be a mere withdrawal or negation, a turning of our back on the world's sufferings, crises, confusions and errors." Kilcourse says it is this Christology that grounds Merton's social criticism and the insights he perceived in the writings of such authors as Pasternak, Camus, and Faulkner. The same inner belief that led Merton to recognize the hiddenness of the kenotic Christ in what some may see as strange places also led him to write, "If organized religion abdicates its mission to disturb man *[sic]* in the depths of his conscience, and seeks instead simply to 'make converts' that will smilingly adjust to the status quo, then it deserves the most serious and uncompromising criticism. Such criticism is not disloyalty.''

A Christology that is so rooted in the exigencies of life not only makes Christ real for us—a person to whom we can genuinely relate—but it also seriously affects our anthropology. Kilcourse recognizes this and devotes a full chapter to Merton's anthropology through an examination of his antipoetry. Many, like me, may not know what is meant by ''antipoetry.'' For us there is an endnote explanation, but I'm not sure, even after reading this, that I know exactly what is meant! However, Kilcourse uses *The Geography of Lograire* and *Cables to the Ace* to give evidence of Merton's theological anthropology.

Perhaps the most challenging test of Merton's Christology comes in his interreligious dialogue. Merton's dialogical exchange included Zen Buddhists, Jews, Sufis, Taoists, Hindus, and Confucianists. The test of his Christology was in the tension between facile syncreticism on the one hand and a triumphalistic portrayal of Christianity on the other. Kilcourse reminds us of how at that last fatal conference in Bangkok, when challenged over the lack of specific reference to Christ in the talks, Merton replied, ''What we are asked to do is not so much to speak any more of Christ as to let him live within us, so that people may feel him by the way he is living in us.'' On a personal note I recall, at an open meeting with some Tibetan Buddhists, how, when aggressively attacked by a fundamentalist Christian on whether they ''knew Christ as their personal Savior'' they gently replied that they did not know Christ personally but had met him through many of his beautiful friends. Kilcourse's chapter on interreligious dialogue primarily focuses on Merton's writings on Zen Buddhism. He offers the criticism that Merton avoids theological rigor by keeping the dialogue at the level of experience. Beneath the ostensible conflicts of doctrine Merton suggests that it may turn out that religions have something in common ''at a deeper level of dialogue.'' Without doubt, says Kilcourse, Merton's own Christology deepened and matured through his many years of involvement in interreligious dialogue: ''Merton insists that he can remain faithful to his Christian commitment and yet learn from the Buddhist and Hindu experience. The unity he seeks is not a newly invented syncretism . . . 'We discover an older unity,' he writes. This 'original unity' means for him that 'what we have to be is what we are.' '' Kilcourse goes on to remark that Merton emphasizes in his notes ''the necessity of a scrupulous respect for important differences.''

In the conclusion Kilcourse restates the movement of Merton from his early naive dualistic Christology to a radically challenging Christ of *kenosis* rooted in the world and the life we live. Merton, he says, "exposed the pretense of what masquerades as Christian spirituality when the 'true self' of Christ's *kenosis* is domesticated, or worse, denied: 'The problem today is that there are no deserts, only dude ranches.' " With Merton, Kilcourse suggests that "[t]he false self can ultimately be liberated only by the 'ace of freedoms,' the Christ of kenosis." "It is this Christ," says Kilcourse, that he has "tried to quarry from the strata of the monk's poetry and antipoetry, his journals, his correspondence, his literary essays."

II

Diana Culbertson, O.P.

Boccaccio once argued on behalf of Dante in an age that privileged theology as a discipline that "theology and poetry can be considered almost one and the same thing when their subject is the same." He thereby aligned himself not only with Dante's own defense of his work but with subsequent readers of John Milton, George Herbert, William Blake, Edward Taylor, T. S. Eliot, W. H. Auden, and now Thomas Merton. He argued further in a burst of enthusiasm that "theology is simply the poetry of God." In this assertion he went beyond Aquinas' more simple observation that figurative language is appropriate to Scripture (*Summa Theol.* I.q.1.art. 9). The imperative to resort to figure and fiction as a strategy for theologizing needs no valiant defense. Paul Ricoeur's comment is pertinent: "Any ethic that addresses the will in order to demand a decision must be subject to a poetry that opens up new dimensions for the imagination" (Paul Ricoeur and Eberhard Jüngel, *Metapher Zür Hermeneutik religiöser Sprache* [Munich, 1974] 70).

What concerns the theological critic of Merton's poetry is whether or not the metapoetic yield can be encompassed in a theological critique or whether it can (or should) be extracted at all. The difficulty is the nature of poetry itself, which, most critics argue along with Cleanth Brooks, is unparaphrasable. To reflect on Merton's Christology using his poetry as source has further obstacles: his corpus is unsystematic, scarcely comparable to the ordered universes of Milton and Dante—or even William Blake—and his modernist style is ironic, parodic, and more dissonant than what we customarily look for in "religious poetry."

Thomas Merton had argued correctly that a poet, even a religious poet, is not a catechist (See "Notes on Sacred and Profane Art," *Jubilee* 4 [1956] 26, 31), and he was consistent in his own theoretical refusal to "prostitute art as propaganda." But Merton, whatever his assertions about the distinctions between religion and art, did use art as a form of preaching. The degree to which his poetry is kerygmatic can be measured in a real sense by the audience he attracts. Readers generally turn to him more for his religious insight than his poetic genius, although Thérèse Lentfoehr in *Words and Silence: On the Poetry of Thomas Merton* has written persuasively of his literary talents. His own literary criticism, however, rarely probes technique but rather the spiritual and religious depths (or nondepths) of the writers he examines: Blake, Pasternak, Camus, Rimbaud, and others. It is appropriate to subject his poetry to the same kind of reading.

George Kilcourse in *Ace of Freedoms: Thomas Merton's Christ* carefully traces Merton's Christological development from poetic reflections on the monastic life and his own spirituality to the world beyond Gethsemani, from the poetry of the choir and the poetry of the desert to what Kilcourse calls the poetry of "paradise consciousness" and the poetry of the forest. "Paradise consciousness" is difficult at first to understand, but Kilcourse sees the term as defining an overarching theme of the self *in Christ*, the *new creation* in Christ symbolized by "wakeful" child innocence, as in the poem "Grace's House."

To examine Merton's understanding of the self and the kenotic Christ, the author consistently integrates Merton's prose reflections with his poetry. As Merton moved beyond poetry expressive of his own spirituality and personal experience, he began to write more complex and, to some extent, more urbane poems, their images drawn from a world of sounds and sights far removed from the quiet Kentucky hills and the hymnody of monks. Those sounds must have come to him as bursts of demonic violence, apocalyptic flashpoints unmitigated by human misgivings or the ambiguities of history. His targets are generals, movie stars, newscasts, television, advertisements, electricity, behavioral scientists, slave-traders, cultural pseudoheroes, clergy, presidents—the whole First World. His denunciation of Western imperialism and decadence becomes so acerbic at times that his own voice is transformed into retaliatory mimesis, sometimes contributory to the noise he attempts to purge. Kilcourse defends Merton on this count by appealing to biblical parable, poetic irony, and "antipoetry." But parables work because of their apparent simplicity, and irony works when it cannot be confounded with its target. The "antipoetry" of Merton (and Nicanor Parra, his model for this style of writing) is not a definable genre. It is, as Merton intended it, a nongenre, an unclassifiable discourse, foreshadowing the shattered narratives and fragmentary art forms of postmodernism.

The question is whether or not Merton's resistance to what he perceived as cultural and linguistic collapse reflects kenotic Christology or a subtle dualism, a Barthian abandonment of all but the Other. Kilcourse, in his *Ace of Freedoms*, aligns Merton with classic kenotic Christology, and he uses as evidence Merton's essays, letters, and diaries. Without the prose counterparts, however, is Merton's poetry theologically explicable? Any attempt to examine his last two volumes of poetry without the endnotes and background information (now mercifully available to us) is daunting. It requires an effort not easily described as pleasurable. And the question then becomes not merely aesthetic but pragmatic. What kind of reader response is elicited by poetry that is so discordant at times as to sound frenetic and uncontrolled? Is the kenotic Christ disclosed in decibels this shrill? These are essential questions. In his late poetry Merton elected to empty his figurative language of God, asserting that "our attempts to reveal God to non-believers border on blasphemous idiocy." A harsh accusation. The attempts of believers may be inept and misdirected, but are they blasphemous and idiotic? That kind of assertion accounts for the sometimes brutal imagery of the Merton who wants to transform and purify poetic diction as well as kerygmatic proclamation. Kilcourse suggests that Merton's distaste for the language and rituals of believers, their "pontifical and organizational routines," loose talk, and activism was the "brew" for Merton's turn to antipoetry and irony. The believers Merton had in mind were those whom Kilcourse describes as "the custodians of the Christian myths and symbols." Merton thus positioned himself in a wilderness between the visible institutional Church and nonbelievers. This wilderness is the environment of both *Cables to the Ace* and *The Geography of Lograire,* his last two poetic volumes. In that emptiness he searched for the hidden Christ.

In the final stanzas of *Cables to the Ace,* as in the tender Cable 78 ("The hidden lovers in the soil become green plants. . . ."), Merton's voice becomes gentle, but after seventy-seven sections parodying those aspects of contemporary civilization that appalled him, Merton's isolated moments of poetic hope appear as afterthoughts rather than a discoverable theme. Cable 80 ("Slowly slowly / Comes Christ through the garden. . . .") concludes with a vision of the Lord of history weeping "into the fire." Kilcourse's observations that Merton was theologically uncomfortable with any image of Christ that is represented as the defender of a certain order is helpful here, as is Merton's criticism of Michelangelo's Christ in the Sistine Chapel "whipping sinners with his great Greek muscles." The monasticism that saw itself as the guardian of the social order was a spirituality Merton had learned to reject. The poet, therefore, clearly saw himself in these last works as an observer of culture, a kind of post-Eliot garbage collector in a postmodern Waste Land. (We read of his requesting advertisements from *Esquire* from his correspondents.) But if he had not finally touched down again into the waters of peace that still flow even in this world, his Christology would be less evident than his apocalypticism. Even with commentary it is sometimes difficult to discover. Boccaccio, perhaps, would have suggested to Merton that he include at the end of his poetic inferno more hints of eschatological beauty, more suggestions that grace is occasionally visible. Dante had escaped from his own dark forest, and his final declarations of faith and an ecstatic vision of love give his poetry its balance and its power. Merton's turn to the theological anthropology of Karl Rahner, of a Church in diaspora, and a Christ whose power is yet concealed dictated a different approach to kerygma.

Poetry can be the theology of God when it is creative and life giving. Kilcourse's argument is predicated on that thesis, and he argues that the antipoet in Merton was a "constructive identity." He interprets Merton's irony as the literary analogue of *kenosis.* As he is careful to acknowledge, he does so by reading Merton's poetry against his prose essays and letters, citing, for example, an important passage from *Zen and the Birds of Appetite:*

> [I]n the heart of anguish are found the gifts of peace and understanding: not simply in personal illumination and liberation, but by commitment and empathy, for the contemplative must assume the universal anguish and the inescapable condition of mortal man.

The author's analysis of Merton's *Cables to the Ace* and *The Geography of Lograire* is an immensely helpful explanation of texts that are not otherwise very comprehensible. One does not have to be a literalist or sentimentalist to conclude that Merton's poetry is often less a mosaic than a clutter. The chapter "A Summa of Offbeat Anthropology: Merton's Antipoetry as Christology" is a clear appraisal of the writer's last poetic testaments in terms of theology. And for that reason *Ace of Freedoms* will be an invaluable source of understanding for those who find in Merton a voice crying in the wilderness of modern culture that Christ has emptied himself for us and is even now hidden among the oppressed of the earth.

III

Donald J. Goergen, O.P.

George Kilcourse has written a stimulating and valuable interpretation of Merton's spirituality as focused on Jesus Christ, "the ace of freedoms," the inner core of that spirituality. I can best be of service to his project by indicating some of its strengths and one of its limitations. I shall mention three of the strengths and then give attention to the limitation, since confronting it will be of more value to Kilcourse.

I myself am not a Merton scholar, although I have been a reader of Merton through the years. The greatest strength of Kilcourse's project is his extensive familiarity with the entire Merton corpus. That means his work must be taken seriously.

A second major strength of *Ace of Freedoms* is the interrelatedness Kilcourse unveils within (1) Merton's spiritual theology of the inner/true self, (2) Merton's image of Christ, and (3) Merton's own autobiographical journey. Merton's own spiritual journey toward his true self is a process of discovering the real Jesus Christ. For Kilcourse, Merton's autobiography is Christology and Merton's Christology is autobiography.

A third strength of Kilcourse's work is his ability to see spirituality as a matrix or source for theology. This point may be controversial. However, as a systematic theologian, I see this as a strength— moving beyond the dichotomy between spirituality and theology that plagues the modern West. Spirituality is theology, and theology is spirituality. True theology is done on one's knees as well as in the library, and spirituality nourishes the head as well as the heart. Along with this strength is Kilcourse's awareness that, for Merton, poetry is a kind of knowledge (cf. 42–45). This is to Kilcourse's and Merton's credit. Not all knowledge is objective, rational, or scientific knowledge. Some knowledge is more personal; some more symbolic. The language of poetry is essential for articulating spiritual experience. Kilcourse's insistence on the theological value of Merton's poetry is related to the first strength mentioned above—his familiarity with the entire Merton corpus, including the poetry and the later Merton. A bottom line is that we must see Merton as a true theologian.

And now to turn to a limitation, or a way in which *Ace of Freedoms* is vulnerable: Kilcourse's tendency toward overstatement, which can then leave one unconvinced. For example, Kilcourse affirms strongly a discontinuity between the early and later Merton. Yet on the basis of the material presented, one could easily argue a more gradual, less dramatic development, at least in his Christology. No one would deny the development. The following is a fairly balanced statement:

> I propose to place in sharp relief the contrast between the early and the late Merton, without overlooking certain continuities. But the emphasis here will be on the contrast between the christological insights of the mature Merton and the earlier disguised voices and contorted postures which he sometimes permitted himself to adopt as a young monk (6).

Fair enough. But the following is exaggeration:

> The distance between the forms and spiritual horizon of *The Seven Storey Mountain*, or the familiar lyric poetry of the 1940s, and the mature Merton's antipoetry, or the christology to be quarried from its deep strata can be measured only in light years (157).

I remained unconvinced by the material presented of a contrast that great. There rather seems to be in Merton a movement from world denial to world affirmation (224), which does not require that strong a break in his Christology.

This tendency toward overstatement surfaces in Kilcourse's sketching of Merton's kenotic Christology, which is at the heart of the book, and thus leaves a very valid insight vulnerable. A valid point is made early by Kilcourse:

> To suggest that Thomas Merton developed a full-blown christol-
> ogy would be to exaggerate his contribution. He remained an es-
> sayist, allergic to all efforts at systematizing or methodological
> expositions (3).

We are dealing more with a Christ-centered spirituality (1, 221) than with an explicit Christology. Why then be so insistent on a "kenotic christology" and "a christology from below"? Such labels make Merton's inchoate Christology (3) seem more self-conscious than it was.

The following is a beautiful, insightful, significant statement that does justice to the data:

> He [Merton] discovers the epiphany of Christ in the human ex-
> perience of poverty, in historical discontinuities, at the margins
> of Christendom, and in the rejection and vulnerability of the
> world's scarred victims and despised outcasts (225).

But is any and every Christology sensitive to "the epiphany of God in weakness and defenselessness" (1) kenotic? How is Kilcourse using the term? How did Merton himself, who used it but not all that fre-quently (cf. 127, 202, 209, 212, 214, 215, 223), understand it? It seems to me that Merton did not have an explicit kenotic Christology as much as a kenotic image of Christ.

I do not think of Merton's mature or later writings as expressive of "a christology from below." Such language is too theologically tech-nical to do justice to Merton's powerful and suggestive insights. Cer-tainly there was a move away from dogmatic efforts. Yet, is every Christology that gives emphasis to the humanity of Jesus a Christol-ogy from below?

There are other adjectives equally accurate to describe Merton's inchoate Christology, all of which Kilcourse uses: monastic, mystical, apophatic, experiential, social. This in no way denies a valid kenotic dimension mined from Merton's writings, but the emphasis on it does appear as overemphasis. Not every reference to emptiness necessar-ily suggests a kenotic Christology as such. One of the best texts in which Merton speaks of his own image of Christ is from one of his letters; Kilcourse quotes this at length (223). The quote seems to be a very apt summary of Merton's Christological directions.

This suggestion that Kilcourse at times tends to overstate does not diminish the strengths of *Ace of Freedoms* with which I began. The overstatements make valuable and suggestive insights vulnerable. Kilcourse must be complimented for his extensive familiarity with the entire Merton corpus; his integration of Merton's autobiographical, Christological, and spiritual insights; and his willingness to see in spiritual/mystical writings and poetry a matrix and source for theology. This latter in particular is perhaps the major achievement of Kilcourse. "Mining" what we might ordinarily think of as nontheological sources such as letters and poetry yields particularly rich theological insights. The book is certainly to be recommended to Merton readers for a fuller and deeper knowledge of his Christology and spirituality.

IV

Jean-Marc Laporte, S.J.

George Kilcourse's book, which beautifully allies theology and imagination, invites comment from many different points of view. Primarily a work of interpretation that takes us through the corpus of Thomas Merton, it offers a fresh Mertonian perspective in which theology, autobiography, and self-identity converge (1–2). It deserves review as a work of interpretation, but the theological themes that emerge out of it are just as deserving of comment. In addition, one could develop a meta-reflection on the interrelation of the personal spiritual quest and authentic theology as it emerges in this work, discerning in Merton not just a spiritual guide but also a contributor to theological method. I have been asked to focus on *kenosis*, an architectonic theological theme that surfaces at many strategic points in the writings of Thomas Merton and runs through the whole of Kilcourse's book. A theme both classical and contemporary, it has elicited theological creativity down through the centuries.[1] It fosters the develop-

1. One would normally evoke the kenotic Christologies of the 19th and early 20th centuries, but more to the point is Luther's creative response to this theme. The Lord/slave dialectic of Philippians 2:6-11 plays a key role in his theology of grace, as we see in *Freedom of a Christian*. The terms he uses to translate two key

ment of a Christology both faithful to the past and incisive as it addresses the present. The image from Merton's antipoems *Cables to the Ace,* from which Kilcourse chooses the title of his work, evokes the origin of this theme in the kenotic Christ (178). In many cardgames, the ace can be either the lowest card, below the deuce, or the highest and most powerful card in the deck. The kenotic Christ is ace in both senses, voluntarily bereft of power but in his powerlessness bringing the unfailing and eventually triumphant power of God's love into an unredeemed creation.

The scriptural passage that roots this theology of the kenotic Christ is the *carmen Christi* of Philippians 2:6-11, a poetic composition whose core is generally recognized as reflecting very early strata of New Testament times. The one who did not consider his rightful status of being recognized as God's equal something to cling to, but rather chose to let go of it in an act of self-emptying, is rewarded by the God who exalts him and gives him the name above all names, enabling the whole creation to recognize him for who he is, Lord, and acclaim him to the glory of God the Father.

This passage has occasioned the spilling of much ink down through the centuries and even to our own day: it is a favorite topic of many monographs and articles. Variant readings abound. It looms large in any effort to piece together the patterns of evolving New Testament thought, and one's preferred interpretation of its verses will contribute decisively to one's view of how New Testament Christology developed and how Christology ought to further unfold in our own day. At times one gets the impression that this sequence is reversed: one's Christological preferences, high or low, Spirit or Word, may lead one to emphasize this or that particular aspect of the passage, to adopt or exclude this or that possible connection with other texts, scriptural or extrascriptural. No matter from which end of the theological spectrum, such hardened choices set aside the multifaceted mystery-laden character of this poetic text. By contrast, Thomas Mer-

---

verbs in that hymn, *Entaüßerung* (self-emptying, alienation) and *Aufhebung* (exaltation, sublation), as well as the Lord/slave dialectic, has had a marked impact on the thought of Hegel, and through Hegel, on that of Karl Marx. Cf. Abraham Rotstein, "The Apocalyptic Tradition: Luther and Marx," *Political Theology in the Canadian Context,* ed. B. Smillie (Waterloo: Wilfrid Laurier University Press, 1982) 147-208.

ton and his interpreter adopt an approach that is open to the paradoxical inclusiveness of this text.

It is not my role to offer a judgment on various interpretations
of this scriptural passage or to judge the accuracy of Kilcourse's interpretation of Merton. Others better qualified can and will do that.
However as a systematic theologian for whom the theme of *kenosis*
has always exercised a keen fascination, I will mainly comment on the
significance for a kenotically based theology of what has emerged in
Kilcourse's interpretation of Merton. In brief, Merton as he appears
in these pages does not offer a fully formed theology of *kenosis* but
does offer precious clues and a powerful stimulus toward the contemplative exploration of the kenotic vein that runs so deeply and constantly throughout Christian thought.

The *Kenosis* of Christ Jesus

Let me begin with a brief comment on the *kenosis* of Jesus Christ
as it emerges in Kilcourse's interpretation of Merton. What I detect
is a classic mainline interpretation quite consistent with Christology
as it has developed through the councils and official Church teaching.
Indeed, *kenosis* emerges as a powerful tool for holding together traditional affirmations about the personal unity and unique divine status
of Christ and the requirements of our age for a Christology that honors
the full humanity of Jesus. One may get the impression that *kenosis*
enables a shift from descending Christology "from above" to ascending Christology "from below," but it is clear from Kilcourse's interpretation that the shift for Merton is not from the former to the latter
but from a perspective that is exclusively descending to a Christology
that embraces both ascending and descending movements. Indeed,
kenosis is at the heart both of the descending dynamic by which God
becomes identified with his chosen Servant in hiddenness, anonymity,
and finally death, and of the ascending dynamic by which that Servant, in the darkest moment of his struggle, totally surrenders to and
finds himself in the mystery of God. The Philippians text clearly speaks
of the second dynamic, offering as model worth imitation Christ Jesus
who chooses to assume and be faithful to the form of the slave, obey-
ing unto death; but it intimates the first dynamic, which roots the
second and which comes to full recognition in the second half of the

kenotic hymn. At the heart of Jesus' ascent to God there is God's condescension, God's irreversible and total choice to be with us rather than against us, for us rather than against us, in the person of Jesus Christ perfectly human and perfectly divine, as Barth tells us in *The Humanity of God*.

Kilcourse, in the footsteps of Rahner, connects the descending and ascending modes of Christology in Merton with metaphysical and salvation-historical approaches to Christology (92). Kilcourse's evident allergy to rigid, static, arthritic, algebraic-like theology may be justified, but I would prefer to emphasize that the recognition of the impact of *kenosis* and the shift to salvation history in Merton are a recovery of an authentic metaphysical outlook in which being, action, and relation are integrally related.[2]

The Wider Range of *Kenosis:* The Self

The kenotic theme in Christology is not limited to the kenotic hymn in Philippians. Other scriptural passages allude to this theme in brief but striking formulas.[3] Those who crafted that hymn drew on an image that resonates widely in Scripture. In Philippians it applies to Jesus Christ and how he chose to live his life. But this text implicitly refers to the counterimage of Adam, who, promised equality with God on God's terms and in God's time, chooses to grasp for what had been

---

2. A recent attractive example of such a retrieval can be found in Norris Clarke's *Person and Being* (*The Aquinas Lecture, 1993*, Milwaukee: Marquette University Press, 1993). Bernard Lonergan pursues the same kind of agenda by his rediscovery of the open-ended intellectualist basis of Aquinas' thought, quite distinct from its rigid conceptualist presentations in many Scholastic manuals of the 19th and early 20th centuries.

3. The two best instances from other Pauline writings are found in 2 Corinthians 8:9 and 2 Corinthians 5:21. These texts delineate the same structure of taking on weakness, but in this case the beneficiaries are not Christ who is exalted but the Christian who receives salvation from Christ in a holy exchange. The theme of the Christ who comes to serve rather than to be served comes up in the Synoptics, in Mark 10:45 and Matt 20:28. John's Gospel makes the same point using the image of the grain of wheat that falls into the ground and dies in order to bear fruit (John 12:24), an intensification and a personalization of the synoptic parable of the sower. Just as *kenosis* is proposed for imitation by Paul, this example of self-gift is proposed by John: cf. the washing of the feet, which occurs soon after the grain of wheat passage in his Gospel.

destined for him in due time as God's free gift. It also applies to the community itself, but that is the theme of the next section of this review.

The reference to Adam urges us to reflect on the import of *kenosis* for Christians of all times. Christ and Adam lay out two paths for us to take, that of Christ, kenotic, in which the acceptance of the self in all its emptiness and poverty leads to the gift of self-fulfillment, and that of Adam, antikenotic, in which the self refuses to accept its own limitations and vainly seeks to bestow fulfillment upon itself, ending up in death rather than life. In his life and ministry Paul seeks to follow the model of Christ; and he himself becomes an example of *kenosis*, urging the followers of Jesus to live their lives kenotically within a world that remains ambiguous and unfinished, waiting for an ultimate fulfillment, which is gift.[4]

This *kenosis* does not, in the illuminating phrase of Karl Barth's commentary, consist in a giving up or a giving away but in a letting go. The inner self—that of Christ as well as ours—is so secure in its identity that it can empty itself out, in the case of Christ of all that to which it is entitled, in ours of the illusory claims for recognition to which we cling. The inner self thus emptied out can without reserve explore totally new ways of objectifying itself, knowing that it will always perdure as the subject, implicitly but ineluctably present as mystery, as generative source.[5] By contrast the person out of touch with this deep source—remember that the counterpoint to Jesus in the kenotic hymn is Adam—is insecure, becomes fixated on a "false self," clings to a pattern of behavior and self-presentation that is familiar, predictable, and subject to the person's own control, that keeps at

4. The themes briefly evoked in this paragraph are more fully developed in my article "Kenosis Old and New" in *The Ecumenist* 12 (1974) 17-21, and in my book *Patience and Power: Grace for the First World* (Mahwah, N.J.: Paulist, 1988) 95-106, 181-85, 267-71.

5. The subject in this sense is a favorite theme within transcendental Thomism. It emerges abundantly in Rahner. A particularly creative instance is his "Dogmatic Reflections on the Knowledge and Self-Consciousness of Christ," in *Theological Investigations* 5:193-215. It is exploited methodically in the works of Lonergan. A parallel to Rahner that summarizes his position is found in "Christ as Subject: A Reply," in *Collection I*, pp. 164-97. The implicit, generative, inescapable subject is the subject as subject. This subject can never be totally objectified. The self as object can be offered a helpful entry into the mystery of the self, but it can also hinder access to it.

bay aspects of the fuller self that, though threatening and disruptive, are invitations to fuller integration and authenticity.[6]

Merton's interest in *kenosis* is not narrowly Christological. Rather, *kenosis* is at the heart of the spiritual quest for authenticity—monastic, Christian, and human—that consumed his life. In his own way Merton follows in the footsteps of Paul, who witnesses to *kenosis* in his own life and urges Christians to embrace it in theirs. The merit of Kilcourse's book is that he brings this out in Merton's work. From the outset he tells us that Merton's questions were

> focused through the effort of aligning Christ, self-identity, and the autobiographical process within a single lens. Jesus' question "who do you say that I am?" (Mark 8:29) perdures as Merton's ultimate question (2).

At heart gift rather than achievement, genuine self-fulfillment is to be found in letting go of our self-willed identity,[7] in relaxing "the psychic and spiritual cramp that knots us in the painful, vulnerable, helpless 'I' that we all know as ourselves" (131). In other words, we are to let go of the sclerotic, neurotic, false self that hinders our authentic development and to allow ourselves to operate from the God-ward emptiness that abides at the very heart of our created selves. Merton's voice in this collaborative and converging quest of authentic subjectivity is well worth hearing.

The Wider Range of *Kenosis:* The Community

The kenotic hymn not only refers to the Servant described in the Song of Isaiah 52 and 53 but also adopts the humiliation/exaltation structure of that passage. The figure of the Isaian Suffering Servant may be a mysterious personal agent of God's provident designs, and that is the meaning that emerges in Philippians 2:6-11, but in its origi-

6. A contemporary development of this theme is found in the writings of R. D. Laing. Cf. his *Politics of Experience* (Harmondsworth: Penguin, 1967) and his *Divided Self: An Existential Study in Sanity and Madness* (Harmondsworth: Penguin, 1965).

7. The theme of wilfulness and willingness, its expressions in contemporary psychological literature, its pertinence for a theology of grace, and its connection with the development of authentic subjectivity are explored in Laporte, *Patience and Power*, 177ff., passim.

nal context it likely also refers to the chosen community itself, which through the insights hammered out on the anvil of its anguish and tribulation becomes a suffering servant community through which a newer religious consciousness dawns on the world.[8]

For all that, the community dimension is far from lacking in the Pauline hymn. Paul's reason for inserting this hymn, probably with adaptations of his own making, was to develop a powerful antidote to the factionalism, the "me first" attitude, that was destructive of the fragile community he had founded. The same concern emerges elsewhere, above all when he deals with the Corinthian community. *Kenosis* vitally affects communities as well as persons because only authentic kenotic persons can make up communities of loving interaction, and only such communities are propitious for the shaping of such persons.

We find this communal concern clearly reflected by Merton when he urges the Church to be more kenotic, especially in the writings of later years that are less subject to Cistercian censorship, and perhaps to the auto-censorship of the younger monk still forging his mature identity (160–69). There is the institutional Church bent on protecting its identity, its claim to authority, for which listening is difficult and teaching easy, which is *a priori* suspicious of any new movement of thought, but there is also the Church that is not afraid to risk losing itself in the *diaspora* because it knows that whatever unanticipated transformations happen, it will essentially perdure because its identity is secure, its charismatic endowment without fail. The Merton who in his later years becomes less concerned with the intrainstitutional issues of monastic life, and more resonant with the currents of thought and experience that shape the world as a whole, is a powerful instance of this shift. In this later phase, monastic life is meant to be not escape from the world but participation in its struggles and sufferings (124).

Merton is not particularly original in this extension of *kenosis* to the Church and its institutions. Kilcourse, however, also shows that

---

8. One of the keenest exponents of the genesis of this heightened religious consciousness in the tribulations of Israel is Eric Voegelin in his *Order and History. Volume One: Israel and Revelation* (Baton Rouge, Louisiana State University Press, 1956). The beauty of the Isaian text, 52:13 to 53:12, which unfolds this image for us, is that its poetic imagery is multivalent and mysterious. One cannot easily exclude from it reference to a mysterious individual destined to play a key role in salvation history, nor reference to Israel itself as a community that achieves redemptive significance through its own sufferings.

for Merton language, which makes community possible, is itself kenotic. His antipoetry unmasks the self-inflated, self-referential speech that characterizes our culture, in which words so often do not speak truth but are used to disguise special interests. Free and unobsessed—that is, kenotic—persons are capable of prophetic speech, of *parrhesia* (172). This dimension is becoming increasingly crucial as power is concentrated in the hands of those who can at their pleasure inform, withhold information, or disinform.

This line of reflection opened up by Merton is well worth pursuing. The quality of our dialogue with one another within the various communities to which we belong is essential if genuine community is to be built and maintained. Further exploration along the following lines may be fruitful. If Christ is the supreme example of *kenosis* for us, if he is the enfleshed Word of God, his use of language and practice of dialogue cannot but be instructive to individuals and communities. The Synoptics present us with a Jesus who speaks by allusion, in image, discreet about himself but clear and firm about the kingdom and its essential nearness. In John's Gospel the one who speaks the word becomes the Word, but nonetheless we find there a Jesus who is a supremely skilled dialogue partner, able to create the space within which people can come to life-shaping commitments in an atmosphere of trust and freedom. Merton explored this kenotic form of speech in his antipoetry and invites us to a more wide-ranging exploration as we seek ways to speak that are more effective because they are more liberating.

The Wider Range of *Kenosis:* Interreligious Dialogue

The theme of dialogue takes on a more precise focus as Merton enters more and more into dialogue with non-Christian monks. Interreligious dialogue has come into the limelight in recent years, with different models vying for supremacy. Are we to remain in the Christological inclusivist position formulated by Karl Rahner and countenanced in the documents of Vatican II, or should we move to a more integral pluralism, a theocentric relativism, as Paul Knitter puts it in *No Other Name*, in our approach to religious truth, mitigating our claims in the interest of making dialogue possible, allowing that what may be ultimately true for me might not be so for someone else? Merton does not appear to make a theoretical contribution to these questions, but his practice of dialogue is instructive because it is open and kenotic. Merton continues to proclaim the Savior, but proclaims him kenotically. No less can be expected if *kenosis* is at the heart of the salvation extended to humankind through Christ, if our assurance comes from seeing through a glass darkly rather than face to face.

If we do not see Truth face to face, we cannot rest until we have encountered every dimension or facet of the truth as present in our fellow human beings and allowed ourselves to be shaped by each of them. If we believe that Christ is at work bringing about total reconciliation in and through our efforts at following in his footsteps, then we can simply let him do his work and not worry about protecting ourselves and the limited truths we have managed to formulate. The Spirit of Christ will prompt us with the dialogical responses that are appropriate to time and circumstance. Paradoxically, kenotic dialogue will be as radical and as authentic as the hope in Christ that anchors it is without flaw or hesitation.

What has been advanced in the above paragraphs draws on the practice of dialogue that became more and more characteristic of Merton rather than with any explicit theory of dialogue he may have devised. Indeed, what Merton begins to articulate as a result of this dialogue is the relationship between the selflessness at the root of Christian *kenosis* and the selflessness at the core of the spiritual quest of the world religions with which he entered into contact. He rejoices in the elements of convergence while remaining firm on maintaining what is specifically Christian, without always being able to formulate it. Interrupted by his death, that dialogue remains incomplete.

Concluding Remarks

George Kilcourse makes a good case for development in the thought of Thomas Merton on kenotic Christology. The rigid structures of manual theology held him back in his years of training as a monk, and he saw the world primarily as something from which to escape through monastic life in order to be shaped into a new identity in Christ. During this period of delicate inner reconfiguration he explored that form of life and the spiritual commitment that animates it in somewhat more conventional terms. But then if one reviews later writings, one finds a more nuanced assessment of the world that he had left, a sharper sense of what was disordered about it, as well as unbounded compassion for those who suffer within it and solidarity with those who have undertaken the struggle for liberation. While Kilcourse is careful not to nail down too precisely the times and circumstances that led to this profound shift, he singles out the year 1958 as a watershed year for Merton (92). I am not in a position to comment on whether or not there is an intimate correspondence between pivotal experiences of that year and the evolution of his thought, but I would like to offer an exploratory comment out of a theology of *kenosis* on the nature of this shift.

This comment is stimulated by a medieval author mentioned incidentally in Kilcourse's book (30) but who evidently does not play a significant role in Merton's thought. I am referring to Richard of St. Victor and his *Four Grades of Violent Love*. Richard offers an account of the kenotic maturation of love within the life of the Christian that appears to fit the development of Merton's thought and practice. This relatively unknown medieval text deserves study on its own terms, but for now the broad pattern it develops will have to suffice. In a first stage (1) the soul returns to itself in meditation, but then (2) it rises above itself in contemplation, and (3) is totally carried into the mystery of God in ecstatic union. So far we have a fairly standard presentation of the three ways: purgative, illuminative, and unitive. But for Richard the pinnacle is not there. In a fourth stage (4) the soul goes out of itself toward God's world in compassion, thirsting for that world as God thirsts for it. Ascent is followed by descent. Escape from the world is followed by return to the world.

The key shift from third to fourth stage helps to articulate the nature of the shift in Merton's thought and practice. At a certain point the need to be correct seems to be superseded by the need to be compassionate. There appears to be a corresponding shift in which the kenotic dimension, at first couched in the pale terms of a conventional Christology that was very reluctant to allow a genuine humanity of Christ that made any difference, becomes gloriously alive for him and enlivens many aspects of his search for truth and fulfillment.

The shift from distraction to ecstasy to compassion in Richard of St. Victor helps us to articulate a twofold *kenosis* in Merton. The earlier *kenosis* entailed in Merton's conversion consisted in the stripping away of the false self and the corresponding emergence of the inner self, a *kenosis* that Jesus, the sinless one, did not undergo, but that Christians seeking to be conformed with Christ must experience.

The second *kenosis* consists in an imitation of the *kenosis* that the earthly Christ did undergo in solidarity with our sin, letting go of the prerogatives and recognition to which he is entitled because of his authentic inner Self. The first *kenosis* leads us from a distracting and seductive world to the inner self fulfilled in God; the second leads us from the inner self to its enfleshment in a complex and messy world. The first is an escape from the world; the second a return to the world.

This distinction is present, for instance, in the life of Augustine, who enthusiastically leaves the world behind in his first conversion but reluctantly returns to it as bishop in his second. Merton writes about the first *kenosis* with some eloquence. The second, at a certain point in his life, appears to take over very powerfully, but he does not articulate it with the same clarity.

What then is Merton's contribution to a theology of *kenosis*? He shows how *kenosis*, rather than remain frozen and lifeless, can regain its original dynamic and function widely throughout the whole range of theology. What speaks most eloquently in Merton's theology of *kenosis* is that it is rooted in image and in praxis rather than in a mere quest for orthodox formulae. One discerns at work deep respect for the received tradition, yes, but also the stirrings of a God-given experience and the challenges of a world deserving of compassion.

What is Kilcourse's contribution to the interpretation of Merton? He has succeeded in bringing out with insight and connaturality Merton's contribution to a theology of *kenosis*, leading the reader to dwell on images and clues that he or she may have hurried past in haste to get to the "theological bits." He has kept together, as is fitting, *kenosis* in thought, *kenosis* in language, and *kenosis* in action, and has illuminated their interrelation in the life and thought of Thomas Merton.

Author's Response

In February of 1994 at the University of Chicago's Thomas Merton Symposium, David Tracy surmised that it was now time for theologians to give a "second reception" to the works of Thomas Merton. I find this an apt description of my own effort in *Ace of Freedoms: Thomas Merton's Christ.* Merton's work has been stereotyped in American Catholic culture. His public image has largely revolved around his autobiography, an early 1940s conversion story and a publishing phenomenon of the post-World War II era. Merton became synonymous with the *persona* of the monk who fled the world for a monastic island of solitude where he let us eavesdrop on his introspective spiritual struggles. Merton studies became an industry preoccupied with this gifted, literate monk as an object of curiosity. But Thomas Merton renegotiated his relationship with himself, with God, and with the world. Theologians have subsequently attended to his writings about war and peacemaking, and they have heralded him as a pioneer in interreligious dialogue with Asian spiritual traditions. However, as a contemplative, monk, poet, and broader social critic, Merton is only just beginning to gain a critical reception from the American theological community.

The reviewers have accurately perceived that I undertook my study of Merton for two major reasons: (1) to situate Merton's sometimes daring reformulations of the Catholic Christian tradition within the context of the developments and changing methods in theology and spirituality studies since Vatican Council II and Merton's death; and (2) to integrate and to discover the underlying sources and influences on Merton's diverse genres and themes, which do not themselves present a system but which, when interpreted systematically, yield an uncanny focus and contemporary insight on what the tradition names as Christ's *kenosis.*

Patrick Eastman's comment on Bernard of Clairvaux's *De diligendo Deo* underscores the ultimate concern of monastic culture with living a life immersed in the mystery of Christ. Christology naturally occupied the center of attention in the monastic reforms of the Cistercian tradition as reflected in the writings of its "golden age," from 1098 to 1250. Bernard McGinn has dubbed this "the Cistercian miracle," because the changes it effected, particularly the emphasis upon experience, awakened Western Christianity to genuine spirituality. Thomas Merton retrieved these dormant sources from beneath the layers of Trappist austerity that had buried his own authentic monastic tradition since De Rancé's reforms of the late seventeenth century.

What Eastman alertly perceives is the importance of method in *Ace of Freedoms*. Where and how does the theologian or the theological critic of imaginative literature turn for the sources of Christology? Diana Culbertson strengthens the case for my including Merton's poetry and prose poems (as well as journals, letters, reading notes, and reviews) as sources for Christology. She identifies the tradition from Boccaccio to Paul Ricoeur as evolving and compelling evidence that the method of turning to poetry "as a strategy for theologizing needs no valiant defense." In the same way, the fifty years since the Catholic Church's encyclical on biblical scholarship, *Divino Afflante Spiritu*, have yielded a myriad of systematic biblical theologies that draw upon and interpret a wide spectrum of literary genres, including an abundance of Hebrew and Greek poetry in the sacred texts.

I take Culbertson's judgment that "[t]o reflect on Merton's Christology, using his poetry as source, has further obstacles: his corpus is unsystematic . . . and his modernist style is ironic, parodic, and more dissonant than what we customarily look for in 'religious poetry' " as a healthy compliment. In *Ace of Freedoms* I have addressed these formidable and challenging "obstacles" and followed the path of Merton's Christ of *kenosis* through his canon, which sometimes looks like a labyrinth. Nathan Scott and Robert Detweiler have been among those championing such methods for a theological criticism of imaginative literature. Scott traces his own theoretical roots to Paul Tillich, whose axiom "Religion is the substance of culture, culture is the form of religion" proves congenial to Merton's efforts as monk and poet. Ricoeur's work argues this thesis even more convincingly and affords new vectors for such attention to an author's metapoetic as a religious text that invites theological reflection.

On the matter of Culbertson's complimenting my consistently integrating Merton's prose and poetry, I would offer a reminiscence. The method of integrating Merton's various genres (and voices) in *Ace of Freedoms* was clarified during a conversation over morning coffee at Michael Mott's home in Bowling Green, Ohio. We were discussing the Pasternak connection and Merton's enthusiasm for the Georgian poet's work. Pasternak, oppressed by Soviet politics, had evoked an extraordinary response from the monk. It was in the course of examining this that Mott, Merton's biographer, argued that the poems at the conclusion of *Doctor Zhivago* were integral to the work, and that a poet like Merton had read them in that way. In this sense, the poems were the hermeneutical key to his prose. In Mott's words, the two—prose and poetry—stood side by side, like panels of a diptych, hinged and matching parts. To separate them would render either piece unintelligible.

In interpreting Merton's antipoetry I have, as Culbertson notes, argued that the antipoet was a "constructive identity" for Merton, with "irony as the literary analogue of kenosis." John Howard Griffin once remarked that *The Geography of Lograire* drew upon the "whole culture of Thomas Merton." In that sense such an imaginative effort challenges a reader like none of his other works. I think of Merton giving voice to a cultural transition like the one announced in T. S. Eliot's highly annotated *The Waste Land*. We will only appreciate the antipoetry as we recover Merton's sense of our world as a "post-Christian" world. Employing that term, he argued that we have abdicated our human freedom, and only as a countercultural "diaspora" Church will we stop relying upon structures and a false sense of our selves and recover our inner spiritual freedom.

Donald Goergen also strikes a chord in harmony with David Tracy's invitation to a "second reception" of Merton when he identifies as a strength of *Ace of Freedoms* my "ability to see spirituality as a matrix or source for theology." Again, the experiential foundations of the Cistercian tradition inform Merton, whose spirituality indeed nourishes heart and head. As for method, Goergen also endorses the turn to poetry as a theological source—as well as my "mining" what might be thought of as the other "nontheological" sources in Merton's canon.

Goergen, however, judges that I overstate when interpreting Merton. He asks if I have overstated a "discontinuity" between the early and later Merton. Anthony Padavano has described the Merton of *The Seven Storey Mountain* as a "Catholic bigot" when comparing him to the later, exploratory spiritual master in dialogue with Buddhist monks. Merton's own self-evaluation, which I have taken from a contrite entry in his notebooks (7), gives evidence of his conversion from a "gnostic" and "manichean" view of the world to a more optimistic and constructive sense of his own "place in the world." I wonder if Goergen's critique is not of Merton himself rather than of my interpretation? As I point out in my introduction (2), Merton's "proclivity to exaggerate'' rivaled his habitual use of irony. On the point of the discontinuity between the early and later Merton, however, I find every evidence of radical and ongoing intellectual, moral, and even religious conversion voiced in autobiographical passages in various genres of his work.

Goergen concludes by recommending *Ace of Freedoms* ''for a fuller and deeper knowledge of [Merton's] Christology.'' Yet earlier he had judged that Merton has ''a kenotic image of Christ'' rather than an explicitly kenotic Christology. Does Goergen do justice to the consistently kenotic patterns and echoes I identify throughout the book when analyzing Merton's Christological language and images? The review by Jean-Marc Laporte suggests an alternative reading from Goergen's. He identifies *kenosis* as an architectonic theological theme ''that surfaces at many strategic points in the writings of Thomas Merton.'' And he suggests that Merton himself contributes to theological method with the interrelation of his personal spiritual quest and the authentic theology emerging from his work. Once again, Tracy's call for a ''second reception'' of Merton gains an endorsement.

As far as the method of *Ace of Freedoms*, Laporte perceives well the distinction I make in Merton's shift from an exclusively ''descending Christology'' to a more complete Christology that embraces ''both ascending and descending movements.'' What he even more alertly picks up is the connection between Merton's theology of the ''true self'' involving a ''disruptive'' invitation to let go of the distortions and fixations with the ''false self''—a central emphasis in the Philippians 2:5-11 text on *kenosis*, which presents Christ and Adam in counterpoint. It yields the very kenotic autobiographical pattern of Merton's own spiritual quest.

Laporte's reflection on the suffering servant community as the subject of the *kenosis* affords a fine connection to Merton's antipoetry and prose of the final years. The suggestion of ''kenotic dialogue'' as a radical recovery of the potential for community across inherited boundaries clarifies the effort I have undertaken in my study of Merton's Christology and his ever-expanding Catholicism. Michael Mott has written on this *parrhesia*, or prophetic speech, as essential for understanding Merton's poetry and his prose. Laporte rightly identifies Jesus as the one who ''is able to create the space in which people can come to life-shaping commitments in an atmosphere of trust and freedom''—thus Christ as the ''ace of freedoms.''

There is an important connection between Merton's mature monastic identity, with his becoming less concerned with intrainstitutional issues, and his embrace of the world with its disruptive moments and discontinuities. Laporte explores such a development in Richard of St. Victor's stages in his *Four Grades of Violent Love*. The fourth and final shift in Richard's thought, from the need to be "correct" (read "orthodox") to the need to be "compassionate," entails a liberating conversion experience. Such was the transition for Merton. Laporte perceives Merton's unrelenting effort to stimulate us in a contemplative exploration of this self-emptying, offering an incipient theology of *kenosis*. He rightly names the first kenosis in Merton's spirituality as the conversion from the false to the true self. The second *kenosis*, compassion, indeed for Merton "led to the risking of that inner self as it found new enfleshment in a complex and ambiguous world."

Diana Culbertson has juxtaposed a pair of images to question whether Merton's antipoetry succeeds or not: is it "clutter" or a "mosaic"? Perhaps we are still standing too close to Merton and the cultural divide of the late 1960s to discern the figure or pattern in what appears to be simply the "clutter" of a complex and ambiguous world. But I wonder if Merton-the-poet's own description of each of his two collections of antipoetry as a "mosaic" does not offer a further kenotic Christological insight for a Church in turmoil but also in renewal. Merton's preference for the apophatic way of "knowing by unknowing," taking the "dark path," is vividly mirrored in the symbols of the Easter Vigil. How appropriate it is that the Church gathers in inky darkness to mark the patient waiting for Christ our Light. From the yawning void of the tomb we emerge into the light of the paschal fire. The paschal candle bears this light and broadcasts it throughout the assembly in the form of tapers held before the diverse faces of humanity. The tapers create a corona of light and color surrounding each face. When seen from this perspective, the gathered body of Christians itself forms a mosaic of light and color, each face being illuminated like the mosaic's single tiles bounded by dark lines. And so the Church becomes the icon of Christ, who is the icon of God. The living body, which has experienced abandonment and oppression, now manifests this hidden Christ through new Easter faith.

I want to express my gratitude to Patrick Eastman, Diana Culbertson, Donald Goergen, and Jean-Marc Laporte for their constructive discourse concerning the interpretations of Merton's Christology and poetry that I have developed in *Ace of Freedoms: Thomas Merton's Christ*. This review-symposium is a genuine example of the scholars' "kenotic dialogue" which Laporte has described as itself a deepening of community.

It is a joy to think that the doctrine of Christ's *kenosis* once again plays a central role in our collective enterprise as theologians and persons of faith. Thomas Merton has articulated this mystery in the images and metaphors of his prose and poetry. The real purpose of our Christian lives finds the energy and freedom Merton proclaims when we are united under the power of the Spirit to the God of Jesus Christ, and when we pour out our lives in healing love and compassionate service.

George Kilcourse

Contributors

Dianne Aprile is a freelance writer who lives in Louisville, Kentucky. Her work has appeared in *Kentucky Voices: A Bicentennial Celebration of Writing*, *The Thinker Review*, and *The Dark Woods I Cross: An Anthology of Contemporary Women Poets*.

Steven L. Baumann is assistant professor of nursing at Hunter College (City University of New York). Baumann has a long-standing interest in the writings of Thomas Merton.

David Belcastro teaches at Capitol University in Columbus, Ohio. He is preparing an extensive investigation of Merton and Albert Camus.

Diana Culbertson, O.P., is professor of English and comparative literature, director of religious studies, and director of the master's program in liberal studies at Kent State University. Her publications include *The Poetics of Revelation: Recognition and the Narrative Tradition* (Mercer UP, 1989), *Rose Hawthorne Lathrop: Selected Writings* (Paulist, 1993).

Patrick Eastman, vicar of spirituality for the Diocese of Tulsa, directs the *Spiritual Life Center* and edits a spirituality newsletter, *Monos*. Eastman's articles have appeared in a number of spiritual and monastic publications.

Roy D. Fuller currently serves as adjunct instructor at Bellarmine College, Indiana University Southeast, and Kentucky State University.

Donald J. Goergen, O.P., is a preacher, teacher, lecturer, author, and theologian. Among the many books he has authored and edited is the recent series on *A Theology of Jesus* (The Liturgical Press).

Timothy J. Johnson, O.F.M. Conv., is currently active in the formation of Franciscans in the United States as well as in Europe and Africa. His areas of interest are the theology of prayer and the renewal of religious life.

George Kilcourse is professor of Theology at Bellarmine College in Louisville. His publications have appeared in numerous journals, and his recent Merton research includes the interview with Jack Ford in vol. 6 of *The Merton Annual* and his *Ace of Freedoms*, reviewed in this volume.

Victor A. Kramer, a founding editor of *The Merton Annual*, has recently published the coedited *More Conversations with Walker Percy*. He is preparing the projected Volume 4 of the complete Merton journals (1960–63).

Jean-Marc Laporte, S.J., joined the Society of Jesus (Upper Canada Province) in 1958. He is on the staff at Regis College and the Toronto School of Theology. Currently he is professor of systematic theology and director of the Toronto School of Theology.

Bruce H. Lescher is a Brother of Holy Cross. He is assistant professor of religious studies at St. Edward's University in Austin, Texas.

Elena Malits, C.S.C., is a professor of Religious Studies at Saint Mary's College, Notre Dame, Indiana. She is author of *The Solitary Explorer, Thomas Merton's Transforming Journey* and a number of articles on Merton.

Elsie F. Mayer is an independent scholar whose articles have appeared in *America, The Explicator,* and *The CEA Critic*. Her book *My Window on the World: The Works of Anne Morrow Lindberg* appeared in 1980.

Matthew McEver is a graduate student at Southern Baptist Theology Seminary in Louisville, Kentucky.

Thomas F. McKenna, C.M., teaches spirituality at St. John's University, New York, at both graduate and undergraduate levels. He has contributed articles on spirituality to various professional journals. His special interest is in the area of renewal in religious life.

Robert F. Morneau, auxiliary bishop of the Diocese of Green Bay, Wisconsin, is involved in pastoral ministry, writing, and conferences on spirituality and poetry. He has published many books and taped lectures. Recently he served as one of the editors of *The Selected Poetry of Jessica Powers.*

Mary Murray is assistant professor of English at Pennsylvania State University at Hazelton. She has published in *The Merton Seasonal* and *Living Prayer.* Her *Artwork of the Mind: An Interdisciplinary Description of Insight and Search for It in Student Writing* was published in 1994.

Patrick F. O'Connell teaches English and Theology at Gannon University in Erie, Pennsylvania and has been a frequent contributor to *The Merton Seasonal* and *The Merton Annual.* He writes a regular column for *Living Prayer.* Also he is editor of the fifth volume of Henry David Thoreau's *Journal,* forthcoming from Princeton University Press, 1995.

John S. Porter teaches at Mohawk College, Hamilton, Ontario. He has published previously in *The Merton Annual* (vol. 5) and is author of *The Thomas Merton Poems: A Caravan of Poems* (1988).

Elaine Prevallet, S.L., is director of Knobs Haven Retreat Center on the grounds of the Motherhouse of the Sisters of Loretto at Nerinx, Kentucky. Previously she taught at Pendle Hill and at Loretto Heights College in Denver.

Sandra M. Schneiders, I.H.M., is currently professor of New Testament and spirituality at the Jesuit School of Theology and the Graduate Theological Union, Berkeley, California. She is the author of five books and numerous articles.

Ron Seitz has published several volumes of poetry, and others are forthcoming. He has taught at Bellarmine College and The University of Louisville. Presently he teaches at St. Catherine's College in Springfield, Kentucky.

Index

Back Issues (Volumes 1-5) of

The Merton
ANNUAL

are available from

AMS Press, Inc.
56 East 13th Street
New York, NY 10003
Fax (212) 995-5413